£44·00

Jav ing
Gla er

The c the
Glass va EE 5
applic

Davi

PUBLISHING

BIRMINGHAM - MUMBAI

Java EE 5 Development using GlassFish Application Server

The complete guide to installing and configuring the GlassFish Application Server and developing Java EE 5 applications to be deployed to this server

First published: October 2007

Production Reference: 1031007

Published by Packt Publishing Ltd.
32 Lincoln Road
Olton
Birmingham, B27 6PA, UK.

ISBN 978-1-847192-60-8

www.packtpub.com

Cover Image by Vinayak Chittar (vinayak.chittar@gmail.com)

Credits

Author

David R. Heffelfinger

Reviewers

Meenakshi Verma

Kim Mark Lewis

Acquisition Editor

Priyanka Baruah

Technical Editor

Ajay.S

Editorial Manager

Dipali Chittar

Project Manager

Patricia Weir

Project Coordinator

Sagara Naik

Indexer

Monica Ajmera

Proofreader

Chris Smith

Production Coordinator

Shantanu Zagade

Cover Designer

Shantanu Zagade

About the Author

David Heffelfinger has been developing software professionally since 1995; he has been using Java as his primary programming language since 1996. He has worked on many large-scale projects for several clients including Freddie Mac, Fannie Mae, and the US Department of Defense. He has a Masters degree in Software Engineering from Southern Methodist University. David is editor in chief of Ensode.net (`http://www.ensode.net`), a website about Java, Linux, and other technology topics.

First and foremost, I would like to thank my family for putting up with me spending several hours a day working on this book; without your support, I wouldn't have been able to accomplish this.

I would also like to thank the Packt Publishing staff for their help and support in getting this book published. I am especially grateful to Priyanka Baruah, who first contacted me regarding this book, Patricia Weir for her patience regarding the several changes to the book's outline, Sagara Naik for keeping track of the schedule. I would also like to thank the technical reviewers, Kim Lewis and Meenakshi Verma for providing excellent suggestions. Last but not least, I would also like to thank Douglas Paterson, who gave me the opportunity to get my first book published (and who wished to work on a second book with me) for supporting my decision to work on this book.

About the Reviewers

Meenakshi Verma has more than nine years of experience in Analysis, Design, Development, and Implementation of stand-alone and web-based applications using various languages like Java-based technologies, C, and BBx. She is proficient in developing applications using J2EE technologies.

Meenakshi has also done the technical review of the Packt book titled *Jasper Reports for Java Developers* by David Heffelfinger.

She is currently working at Sapient's Toronto Office.

Kim Mark Lewis has been a consultant since 1991 to the US Federal Government, working on financial and human resource systems for a variety of agencies such as NASA, the Federal Communications Commission, the Federal Reserve Board, the Department of the Army, and the Department of the Navy. Kim divides his professional programming life between Java and .NET. He is married and has one daughter and is currently living in the Washington D.C. area.

Table of Contents

Preface

Project GlassFish was formally announced at the 2005 JavaOne conference. Version one of the GlassFish application server was released to the public approximately a year later, at the 2006 JavaOne conference. GlassFish version one became the reference implementation for the Java EE 5 specification, and as such, was the first available application server compliant with this specification.

While releasing the first available Java EE 5 application server was a tremendous accomplishment, the first version of GlassFish lacked some enterprise features such as clustering and High Availability. GlassFish version 2, released in September 2007, added these and other enterprise features, in addition to other features such as an enhanced web based administration console.

This book will guide you through the development and deployment of Java EE 5-compliant application on GlassFish version 2. It also covers application development using frameworks that build on top of the Java EE 5 specification, including Facelets, Ajax4jsf, and Seam.

What This Book Covers

Chapter 1 provides an overview of Glassfish, including how to install it, configure it, and verify the installation.

Chapter 2 covers how to develop server-side web applications using the Servlet API.

Chapter 3 explains how to develop web applications using JavaServer Pages (JSPs), including how to develop and use JSP custom tags.

Chapter 4 discusses how to develop Java EE applications that interact with a relational database system through the Java Persistence API (JPA) and through the Java Database Connectivity API (JDBC).

Chapter 5 explains how to use the JSP Standard Tag Library (JSTL) when developing JavaServer Pages.

Chapter 6 covers how to develop applications using the JavaServer Faces (JSF) component framework to build web applications.

Chapter 7 explains how to develop messaging applications though the Java Messaging Service (JMS) API.

Chapter 8 covers securing J2EE applications through the Java Authentication and Authorization Service (JAAS).

Chapter 9 discusses how to develop Enterprise Java Beans that adhere to the EJB 3 specification.

Chapter 10 explains how to develop and deploy web services that conform to the JAX-WS 2.1 specification.

Chapter 11 covers frameworks that build on top of the Java EE 5 specification, including Seam, Facelets, and Ajax4Jsf.

Appendix A covers sending email from Java EE Applications.

Appendix B covers IDE integration.

Who is This Book for

This book is aimed at Java developers wishing to become proficient with Java EE 5, who are expected to have some experience with Java and to have developed and deployed applications in the past, but need no previous knowledge of Java EE or J2EE. It teaches the reader how to use GlassFish to develop and deploy applications.

Conventions

In this book, you will find a number of styles of text that distinguish between different kinds of information. Here are some examples of these styles, and an explanation of their meaning.

There are three styles for code. Code words in text are shown as follows: "We can include other contexts through the use of the `include` directive."

A block of code will be set as follows:

```
<head>
<meta http-equiv="Content-Type" content="text/html; charset=UTF-8">
<title>Server Date And Time</title>
</head>
```

When we wish to draw your attention to a particular part of a code block, the relevant lines or items will be made bold:

```
</head>
<body>
<p>Server date and time: <% out.print(new Date()); %>
</p>
</body>
```

New terms and **important words** are introduced in a bold-type font. Words that you see on the screen, in menus or dialog boxes for example, appear in our text like this: "clicking the **Next** button moves you to the next screen".

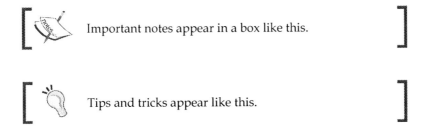

Important notes appear in a box like this.

Tips and tricks appear like this.

Reader Feedback

Feedback from our readers is always welcome. Let us know what you think about this book, what you liked or may have disliked. Reader feedback is important for us to develop titles that you really get the most out of.

To send us general feedback, simply drop an email to feedback@packtpub.com, making sure to mention the book title in the subject of your message.

If there is a book that you need and would like to see us publish, please send us a note in the **SUGGEST A TITLE** form on www.packtpub.com or email suggest@packtpub.com.

If there is a topic that you have expertise in and you are interested in either writing or contributing to a book, see our author guide on www.packtpub.com/authors.

Customer Support

Now that you are the proud owner of a Packt book, we have a number of things to help you to get the most from your purchase.

Downloading the Example Code for the Book

Visit `http://www.packtpub.com/support`, and select this book from the list of titles to download any example code or extra resources for this book. The files available for download will then be displayed.

The downloadable files contain instructions on how to use them.

Errata

Although we have taken every care to ensure the accuracy of our contents, mistakes do happen. If you find a mistake in one of our books—maybe a mistake in text or code—we would be grateful if you would report this to us. By doing this you can save other readers from frustration, and help to improve subsequent versions of this book. If you find any errata, report them by visiting `http://www.packtpub.com/support`, selecting your book, clicking on the **Submit Errata** link, and entering the details of your errata. Once your errata are verified, your submission will be accepted and the errata added to the list of existing errata. The existing errata can be viewed by selecting your title from `http://www.packtpub.com/support`.

Questions

You can contact us at `questions@packtpub.com` if you are having a problem with some aspect of the book, and we will do our best to address it.

1
Getting Started with GlassFish

In this chapter, we will discuss how to get started with GlassFish. Some of the topics discussed in this chapter are:

- An overview of Java EE and GlassFish
- Obtaining GlassFish
- Installing GlassFish
- Verifying the GlassFish Installation
- Deploying Java EE Applications
- Setting Up Database Connectivity

Overview of Java EE and GlassFish

Java EE (formerly called J2EE) is a standard set of technologies for server-side Java development. Java EE technologies include Servlets, JavaServer Pages (JSPs), JavaServer Faces (JSF), Enterprise JavaBeans (EJBs), and the Java Messaging Service (JMS).

Several commercial and open-source application Java EE servers exist. Java EE application servers, such as GlassFish, allow application developers to develop and deploy Java EE-compliant applications. Other open-source Java EE application servers include Red Hat's JBoss, the Apache Software Foundation's Geronimo, and ObjectWeb's JOnAS.

Commercial application servers include BEA's Weblogic, IBM's Websphere, and the Oracle Application Server.

GlassFish is an open-source, freely available, Java EE application server. GlassFish is dual licensed under the Common Development and Distribution License (CDDL) and the GNU Public License (GPL) version 2.

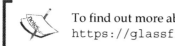 To find out more about GlassFish's license, see
`https://glassfish.dev.java.net/public/CDDL+GPL.html`.

Like all Java EE-compliant application servers, GlassFish provides the necessary libraries to allow us to develop and deploy Java applications compliant with Java EE specifications.

GlassFish Advantages

With so many options in Java EE application servers, why choose GlassFish? Besides the obvious advantage of GlassFish being available free of charge, it offers the following benefits:

- It is made by Sun Microsystems
  - Sun Microsystems is the steward of Java language, and the Java EE specification.

- Commercial support is available
  - Sun Microsystems sells a re-packaged version of GlassFish called the Sun Java System Application Server. Commercial support is available (at a cost) from Sun Microsystems for this re-packaged GlassFish version. Many software development shops will not use any software for which commercial support is not available; therefore commercial support availability allows GlassFish to be used in environments where it otherwise wouldn't be.

- It is the Java EE reference Implementation
  - GlassFish is the Java EE Reference implementation. What this means is that other application servers may use GlassFish to make sure their product complies with the specification. GlassFish could theoretically be used to debug other application servers. If an application deployed under another application server is not behaving properly, but it does behave properly when deployed under GlassFish, then it is more than likely that the improper behavior is due to a bug in the other application server.

- It supports the latest versions of the Java EE specification
  - ○ GlassFish is the reference Java EE specification, so it tends to implement the latest specifications before any other application server in the market.

Obtaining GlassFish

GlassFish can be downloaded from `https://glassfish.dev.java.net` by clicking an image that looks like this:

The image should be near the top right window of the page.

After clicking on the image, and scrolling down to a section titled **Binary builds** around the middle of the resulting page, you should see links to download GlassFish for several different architectures. Currently Solaris Sparc, Solaris x86, Windows, Linux, and MacOS are supported.

To download GlassFish, simply click on the link for your platform; the file should start downloading immediately. After the file finishes downloading, you should have a file called something like `glassfish-installer-v2-b58g.jar`; the exact file name will depend on the exact GlassFish version and platform.

Installing GlassFish

Installing GlassFish is an easy process; however, GlassFish assumes that some dependencies are present in your system.

GlassFish Dependencies

Before GlassFish can be installed, a recent version of the Java Development Kit must be present in your system and (optionally) the Apache ANT tool.

- Java Development Kit
    - In order to install GlassFish, a recent version of the Java Development Kit (JDK) must be installed on your workstation (JDK 1.5 or newer required), and the `java` executable must be in your system PATH. The latest JDK can be downloaded from `http://java.sun.com/`. Please refer to the JDK installation instructions for your particular platform at `http://java.sun.com/javase/6/webnotes/install/index.html`.
- ANT (Optional)
    - Ant is a very popular build tool; it can be downloaded from `http://ant.apache.org`. A version of ANT is included with GlassFish, therefore this step is optional. If you already have ANT installed on your system you can use it to install GlassFish. Just make sure that the ant script is executable and in your system's PATH. Please note that GlassFish requires ANT 1.6.5 or later.

Performing the Installation

Once the dependencies have been installed, copy the file downloaded in the previous section to an appropriate installation location and run the following command from a terminal window:

```
java -Xmx256m -jar glassfish-installer-v2-b58g.jar
```

The actual file name at the end of the command will depend on the version of GlassFish downloaded.

After running this command, a window prompting you to accept the license terms will show up.

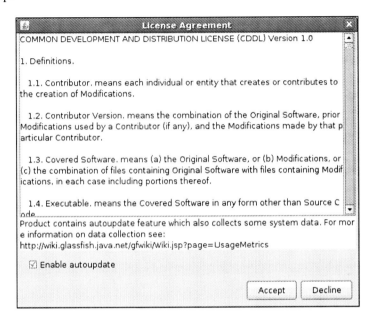

Scroll all the way down and click on the button labeled **Accept**.

You should see a lot of text scrolling on your terminal window, after the text stops scrolling, you should see the following text at the bottom of your terminal window:

installation complete.

The installer creates a directory called `glassfish` at the location where we ran the above command from.

Although we saw the above message when we completed the step required in the previous paragraph, we are not quite done installing GlassFish. Inside the `glassfish` directory, there is an ANT build script that must be executed to complete the installation. The file name for this build script is `setup.xml`. This script can be executed from the command line by changing to the GlassFish installation directory and typing the following command:

```
ant -f setup.xml
```

After executing this command you should see the following message at the bottom of the terminal the time taken may vary:

```
BUILD SUCCESSFUL

Total time: 43 seconds
```

 The above command assumes that ANT 1.6.5 or newer is installed in the system, and that the ant executable is in the system PATH. GlassFish includes ANT; to access it from any directory add [glassfish installation directory]/glassfish/lib/ant/bin to your system PATH.

We have now successfully installed GlassFish and we are ready to start it for the first time.

Verifying the Installation

To start GlassFish, change directory to [glassfish installation directory]/glassfish/bin, and execute the following command:

```
./asadmin start-domain domain1
```

 The above command and most commands shown in this chapter assume a Unix or Unix-like operating system. For Windows systems, the initial "./" is not necessary.

After executing the above command you should see a message similar to the following in the command line console:

Domain domain1 is ready to receive client requests. Additional services are being started in background.

The above message will be followed by additional information indicating the ports that GlassFish listens to and other information.

We can then open a browser window and type the following URL in the browser's location text field: http://localhost:8080.

If everything went well you should see a page similar to the following:

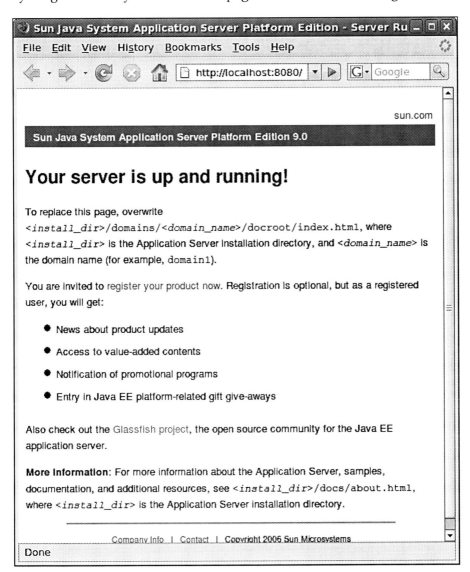

 Getting Help

If any of the above steps fail, a good place to ask for help is the GlassFish forums at http://forums.java.net/jive/forum.jspa?forumID=56.

Deploying Our First Java EE Application

To further test that our GlassFish installation is running properly, we will deploy a war (Web ARchive) file and make sure it deploys and executes properly. Before moving on, please download the file simpleapp.war from this book's website.

Deploying an Application through the Web Console

To deploy simpleapp.war, open a browser and navigate to the following URL: http://localhost:4848; you should be greeted with a login screen that looks like the following:

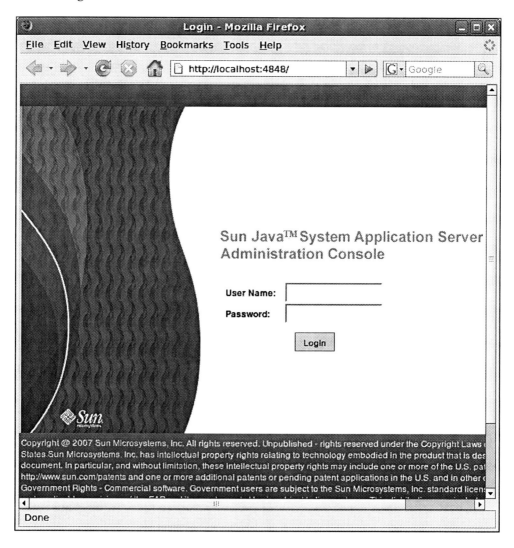

The default administrator user name/password combination is **admin/adminadmin** and log in using these credentials; you should see a page like the following:

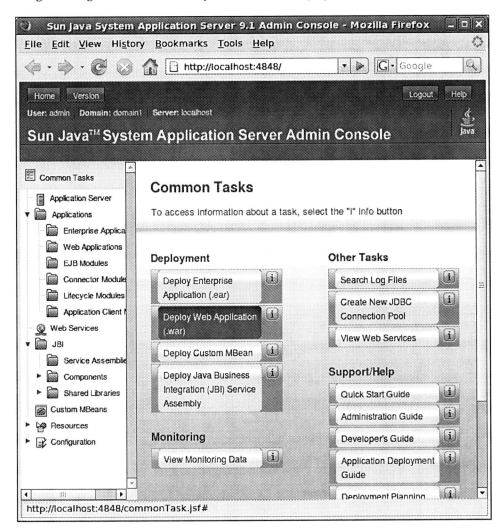

Changing the Administrator Password

It is good practice to change the default administrator password. To change your administrator password click on the **Application Server** menu item at the top left, then click on the **Administrator Password** tab. Then enter and confirm the new administrator password and click on the Save button.

Now, click on the **Deploy Web Application** item on the main page (highlighted in the previous screenshot). You should now see a screen like the following:

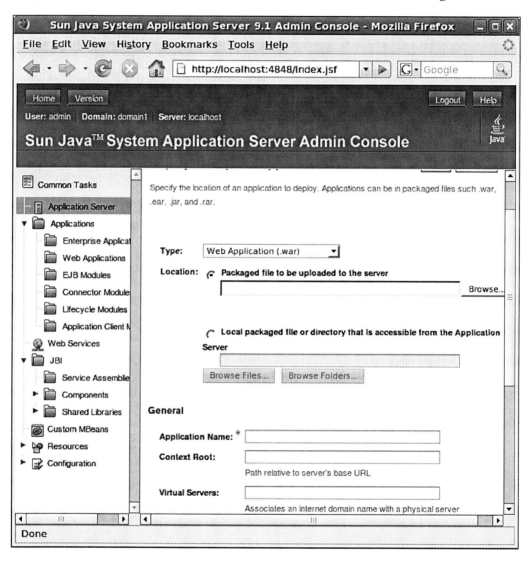

The war file can either be deployed by "uploading it" to the server (this functionality is there to upload files to remote servers; in our case the workstation and server are one and the same), or by navigating the file system to select the desired war file.

Even though our server and workstation are one and the same, we will use the upload option as navigation is much easier (selecting the local packaged file option will result in us having to navigate through the whole directory tree; by selecting the upload option we only have to navigate from our home directory).

After clicking on the **Browse** button and navigating to the location of `simpleapp.war`, the screen will look similar to this:

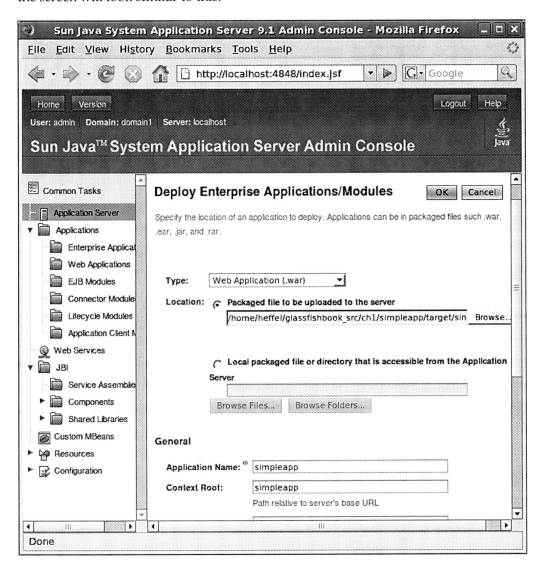

Notice how the **Application Name** and **Context Root** text fields are automatically filled out.

Clicking on the **OK** button at the top right of the page will deploy the application.

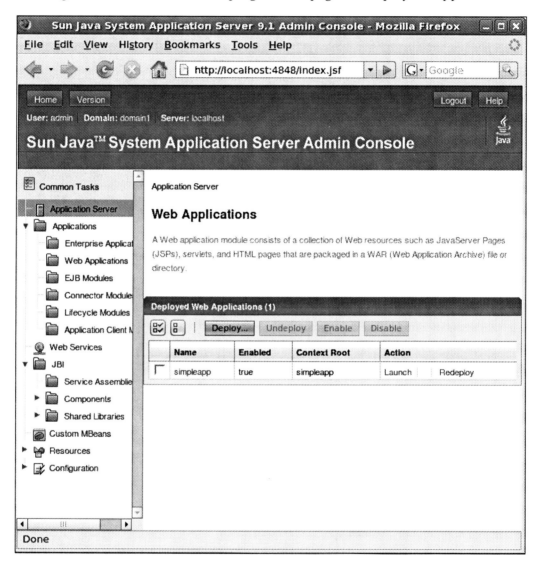

As can be seen in the screenshot above, our `simpleapp` application now has been deployed.

To execute the `simpleapp` application, type the following URL in the browser's location text field: `http://localhost:8080/simpleapp/simpleservlet`. The resulting page should look like this:

That's it! We have successfully deployed our first Java EE application.

Undeploying an Application through the Web Console

In the next section, we explain how to deploy a web application through the command line. In order for the instructions in the next section to work, we need to undeploy `simpleapp.war`.

To undeploy the application that we deployed in the previous section, log in to the GlassFish web console by typing the following URL in the browser: `http://localhost:4040` and entering the admin user name and corresponding password.

Then click on the **Web Applications** menu item near the top left of the page and click on the checkbox by **simpleapp** web application.

Then click on the **Undeploy** button; the application will be undeployed and removed from the list of deployed applications.

Deploying an Application through the Command Line

Now that we have undeployed the `simpleapp` file, we are ready to deploy it using the command line. To deploy the application in this manner, simply copy `simpleapp.war` to `[glassfish installation directory]/glassfish/domains/domain1/autodeploy`. The application will automatically be deployed just by copying it to this directory.

We can verify that the application has successfully been deployed by looking at the server log. The server log can be found at `[glassfish installation directory]/glassfish/domains/domain1/logs/server.log`. The last few lines on this file should look something like this:

```
[#|2007-02-13T20:57:41.825-0500|INFO|sun-appserver9.1|javax.enterprise.
system.tools.deployment|_ThreadID=23;_ThreadName=Timer-4;|deployed with
moduleid = simpleapp|#]
```

```
[#|2007-02-13T20:57:42.100-0500|INFO|sun-appserver9.1|javax.enterprise.
system.tools.deployment|_ThreadID=23;_ThreadName=Timer-4;|[AutoDeploy]
Successfully autodeployed : /opt/glassfish/domains/domain1/autodeploy/
simpleapp.war.|#]
```

Of course, we can also verify the deployment by navigating to the URL for the application, which will be the same one that we used when deploying through the web console: `http://localhost:8080/simpleapp/simpleservlet`; the application should execute properly.

An alternative way of deploying an application through the command line is to use the following command:

```
asadmin deploy [path to file]/simpleapp.war
```

The server log file should show a message similar to the following:

```
[#|2007-02-15T18:03:13.879-0500|INFO|sun-appserver9.1|javax.enterprise.
system.tools.deployment|_ThreadID=15;_ThreadName=Thread-25;|deployed with
moduleid = simpleapp|#]
```

Undeploying an Application through the Command Line

To undeploy an application from the command line simply delete it from the `[glassfish installation directory]/glassfish/domains/domain1/autodeploy` directory. It will be automatically undeployed; this can be verified by looking at the server log, which should have some lines that look something like this:

```
[#|2007-02-13T21:04:43.753-0500|INFO|sun-appserver9.1|javax.enterprise.
system.tools.deployment|_ThreadID=23;_ThreadName=Timer-4;|Autoundeploying
application :simpleapp|#]
```

```
[#|2007-02-13T21:04:44.023-0500|INFO|sun-appserver9.1|javax.enterprise.
system.tools.deployment|_ThreadID=23;_ThreadName=Timer-4;|[AutoDeploy]
Successfully autoundeployed : /opt/glassfish/domains/domain1/autodeploy/
simpleapp.war.|#]
```

As can be seen from this section and the previous one, deploying and undeploying an application through the command line is a very simple and fast process that saves a lot of time when testing applications. All future examples in this book will be deployed by copying the appropriate files to the `autodeploy` directory.

The `asadmin` executable can be used to undeploy an application as well, by issuing a command like the following:

```
asadmin undeploy simpleapp
```

The following message should be shown at the bottom of the terminal window:

```
Command undeploy executed successfully.
```

Please note that the file extension is not used to undeploy the application, the argument to `asadmin undeploy` should be the context root for the application (which is typed right after `http://localhost:4848` to access the application through the browser), which defaults to the `war` file name.

[In the next chapter, we will see how to change the default context root for an application.]

GlassFish Domains Explained

The alert reader might have noticed that the `autodeploy` directory is under a `domains/domain1` subdirectory. GlassFish has a concept of **domains**. Domains allow a collection of related applications to be deployed together. A default domain called `domain1` is created when installing GlassFish.

Creating Domains

Additional domains can be created from the command line by issuing the following command:

```
asadmin create-domain domainname
```

The above command takes several parameters to specify ports where the domain will listen to for several services (HTTP, Admin, JMS, IIOP, secure HTTP, etc.); type the following command in the command line to see this parameters:

```
asadmin create-domain --help
```

If we want several domains to execute concurrently on the same server, these ports must be chosen carefully, because specifying the same ports for different services (or even the same service across domains) will prevent one of the domains from working properly.

The default ports for the default `domain1` domain are listed in the following table:

Service	Port
Admin	4848
HTTP	8080
Java Messaging System (JMS)	7676
Internet Inter-ORB Protocol (IIOP)	3700
Secure HTTP (HTTPS)	8181
Secure IIOP	3820
Mutual Authorization IIOP	3920
Java Management Extensions (JMX) Administration	8686

Please note that when creating a domain, the only port that needs to be specified is the admin port; if the other ports are not specified, the default ports listed in the table above will be used. Care must be taken when creating a domain, because, as explained above, two domains cannot run concurrently in the same server if any of their services listen for connections on the same port.

An alternative method of creating a domain, without having to specify ports for every service, is to issue the following command:

```
asadmin createdomain --portbase [port number] domainname
```

The value of the `--portbase` parameter dictates the base port for the domain; ports for the different services will be offsets of the given port number. The following table lists the ports assigned to all the different services.

Service	Port
Admin	portbase + 48
HTTP	portbase + 80
Java Messaging System (JMS)	portbase + 76
Internet Inter-ORB Protocol (IIOP)	portbase + 37
Secure HTTP (HTTPS)	portbase + 81
Secure IIOP	portbase + 38
Mutual Authorization IIOP	portbase + 39
Java Management Extensions (JMX) Administration	portbase + 86

Of course, care must be taken when choosing the value for portbase, making sure that none of the assigned ports collide with any other domain.

As a rule of thumb, creating domains using a portbase number greater than 8000 and divisible by 1000 should create domains that don't conflict with each other; for example, it should be safe to create a domain using a portbase of 9000, another one using a portbase of 10000, so on and so forth.

Deleting Domains

Deleting a domain is very simple; it can be accomplished by issuing the following command in the command line:

```
asadmin delete-domain domainname
```

We should see a message like the following on the terminal window:

```
Domain domainname deleted.
```

Please use the above command with care; once a domain is deleted, it cannot be easily recreated (all deployed applications will be gone, as well as any connection pools, data sources, etc.).

Stopping a Domain

A domain that is executing can be stopped by issuing the following command:

```
asadmin stop-domain domainname
```

The above command will stop the domain named `domainname`.

If only one domain is running, the domain name argument is optional.

This book will assume the reader is working with the default domain called `domain1` and the default ports. If this is not the case, instructions given need to be modified to match the appropriate domain and port.

Setting Up Database Connectivity

Any non-trivial Java EE application will connect to a Relational Database Management Server (RDBMS). Supported RDBMS systems include JavaDB, Oracle, Derby, Sybase, DB2, Pointbase, MySQL, PostgreSQL, Informix, Cloudscape, and SQL Server. In this section, we will demonstrate how to set up GlassFish to communicate with PostgreSQL; the procedure is similar for others.

 GlassFish comes bundled with an RDBMS called JavaDB. This RDBMS is based on Apache Derby. To limit the downloads and configuration needed to follow this book's code, all examples needing an RDBMS will use the embedded JavaDB RDBMS.

Setting Up Connection Pools

The first step to follow when setting up a connection pool is to copy the JAR file containing the JDBC driver for our RDBMS in the `lib` directory of the domain (consult your RDBMS documentation for information on where to obtain this JAR file). If the GlassFish domain where we want to add the connection pool is running when copying the JDBC driver, it must be restarted for the change to take effect.

The domain can be restarted by executing `asadmin stop-domain domain1` followed by executing `asadmin start-domain domain1`.

Once the JDBC driver has been copied to the appropriate location and the application server has been restarted, log in to the admin console by pointing the browser to `http://localhost:4848` (assuming the current domain is listening on the default admin port).

Then click on **Resources->JDBC->Connection Pools**; the browser should now look something like this:

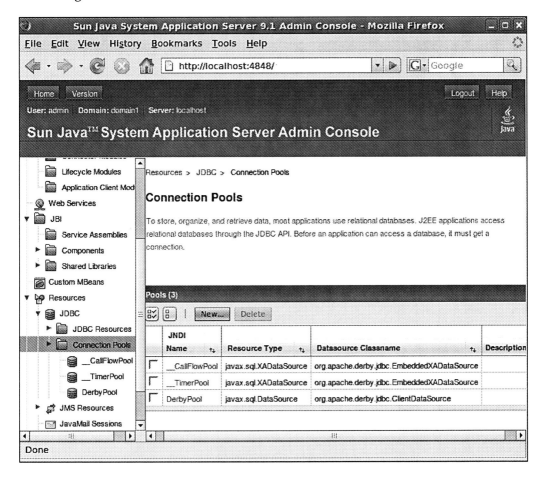

Click on the **New...** button; after entering the appropriate values for our RDBMS, the page should look something like this:

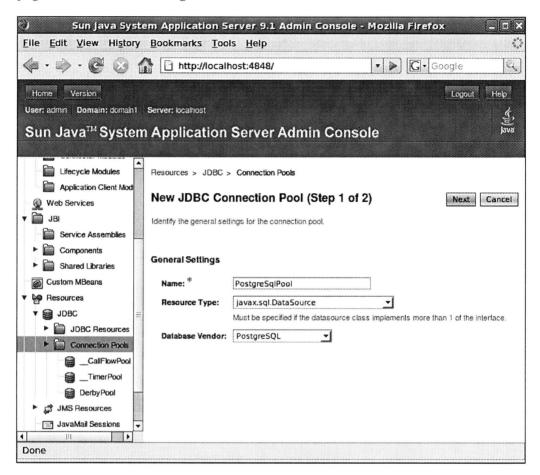

After entering the appropriate data for the RDBMS and clicking the **Next** button, you should see a page like the following:

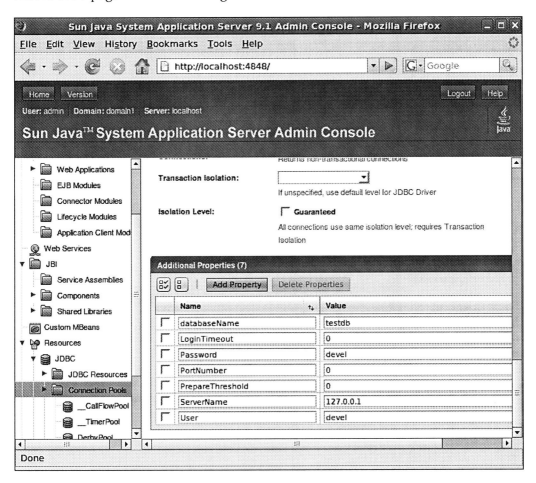

Most of the default values on this page are sensible; scroll all the way down and enter the appropriate data for our RDBMS, then click on the **Finish** button at the top right of the screen.

Our newly created connection pool should now be visible in the list of connection pools.

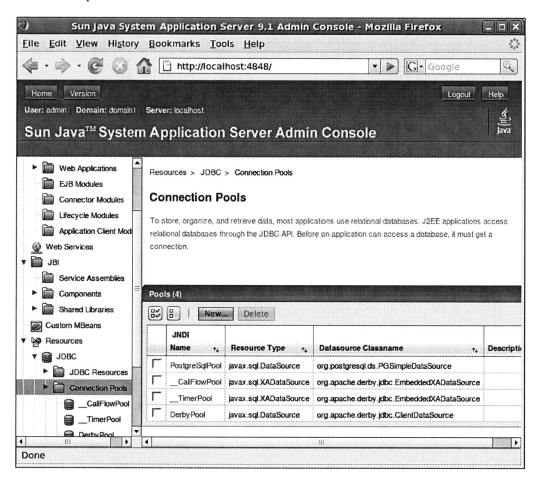

After clicking on the JNDI name for the new connection pool, and clicking on the
Ping button, you should see a message like the following:

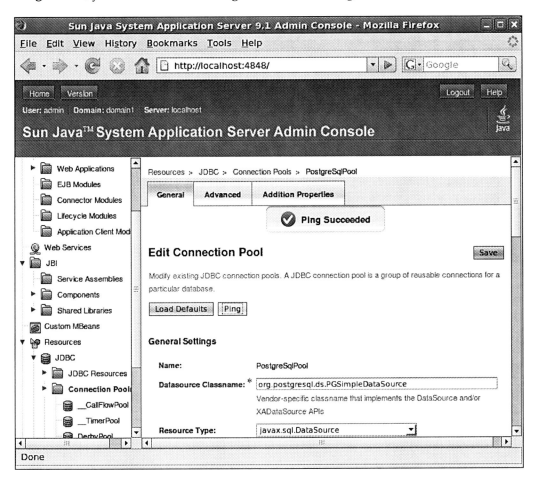

Our connection pool is now ready to be used by our applications.

Setting Up Data Sources

Java EE applications don't access connection pools directly, instead they access a data
source, which points to a connection pool. To set up a new data source, click on the
JDBC Resources menu item on the left-hand side of the web console, then click on
the **New...** button.

After filling out the appropriate information for our new data source, you should see a page like this:

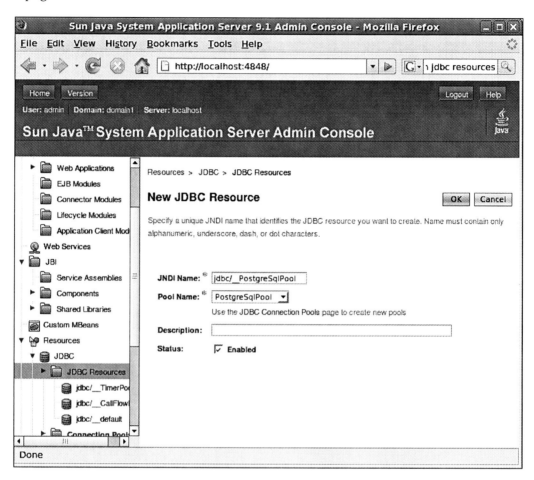

After clicking the **OK** button, you can see our newly created data source:

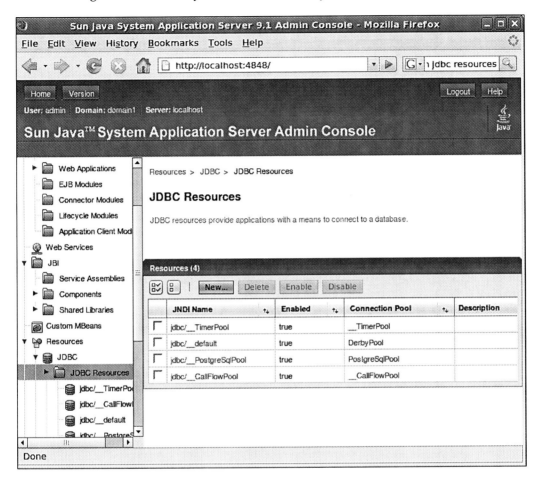

Summary

In this chapter, we discussed how to download and install GlassFish. We also discussed several methods of deploying Java EE application: through the GlassFish web console, through the `asadmin` command, and by copying the file to the `autodeploy` directory. We also discussed basic GlassFish administration tasks like setting up domains and setting up database connectivity by adding connection pools and data sources.

2
Servlet Development and Deployment

In this chapter, we will discuss how to develop and deploy Java servlets. Some of the topics covered are:

- An explanation of what servlets are
- Developing, configuring, packaging and deploying our first servlet
- HTML form processing
- Forwarding HTTP requests
- Redirecting HTTP responses
- Persisting data across HTTP requests

What is a Servlet? A servlet is a Java class that is used to extend the capabilities of servers that host applications. Servlets can respond to requests and generate responses. The base class for all servlets is `javax.servlet.GenericServlet`, this class defines a generic, protocol-independent servlet.

By far, the most common type of servlet is an HTTP servlet; this type of servlet is used in handling HTTP requests and generating HTTP responses. An HTTP servlet is a class that extends the `javax.servlet.http.HttpServlet` class, which is a subclass of `javax.servlet.GenericServlet`.

A servlet must implement one or more methods to respond to specific HTTP requests. These methods are overridden from the parent `HttpServlet` class. As can be seen in the following table, these methods are named so that knowing which one to use is intuitive.

HTTP Request	HttpServlet Method
GET	`doGet(HttpServletRequest request, HttpServletResponse response)`
POST	`doPost(HttpServletRequest request, HttpServletResponse response)`
PUT	`doPut(HttpServletRequest request, HttpServletResponse response)`
DELETE	`doDelete(HttpServletRequest request, HttpServletResponse response)`

Each of these methods take the same two parameters, namely an instance of a class implementing the `javax.servlet.http.HttpServletRequest` interface and an instance of a class implementing the `javax.servlet.http.HttpServletResponse`. These interfaces will be covered in detail, later in this chapter.

Application developers never call the above methods directly; they are called automatically by the application server whenever it receives the corresponding HTTP request.

Of the four methods listed above, `doGet()` and `doPost()` are, by far, the most commonly used.

An HTTP GET request is generated whenever a user types the servlet's URL in the browser, when a user clicks on a link pointing to the servlet's URL, or when a user submits an HTML form using the GET method that has an action pointing to the servlet's URL. In any of these cases, the code inside the servlet's `doGet()` method gets executed.

An HTTP POST request is typically generated when a user submits an HTML form using the POST method and an action pointing to the servlet's URL. In this case, the servlet's code inside the `doPost()` method gets executed.

Writing Our First Servlet

In chapter 1, we deployed a simple application that printed a message on the browser window. That application basically consisted of a single servlet. In this section, we will see how that servlet was developed, configured, and packaged.

The code for the servlet is as follows:

```
package net.ensode.glassfishbook.simpleapp;

import java.io.IOException;
import java.io.PrintWriter;

import javax.servlet.http.HttpServlet;
import javax.servlet.http.HttpServletRequest;
import javax.servlet.http.HttpServletResponse;

public class SimpleServlet extends HttpServlet
{
  protected void doGet(HttpServletRequest request, HttpServletResponse
response)
  {
    try
    {
      response.setContentType("text/html");
      PrintWriter printWriter = response.getWriter();
      printWriter.println("<h2>");
      printWriter
          .println("If you are reading this,
                             your application server is good to go!");
      printWriter.println("</h2>");
    }
    catch (IOException ioException)
    {
      ioException.printStackTrace();
    }
  }
}
```

As this servlet is meant to execute when a user enters its URL in the browser
window, we need to override the doGet() method from the parent HttpServlet
class. As we explained, this method takes two parameters: an instance of a class
implementing the javax.servlet.http.HttpServletRequest interface, and an
instance of a class implementing the javax.servlet.http.HttpServletResponse
interface.

Even though HttpServletRequest and HttpServletResponse are interfaces,
application developers don't typically write classes implementing them. When
control goes to a servlet from an HTTP request, the application server (GlassFish, in
our case) provides objects implementing these interfaces.

The first thing our `doGet()` method does is to set the content type for the `HttpServletResponse` object to "text/html". If we forget to do this, the default content type used is "text/plain", which means that the HTML tags used a couple of lines down will be displayed on the browser, as opposed to them being interpreted as HTML tags.

Then we obtain an instance of `java.io.PrintWriter` by calling the `HttpServletResponse.getWriter()` method. We can then send text output to the browser by calling the `PrintWriter.print()` and `PrintWriter.println()` methods (the previous example uses `println()` exclusively). As we set the content type to "text/html", any HTML tags are interpreted properly by the browser.

Compiling the Servlet

To compile the servlet, the Java library included with GlassFish must be in the CLASSPATH. This library is called `javaee.jar`, it can be found under `[glassfish installation directory]/glassfish/lib`.

To compile from the command line using the `javac` compiler, a command like the following must be issued (all in one line):

```
javac -cp /opt/glassfish/lib/javaee.jar:. net/ensode/glassfishbook/
simpleapp/SimpleServlet.java
```

Of course, these days very few developers compile code with the "raw" `javac` compiler; instead, either a graphical IDE or a command line build tool like Apache ANT or Apache Maven is used. Consult your IDE or build tool documentation for information on how to add the `javaee.jar` library to its CLASSPATH.

Maven

Apache Maven is a build tool similar to ANT. However, Maven offers a number of advantages over ANT including automatic download of dependencies and standard commands for compilation and packaging of applications. Maven was the build tool used to compile and package most of the examples in this book, therefore it is recommended to have Maven installed in order to easily build the examples.

When using Maven, the code can be compiled and packaged by issuing the following command at the project's root directory (`simpleapp` in this case): `mvn package`.

Maven can be downloaded from `http://maven.apache.org/`.

Configuring the Servlet

Before we can deploy our servlet, we need to configure it. All Java EE web applications are configured via an XML deployment descriptor named `web.xml`. The `web.xml` deployment descriptor for our servlet is as follows:

```xml
<?xml version="1.0" encoding="UTF-8"?>
"<web-app xmlns="http://java.sun.com/xml/ns/javaee" version="2.5"
    xmlns:xsi=" http://www.w3.org/2001/XMLSchema-instance"
    xsi:schemaLocation=" http://java.sun.com/xml/ns/
    javaee http://java.sun.com/xml/ns/javaee/web-app_2_5.xsd">"
  <servlet>
    <servlet-name>SimpleServlet</servlet-name>
    <servlet-class>
      net.ensode.glassfishbook.simpleapp.SimpleServlet
    </servlet-class>
   </servlet>
  <servlet-mapping>
    <servlet-name>SimpleServlet</servlet-name>
    <url-pattern>/simpleservlet</url-pattern>
  </servlet-mapping>
</web-app>
```

The first few lines are boilerplate XML stating the XML version and encoding, plus the schema used for the XML file and other information. It is safe to just copy and paste these lines and reuse them across applications. The `<servlet>` and `<servlet-mapping>` XML tags above are used to actually configure our servlet.

The `<servlet>` tag contains two nested tags. `<servlet-name>` defines a logical name for the servlet, and `<servlet-class>` indicates the Java class defining the servlet.

The `<servlet-mapping>` tag also contains two nested tags: `<servlet-name>`, which must match the value set inside the `<servlet>` tag and `<url-pattern>`, which sets the URL pattern for which the servlet will execute.

`<url-pattern>` can be specified in one of two ways, by using a path prefix (which is what the example above does), or by specifying an extension suffix.

Path prefix values for `<url-pattern>` indicate that any URL paths starting with the given path will be serviced by the corresponding servlet. Path prefix values must start with a forward slash.

Java EE web applications run from within a context root. The context root is the first string in the URL that is not the server name or IP address, nor the port. For example, in the URL `http://localhost:8080/simpleapp/simpleservlet`, the string `simpleapp` is the context root. The value for `<url-pattern>` is relative to the application's context root.

Extension suffix values for `<url-pattern>` indicate that any URLs ending in the given suffix will be serviced by the corresponding servlet. In the above example, we chose to use a path prefix. Had we chosen to use an extension suffix, the `<servlet-mapping>` tag would have looked something like this:

```
<servlet-mapping>
  <servlet>SimpleServlet</servlet>
  <url-pattern>*.foo</url-pattern>
</servlet-mapping>
```

This would direct any URLs ending with the string `.foo` to our servlet.

The reason the `<servlet-name>` tag is specified twice (once inside the `<servlet>` tag and again inside the `<servlet-mapping>` tag) is because a Java EE 5 web application can have more than one servlet, each of which must have a `<servlet>` tag in the application's `web.xml`. The `<servlet>` tag for each must have a corresponding `<servlet-mapping>` tag, and the `<servlet-name>` nested tag is used to indicate which `<servlet>` tag corresponds to which `<servlet-mapping>` tag.

A Java EE 5 `web.xml` file can contain many additional XML tags. However, these additional tags are not needed for this simple example. Additional tags will be discussed in future examples when they are needed.

Before we can execute our servlet, we need to package it as part of a web application in a WAR (Web ARchive) file.

Packaging the Web Application

All Java EE 5 web applications must be packaged in a WAR (Web ARchive) file before they can be deployed. A WAR file is nothing but a compressed file containing our code and configuration. WAR files can be created by any utility that can create files in ZIP format (for example, WinZip, 7-Zip, etc.). Also, many Java IDEs and build tools such as ANT and Maven automate WAR file creation.

A WAR file must contain the following directories (in addition to its root directory)

```
WEB-INF
```

```
WEB-INF/classes
```

```
WEB-INF/lib
```

The root directory contains JSPs (covered in the next chapter), HTML files, JavaScript files, and CSS files.

`WEB-INF` contains deployment descriptors such as `web.xml`.

`WEB-INF/classes` contains the compiled code (`.class` files) and may optionally contain property files. Just as with any Java classes, the directory structure must match the package structure, therefore this directory typically contains several subdirectories corresponding to the classes contained in it.

`WEB-INF/lib` contains JAR files containing any library dependencies our code might have.

The root directory, `WEB-INF`, and `WEB-INF/classes` directories can have sub directories. Any resources on a subdirectory of the root directory (other than `WEB-INF`) can be accessed by prepending the subdirectory name to its file name. For example, if there was a subdirectory called `css` containing a CSS file called `style.css`, this CSS file could be accessed in JSPs and HTML files in the root directory by the following line:

```
<link rel="stylesheet" type="text/css" media="screen" href="css/style.css" />
```

Notice the `css` prefix to the file name, corresponding to the directory where the CSS file resides.

To create our WAR file "from scratch", create the above directory structure in any directory in your system, then follow the following steps:

1. Copy the `web.xml` file to `WEB-INF`.
2. Create the following directory structure under `WEB-INF/classes`: `net/ensode/glassfishbook/simpleapp`.
3. Copy `SimpleServlet.class` to the `simpleapp` directory from step 2.
4. From the command line, issue the following command from the directory right above `WEB-INF`: `jar cvf simpleapp.war`.

You should now have a WAR file ready for deployment.

 When using Maven to build the code, the WAR file is automatically generated when issuing the `mvn package` command. The WAR file can be found under the `target` directory, it is named `simpleapp.war`.

Before we can execute our application, it needs to be deployed.

Deploying the Web Application

As we discussed in Chapter 1, there are several ways of deploying an application. The easiest and most straightforward way to deploy any Java EE application is to copy the deployment file (WAR file in this case) to the `[glassfish installation directory]/glassfish/domains/domain1/autodeploy` directory.

After copying the WAR file to the `autodeploy` directory, the system log should show a message similar to the following:

```
[#|2007-02-17T11:36:22.906-0500|INFO|sun-appserver9.1|javax.enterprise.
system.tools.deployment|_ThreadID=12;_ThreadName=Timer-4;|deployed with
moduleid = simpleapp|#]


[#|2007-02-17T11:36:23.424-0500|INFO|sun-appserver9.1|javax.enterprise.
system.tools.deployment|_ThreadID=12;_ThreadName=Timer-4;|[AutoDeploy]
Successfully autodeployed : /opt/glassfish/domains/domain1/autodeploy/
simpleapp.war.|#]
```

 The system log can be found under `[glassfish installation directory]/glassfish/domains/domain1/logs/server.log`.

The last line should contain the string "Successfully autodeployed" indicating that our WAR file was deployed successfully.

Testing the Web Application

To verify that the servlet has been properly deployed, we need to point our browser to `http://localhost:8080/simpleapp/simpleservlet`; after doing so, we should see a page like the one shown in the following screenshot.

Unsurprisingly, this is the same message as we saw when deploying the application in Chapter 1, as this is the same application as we deployed then.

Earlier in this chapter, we mentioned that URL paths for a Java EE 5 application are relative to their context root. The default context root for a WAR file is the name of the WAR file itself (minus the .war extension). As can be seen in the screenshot above, the context root for our application is simpleapp, which happens to match the name of the WAR file. This default can be changed by adding an additional configuration file to the WEB-INF directory of the WAR file. The name of this file must be sun-web.xml. An example sun-web.xml that will change the context root of our application from the default simpleapp to simple would look like this:

```
<?xml version="1.0" encoding="UTF-8"?>
<!DOCTYPE sun-web-app PUBLIC "-//Sun Microsystems, Inc.//DTD
Application Server 8.1 Servlet 2.4//EN" "http://www.sun.com/software/
appserver/dtds/sun-web-app_2_4-1.dtd">
<sun-web-app>
  <context-root>/simple</context-root>
</sun-web-app>
```

As can be seen in the above example, the context root for the application must be in the <context-root> tag of the sun-web.xml configuration file. After redeploying the simpleapp.war, directing the browser to http://localhost:8080/simple/simpleservlet will execute our servlet.

 The sun-web.xml file can contain a number of additional tags to configure several aspects of the application. Additional tags will be discussed in the relevant sections of this book.

Processing HTML Forms

Servlets are rarely accessed by typing their URL directly in the browser. The most common use for servlets is to process data entered by users in an HTML form. In this section, we illustrate this process.

Before digging into the servlet code and HTML markup, let's take a look at the web. xml file for this new application.

```xml
<?xml version="1.0" encoding="UTF-8"?>
<web-app version="2.4" xmlns="http://java.sun.com/xml/ns/j2ee"
  xmlns:xsi="http://www.w3.org/2001/XMLSchema-instance"
  xsi:schemaLocation="http://java.sun.com/xml/ns/j2ee http://java.sun.
com/xml/ns/j2ee/web-app_2_4.xsd">
  <servlet>
    <servlet-name>FormHandlerServlet</servlet-name>
    <servlet-class>
      net.ensode.glassfishbook.formhandling.FormHandlerServlet
    </servlet-class>
  </servlet>
  <servlet-mapping>
    <servlet-name>FormHandlerServlet</servlet-name>
    <url-pattern>/formhandlerservlet</url-pattern>
  </servlet-mapping>
  <welcome-file-list>
    <welcome-file>dataentry.html</welcome-file>
  </welcome-file-list>
</web-app>
```

The above web.xml file is very similar to the one we saw in the previous section; however, it contains an XML tag we haven't seen before, namely the <welcome-file> tag. The <welcome-file> tag determines what file to direct to when a user types a URL ending in the application's context root (for this example, the URL would be http://localhost:8080/formhandling, as we are naming our WAR file formhandling.war and not specifying a custom context root). We will name the HTML file containing the form dataentry.html; this will cause GlassFish to render it in the browser when the user types our application's URL and does not specify a file name.

 If no <welcome-file> is specified in the application's web.xml file, GlassFish will look for a file named index.html and use it as the welcome file. If it can't find it, it will look for a file named index.jsp and use it as a welcome file. If it can't find it either one, it will display a directory listing.

The HTML file containing the form for our application looks like this:

```
<!DOCTYPE html PUBLIC "-//W3C//DTD HTML 4.01 Transitional//EN"
"http://www.w3.org/TR/html4/loose.dtd">
<html>
<head>
<meta http-equiv="Content-Type" content="text/html; charset=UTF-8">
<title>Data Entry Page</title>
</head>
<body>
<form method="post" action="formhandlerservlet">
<table cellpadding="0" cellspacing="0" border="0">
  <tr>
    <td>Please enter some text:</td>
    <td>
      <input type="text" name="enteredValue" />
    </td>
  </tr>
  <tr>
    <td></td>
    <td><input type="submit" value="Submit"></td>
  </tr>
</table>
</form>
</body>
</html>
```

Notice how the value for the form's `action` attribute matches the value of the servlet's `<url-pattern>` in the application's `web.xml` (minus the initial slash). As the value of the form's `method` attribute is "post", our servlet's `doPost()` method will be executed when the form is submitted.

Now let's take a look at our servlet's code:

```
package net.ensode.glassfishbook.formhandling;

import java.io.IOException;
import java.io.PrintWriter;

import javax.servlet.http.HttpServlet;
import javax.servlet.http.HttpServletRequest;
import javax.servlet.http.HttpServletResponse;

public class FormHandlerServlet extends HttpServlet
{
  protected void doPost(HttpServletRequest request,
```

```
        HttpServletResponse response)
    {
      String enteredValue;

      enteredValue = request.getParameter("enteredValue");

      response.setContentType("text/html");

      PrintWriter printWriter;
      try
      {
        printWriter = response.getWriter();

        printWriter.println("<p>");
        printWriter.print("You entered: ");
        printWriter.print(enteredValue);
        printWriter.print("</p>");
      }
      catch (IOException e)
      {
        e.printStackTrace();
      }
    }

}
```

As can be seen in the above example, we obtain a reference to the value the user typed by calling the `request.getParameter()` method. This method takes a single `String` object as its sole parameter; the value of this string must match the name of the input field in the HTML file. In this case, the HTML file has a text field named "enteredValue":

```
<input type="text" name="enteredValue" />
```

Therefore the servlet has a corresponding line:

```
enteredValue = request.getParameter("enteredValue");
```

to obtain the text entered by the user and store it in the string variable named `enteredValue` (the name of the variable does not need to match the input field name, but naming it that way is good practice to make it easy to remember what value the variable is holding).

After packaging the preceding three files in a WAR file called `formhandling.war`, then deploying the WAR file, we can see the rendered `dataentry.html` file by entering the following URL in the browser: `http://localhost:8080/formhandling`.

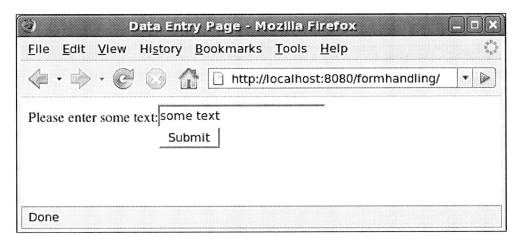

After we enter "some text" in the text field and submit the form (either by hitting "enter" or clicking on the **Submit** button), we should see the output of the servlet.

The `HttpServletRequest.getParameter()` method can be used to obtain the value of any HTML input field that can only return one value (text boxes, text areas, single selects, radio buttons, hidden fields, etc.). The procedure to obtain any of these fields values is identical, in other words, the servlet doesn't care if the user typed in the value in a text field, selected it from a set of radio buttons, etc. As long as the input field's name matches the value passed to the `getParameter()` method, this code will work.

When dealing with radio buttons, all related radio buttons must have the same name. Calling the `HttpServletRequest.getParameter()` method and passing the name of the radio buttons will return the value of the selected radio button.

Some HTML input fields like checkboxes and multiple select boxes allow the user to select more than one value. For these fields, instead of using the `HttpServletRequest.getParameter()` method, the `HttpServletRequest.getParameterValues()` method is used. This method also takes a string containing the input field's name as its only parameter, and returns an array of strings containing all the values that were selected by the user.

Let's add a second HTML file and a second servlet to our application to illustrate this case. The relevant sections of this HTML are shown below.

```html
<form method="post" action="multiplevaluefieldhandlerservlet">
<p>Please enter one or more options.</p>
<table cellpadding="0" cellspacing="0" border="0">
  <tr>
    <td><input name="options" type="checkbox" value="option1" />
    Option 1</td>
  </tr>
  <tr>
    <td><input name="options" type="checkbox" value="option2" />
    Option 2</td>
  </tr>
  <tr>
    <td><input name="options" type="checkbox" value="option3" />
    Option 3</td>
  </tr>
  <tr>
    <td><input type="submit" value="Submit" /></td>
    <td></td>
  </tr>
</table>
</form>
```

The new HTML file contains a simple form having three checkboxes and a submit button. Notice how every checkbox has the same value for its `name` attribute. As we mentioned before, any checkboxes that are clicked by the user will be sent to the servlet.

Let's now take a look at the servlet that will handle the above HTML form.

```java
package net.ensode.glassfishbook.formhandling;

import java.io.IOException;
import java.io.PrintWriter;
```

```java
import javax.servlet.http.HttpServlet;
import javax.servlet.http.HttpServletRequest;
import javax.servlet.http.HttpServletResponse;

public class MultipleValueFieldHandlerServlet extends HttpServlet
{
  protected void doPost(HttpServletRequest request,
      HttpServletResponse response)
  {
    String[] selectedOptions = request.getParameterValues("options");

    response.setContentType("text/html");

    try
    {
      PrintWriter printWriter = response.getWriter();

      printWriter.println("<p>");
      printWriter.print("The following options were selected:");
      printWriter.println("<br/>");

      if (selectedOptions != null)
      {
        for (String option : selectedOptions)
        {
          printWriter.print(option);
          printWriter.println("<br/>");
        }
      }
      else
      {
        printWriter.println("None");
      }
      printWriter.println("</p>");
    }
    catch (IOException e)
    {
      e.printStackTrace();
    }
  }
}
```

The above code calls the `request.getParameterValues()` method and assigns its return value to the `selectedOptions` variable. Farther down the `doPost()` method, the code traverses the `selectedOptions` array and prints the selected values in the browser.

This code uses the enhanced `for` loop introduced in JDK 1.5. Refer to `http://java.sun.com/j2se/1.5.0/docs/guide/language/foreach.html` for more information.

If no checkboxes are clicked, the `request.getParameterValues()` method will return null; therefore it is a good idea to check for null before attempting to traverse through this method's return values.

Before this new servlet can be deployed, the following lines need to be added to the application's `web.xml` file:

```
<servlet>
    <servlet-name>MultipleValueFieldHandlerServlet</servlet-name>
    <servlet-class>
       net.ensode.glassfishbook.formhandling.
MultipleValueFieldHandlerServlet
    </servlet-class>
  </servlet>
```

and:

```
<servlet-mapping>
    <servlet-name>MultipleValueFieldHandlerServlet</servlet-name>
    <url-pattern>/multiplevaluefieldhandlerservlet</url-pattern>
  </servlet-mapping>
```

to assign a logical name and URL to the new servlet.

After re-creating the `formhandling.war` file by adding the compiled servlet and the HTML file and redeploying it, we can see the changes in action by typing the following URL in the browser window: `http://localhost:8080/formhandling/multiplevaluedataentry.html`.

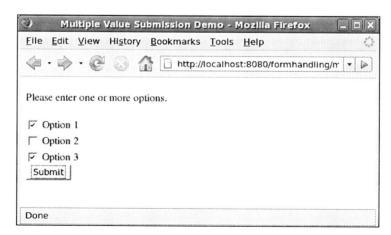

After submitting the form, control goes to our servlet, and the browser window should look something like this:

Of course, the actual message seen in the browser window will depend on what checkboxes the user clicked on.

Request Forwarding and Response Redirection

In many cases, one servlet processes form data, then transfers control to another servlet or JSP to do some more processing or display a confirmation message on the screen. There are two ways of doing this: either the request can be forwarded or the response can be redirected to another servlet or page.

Request Forwarding

Notice how the text displayed in the previous sections' example matches the value of the value attribute of the checkboxes that were clicked, and not the labels displayed on the previous page. This might confuse the users. Let's modify the servlet to change these values so that they match the labels, then forward the request to another servlet that will display the confirmation message on the browser.

The new version of `MultipleValueFieldHandlerServlet` is shown next.

```
package net.ensode.glassfishbook.formhandling;

import java.io.IOException;
import java.util.ArrayList;
```

```
import javax.servlet.ServletException;
import javax.servlet.http.HttpServlet;
import javax.servlet.http.HttpServletRequest;
import javax.servlet.http.HttpServletResponse;
public class MultipleValueFieldHandlerServlet extends HttpServlet
{
  protected void doPost(HttpServletRequest request,
      HttpServletResponse response)
  {
    String[] selectedOptions = request.getParameterValues("options");
    ArrayList<String> selectedOptionLabels = null;

    if (selectedOptions != null)
    {
      selectedOptionLabels = new
          ArrayList<String>(selectedOptions.length);

      for (String selectedOption : selectedOptions)
      {
        if (selectedOption.equals("option1"))
        {
          selectedOptionLabels.add("Option 1");
        }
        else if (selectedOption.equals("option2"))
        {
          selectedOptionLabels.add("Option 2");
        }
        else if (selectedOption.equals("option3"))
        {
          selectedOptionLabels.add("Option 3");
        }
      }
    }

    request.setAttribute("checkedLabels", selectedOptionLabels);
    try
    {
      request.getRequestDispatcher("confirmationservlet").
          forward(request, response);
    }
    catch (ServletException e)
    {
      e.printStackTrace();
    }
    catch (IOException e)
    {
      e.printStackTrace();
    }
  }
}
```

This version of the servlet iterates through the selected options and adds the corresponding label to an `ArrayList` of Strings. This `ArrayList` is then attached to the request object by calling the `request.setAttribute()` method. This method is used to attach any object to the request so that any other code we forward the request to can have access to it later.

> This code uses generics, a feature introduced to the Java language in JDK 1.5, see `http://java.sun.com/j2se/1.5.0/docs/guide/language/generics.html` for details.

After attaching the `ArrayList` to the request, we then forward the request to the new servlet in the following line of code:

```
request.getRequestDispatcher("confirmationservlet").forward(
        request, response);
```

The `String` argument to this method must match the value of the `<url-pattern>` tag of the servlet in the application's `web.xml` file.

At this point, control goes to our new servlet. The code for this new servlet is shown below:

```
package net.ensode.glassfishbook.requestforward;
import java.io.IOException;
import java.io.PrintWriter;
import java.util.List;
import javax.servlet.http.HttpServlet;
import javax.servlet.http.HttpServletRequest;
import javax.servlet.http.HttpServletResponse;
public class ConfirmationServlet extends HttpServlet
{
  @Override
  protected void doPost(HttpServletRequest request,
HttpServletResponse response)
  {
    try
    {
      PrintWriter printWriter;
      List<String> checkedLabels = (List<String>) request
          .getAttribute("checkedLabels");

      response.setContentType("text/html");
      printWriter = response.getWriter();
      printWriter.println("<p>");
      printWriter.print("The following options were selected:");
```

```
            printWriter.println("<br/>");
            if (checkedLabels != null)
            {
              for (String optionLabel : checkedLabels)
              {
                printWriter.print(optionLabel);
                printWriter.println("<br/>");
              }
            }
            else
            {
              printWriter.println("None");
            }
            printWriter.println("</p>");
          }
        catch (IOException ioException)
        {
          ioException.printStackTrace();
        }
      }
    }
}
```

This code obtains the `ArrayList` that was attached to the request by the previous servlet. This is accomplished by calling the `request.getAttribute()` method; the parameter for this method must match the value used to attach the object to the request.

Once this servlet obtains the list of option labels, it traverses through it and displays them on the browser.

Forwarding a request as described above only works for other resources (servlets and JSP pages) in the same context as the code doing the forwarding. In simple terms, the servlet or JSP that we want to forward to must be packaged in the same WAR file as the code that is invoking the `request.getRequestDispatcher().` `forward()` method. If we need to direct the user to a page in another context (or even another server), we can do it by redirecting the response object.

Response Redirection

One disadvantage of forwarding a request as described in the previous section is that requests can only be forwarded to other servlets or JSPs in the same context. If we need to direct the user to a page on a different context (deployed in another WAR file in the same server or deployed in a different server) we need to use the `HttpServletResponse.sendRedirect()` method.

To illustrate response redirection, let's develop a simple web application that asks the user to select their favorite search engine, then directs the user to his/her search engine of choice. The HTML page for this application would look like this:

```
<!DOCTYPE html PUBLIC "-//W3C//DTD HTML 4.01 Transitional//EN"
"http://www.w3.org/TR/html4/loose.dtd">
<html>
<head>
<meta http-equiv="Content-Type" content="text/html; charset=UTF-8">
<title>Response Redirection Demo</title>
</head>
<body>
<form method="post" action="responseredirectionservlet">
Please indicate your favorite search engine.
<table>
  <tr>
    <td><input type="radio" name="searchEngine"
      value="http://www.google.com">Google</td>
  </tr>
  <tr>
    <td><input type="radio" name="searchEngine"
      value="http://www.msn.com">MSN</td>
  </tr>
  <tr>
    <td><input type="radio" name="searchEngine"
      value="http://www.yahoo.com">Yahoo!</td>
  </tr>
  <tr>
```

```
      <td colspan="2"><input type="submit" value="Submit" /></td>
    </tr>
  </table>
  </form>
  </body>
  </html>
```

The HTML form in this markup code contains three radio buttons; the value for each of them is the URL for the search engine corresponding to the user's selection. Notice how the value for the name attribute of each radio button is the same, namely "searchEngine". The servlet will obtain the value of the selected radio button by calling the request.getParameter() method and passing the string "searchEngine" as a parameter, as demonstrated in the code below:

```
package net.ensode.glassfishbook.responseredirection;

import java.io.IOException;
import java.io.PrintWriter;

import javax.servlet.http.HttpServlet;
import javax.servlet.http.HttpServletRequest;
import javax.servlet.http.HttpServletResponse;

public class ResponseRedirectionServlet extends HttpServlet
{
  @Override
  protected void doPost(HttpServletRequest request,
HttpServletResponse response) throws IOException
  {
    String url = request.getParameter("searchEngine");

    if (url != null)
    {
      response.sendRedirect(url);
    }
    else
    {
      PrintWriter printWriter = response.getWriter();

      printWriter.println("No search engine was selected.");
    }
  }
}
```

By calling `request.getParameter("searchEngine")`, this code assigns the URL of the selected search engine to the variable `url`. Then, (after checking for `null`, in case the user clicked on the submit button without selecting a search engine), it directs the user to the selected search engine by calling `response.sendRedirect()` and passing the `url` variable as a parameter.

The `web.xml` file for this application should be fairly straightforward and is not shown (it is part of this book's code download).

After packaging the code and deploying it, we can see it in action by typing the following URL in the browser: `http://localhost:8080/responseredirection/`.

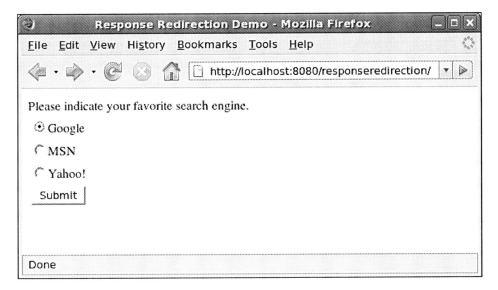

After clicking the **submit** button, the user is directed to their favorite search engine.

It should be noted that redirecting the response as just illustrated creates a new HTTP request to the page we are redirecting to; therefore any request parameters and attributes are lost.

Persisting Application Data across Requests

In the previous section, we saw how it is possible to store an object in the request by invoking the HttpRequest.setAttribute() method and how later this object can be retrieved by invoking the HttpRequest.getAttribute() method. This approach only works if the request was forwarded to the servlet invoking the getAttribute() method. If this is not the case, the getAttribute() method will return null.

It is possible to persist an object across requests. In addition to attaching an object to the request object, an object can also be attached to the session object or to the servlet context. The difference between these two is that objects attached to the session will not be visible to different users, whereas objects attached to the servlet context are.

Attaching objects to the session and servlet context is very similar to attaching objects to the request. To attach an object to the session, the `HttpServletRequest.getSession()` method must be invoked. This method returns an instance of `javax.servlet.http.HttpSession`, we then call the `HttpSession.setAttribute()` method to attach the object to the session. The following code fragment illustrates the process:

```
protected void doPost(HttpServletRequest request, HttpServletResponse
response)
{
    .
    .
    .
    Foo foo = new Foo(); //theoretical object
    HttpSession session = request.getSession();

    session.setAttribute("foo", foo);
    .
    .
    .
}
```

We can then retrieve the object from the session by calling the `HttpSession.getAttribute()` method.

```
protected void doPost(HttpServletRequest request, HttpServletResponse
response)
{
    HttpSession session = request.getSession();

    Foo foo = (Foo)session.getAttribute("foo");
}
```

Notice how the return value of `session.getAttribute()` needs to be cast to the appropriate type. This is necessary because the return value of this method is `java.lang.Object`.

The procedure to attach objects to and retrieve objects from the servlet context is very similar. The servlet needs to call the getServletContext() method (defined in the class called GenericServlet, which is the parent class of HttpServlet, which in turn is the parent class of our servlets). This method returns an instance of javax. servlet.ServletContext, which defines a setAttribute() and a getAttribute() method. These methods work in the same way as their HttpServletRequest and HttpSessionResponse counterparts.

The procedure to attach an object to the servlet context is illustrated in the following code snippet:

```
protected void doPost(HttpServletRequest request, HttpServletResponse
response)
{
  //The getServletContext() method is defined higher in
  //the inheritance hierarchy.
  ServletContext servletContext = getServletContext();

  Foo foo = new Foo();
  servletContext.setAttribute("foo", foo);
  .
  .
  .
}
```

The above code attaches the foo object to the servlet context; this object will be available to any servlet in our application, and will be the same across sessions. It can be retrieved by calling the ServletContext.getAttribute() method, as is illustrated next.

```
protected void doPost(HttpServletRequest request, HttpServletResponse
response)
{
  ServletContext servletContext = getServletContext();
  Foo foo = (Foo)servletContext.getAttribute("foo");
  .
  .
  .
}
```

This code obtains the foo object from the request context; again a cast is needed because the ServletContext.getAttribute() method, like its counterparts, returns an instance of java.lang.Object.

Objects attached to the servlet context are said to have a scope of application. Similarly, objects attached to the session are said to have a scope of session, and objects attached to the request are said to have a scope of request.

Summary

This chapter covered how to develop, configure, package, and deploy servlets. We also covered how to process HTML form information by accessing the HTTP request object. Additionally, we covered forwarding HTTP requests from one servlet to another, as well as redirecting the HTTP response to a different server. Lastly, we discussed how to persist objects in memory across requests by attaching them to the servlet context and the HTTP session.

3
JavaServer Pages

In the previous chapter, we saw how to develop Java servlets. Servlets are great for handling form input, but servlet code that outputs HTML markup to the browser tends to be cumbersome to write, read, and debug. A better way to send output to the browser is through JavaServer Pages (JSPs).

The following topics will be covered in this chapter:

- Developing our first JSP
- Implicit JSP objects
- JSPs and JavaBeans
- Reusing JSP content
- Writing custom tags

Introduction to JavaServer Pages

In the early days, servlets were the only API available to develop server-side web applications in Java. Servlets had a number of advantages over CGI scripts, which were prevalent in those days (and to some extent, still are). Some of the advantages of servlets over CGI scripts included increased performance and enhanced security.

However, servlets also had one major disadvantage: as the HTML code to be rendered in the browser needed to be embedded in Java code, most servlet code was very hard to maintain. To overcome these limitations, JavaServer Pages (JSPs) technology was created. JSPs use a combination of static HTML content and dynamic content to generate web pages. As the static content is separate from the dynamic content, JSP pages are a lot easier to maintain than servlets that generate HTML output.

In most modern applications using JSPs, servlets are still used; however, they typically assume the role of a controller in the Model-View-Controller (MVC) design pattern, with JSPs assuming the role of the view. As controller servlets have no user interface, we don't run into the issue of having HTML markup inside Java code.

In this chapter, we will cover how to develop server-side web applications using JavaServer Pages technology.

Developing Our First JSP

JSPs are basically pages containing both static HTML markup and dynamic content. Dynamic content can be generated by using snippets of Java code called scriptlets or by using standard or custom JSP tags. Let's look at a very simple JSP that displays the current server time in the browser.

```
<%@ page language="java" contentType="text/html; charset=UTF-8"
  pageEncoding="UTF-8"%>
<%@ page import="java.util.Date" %>
<!DOCTYPE html PUBLIC "-//W3C//DTD HTML 4.01 Transitional//EN"
"http://www.w3.org/TR/html4/loose.dtd">
<html>
<head>
<meta http-equiv="Content-Type" content="text/html; charset=UTF-8">
<title>Server Date And Time</title>
</head>
<body>
<p>Server date and time: <% out.print(new Date()); %>
</p>
</body>
</html>
```

To deploy the above JSP, all that needs to be done is to put it in a WAR file. When a WAR file contains no servlets, the `web.xml` file is optional. As we mentioned before, the easiest way to deploy the WAR file is to copy it to `[glassfish installation directory]/glassfish/domains/domain1/autodeploy`. After a successful deployment, pointing the browser to `http://localhost:8080/firstjsp/first.jsp` should result in a page like the following:

The "**Server date and time:**" string came for the static text immediately following the <p> tag in the JSP page. The actual date and time displayed came from the output of the code between the <% and %> delimiters. We can place any valid Java code between these two delimiters. Code inside these delimiters is known as a **scriptlet**. The scriptlet in the above JSP makes use of the out implicit object. JSP implicit objects are objects that can be readily used in any JSP, with no need to declare or initialize them. The out implicit object is an instance of javax.servlet.jsp.JspWriter. It can be thought of as an equivalent of calling the HttpServletResponse.getWriter() method.

The first two lines in this JSP are **JSP page directives**. A JSP page directive defines attributes that apply to the entire JSP page. A **JSP page directive** can have several attributes. In this example, the first page directive sets the language, contentType, charset, and PageEncoding attributes. The second one adds an import statement to the page.

As can be seen in the example, JSP page directive attributes can be combined in a single directive, or a separate page directive can be used for each attribute. Using a separate page directive for each attribute is possible, as well as combining all page directive attributes in a single page directive.

The following table lists all attributes for the page directive:

Attribute	Description	Valid Values	Default Value
autoFlush	Determines whether the output buffer should be flushed automatically when it is full.	true or false	true
buffer	The output buffer size in kilobytes.	Nkb where N is an integer number. "none" is also a valid value.	8kb
contentType	Determines the page's HTTP response, MIME type, and character encoding.	Any valid MIME type and character encoding combination	text/html; charset= ISO-8859-1
errorPage	Indicates to what page to navigate when the JSP throws an exception.	Any valid relative URL to another JSP.	N/A
extends	Indicates the class this JSP extends.	The fully qualified name for the JSP's parent class.	N/A

Attribute	Description	Valid Values	Default Value
`import`	Imports one or more classes to be used in scriptlets.	A fully qualified name of a class to import, or the full package name + ".*" to import all necessary classes from the package (e.g., `<%@ page import java.util.*" %>`).	N/A
`info`	The value for this attribute is incorporated into the compiled JSP. It can later be retrieved by calling the page's `getServletInfo()` method.	Any string.	N/A
`isErrorPage`	Determines if this page is an error page.	`true` or `false`	`false`
`isThreadSafe`	Determines whether the page is thread safe.	`true` or `false`	`true`
`language`	Determines the scripting language used in scriptlets, declarations, and expressions in the JSP page.	Any scripting language that can execute in the Java Virtual Machine (groovy, jruby, etc.).	`java`
`pageEncoding`	Determines the page encoding, for example, "UTF-8".	Any valid page encoding.	N/A
`session`	Determines whether the page has access to the HTTP session.	`true` or `false`	`True`

Of the attributes on the table, `errorPage`, `import`, and `isErrorPage` are the most commonly used. The others have sensible defaults.

When deployed to the application server, JSPs are translated (compiled into) servlets. The `extends` attribute of the page directive indicates the generated servlet's parent class. The value of this attribute must be a subclass of `javax.servlet.GenericServlet`.

Although the `language` attribute can accept any language that can execute in the Java Virtual Machine, it is extremely rare to use any language other than Java.

JSP Implicit Objects

JSP implicit objects are objects that can be used in a JSP without having to be declared or initialized. They are actually declared and initialized behind the scenes by the application server when the JSP is deployed.

In the example in the previous section, we used the JSP implicit object `out`, this object, for all practical purposes is equivalent to calling the `HttpResponse.getWriter()` in a servlet. In addition to the `out` object, there are several other implicit objects that can be used in JSP scriptlets. These implicit objects are listed in the following table:

Implicit Object	Implicit Object Class	Description
application	`javax.servlet.ServletContext`	Equivalent to calling the `getServletContext()` method in a servlet.
config	`javax.servlet.ServletConfig`	Equivalent to invoking the `getServletConfig()` method in a servlet.
exception	`java.lang.Throwable`	Only accessible if the page directive's `isErrorPage` attribute is set to true. Provides access to the exception that was thrown that led to the page being invoked.
out	`javax.servlet.jsp.JspWriter`	Equivalent to the return value of `HttpServletResponse.getWriter()`.
page	`java.lang.Object`	Provides access to the page's generated servlet.
pageContext	`javax.servlet.jsp.PageContext`	Provides several methods for managing the various web application scopes (request, session, application). Refer to the JavaDoc for PageContext at `http://java.sun.com/javaee/5/docs/api/javax/servlet/jsp/PageContext.html`.
request	`javax.servlet.ServletRequest`	Equivalent to the instance of `HttpServletRequest` we obtain as a parameter of the `doGet()` and `doPost()` methods in a servlet.

Implicit Object	Implicit Object Class	Description
response	javax.servlet. ServletResponse	Equivalent to the instance of HttpServletResponse we obtain as a parameter of the doGet() and doPost() methods in a servlet.
session	javax.servlet.http. HttpSession	Equivalent to the return value of the HttpServletRequest. getSession() method.

The following example JSP illustrates the use of several of the JSP implicit objects:

```
<%@ page language="java" contentType="text/html; charset=UTF-8"
  pageEncoding="UTF-8"%>
<!DOCTYPE html PUBLIC "-//W3C//DTD HTML 4.01 Transitional//EN"
"http://www.w3.org/TR/html4/loose.dtd">
<%@page import="java.util.Enumeration"%>
<html>
<head>
<meta http-equiv="Content-Type" content="text/html; charset=UTF-8">
<title>Implicit Objects Demo</title>
</head>
<body>
<p>This page uses JSP Implicit objects to attach objects to the
request, session, and application scopes.<br />
It also retrieves some initialization parameters sent in the web.xml
configuration file.<br />
The third thing it does is get the buffer size from the implicit
response object.<br />
</p>
<p>
<%

    application.setAttribute("applicationAttribute", new String(
        "This string is accessible accross sessions."));

    session.setAttribute("sessionAttribute", new String(
        "This string is accessible accross requests"));

    request.setAttribute("requestAttribute", new String(
        "This string is accessible in a single request"));

    Enumeration initParameterNames =
        config.getInitParameterNames();

    out.print("Initialization parameters obtained ");
    out.print("from the implicit <br/>");
```

```
        out.println("config object:<br/><br/>");
        while (initParameterNames.hasMoreElements())
        {
          String parameterName =
              (String) initParameterNames.nextElement();
          out.print(parameterName + " = ");
          out.print(config.getInitParameter(
              (String) parameterName));
          out.print("<br/>");
        }

        out.println("<br/>");

        out.println("Implicit object <b>page</b> is of type "
            + page.getClass().getName() + "<br/><br/>");

        out.println("Buffer size is: " + response.getBufferSize()
            + " bytes");
%>
</p>
<p><a href="implicitobjects2.jsp">
        Click here to continue.
    </a></p>
</body>
</html>
```

The above JSP utilizes most of the implicit objects available to JSP scriptlets. The first thing it does is attach objects to the `application`, `session`, and `request` implicit objects. It then gets all initialization parameters' implicit `config` objects and displays their name and values on the browser by using the implicit `out` object. Next, it displays the fully qualified name of the implicit `page` object. Finally, it displays the buffer size by accessing the implicit `response` object.

JSP (and servlet) initialization parameters are declared in the application's `web.xml` file. For this application, the `web.xml` looks like this:

```
<?xml version="1.0" encoding="UTF-8"?>
<web-app version="2.4" xmlns="http://java.sun.com/xml/ns/j2ee"
  xmlns:xsi="http://www.w3.org/2001/XMLSchema-instance"
  xsi:schemaLocation="http://java.sun.com/xml/ns/j2ee http://java.sun.
com/xml/ns/j2ee/web-app_2_4.xsd">

  <servlet>
    <servlet-name>ImplicitObjectsJsp</servlet-name>
    <jsp-file>/implicitobjects.jsp</jsp-file>
    <init-param>
      <param-name>webxmlparam</param-name>
```

```
        <param-value>
          This is set in the web.xml file
        </param-value>
      </init-param>
    </servlet>

    <servlet-mapping>
      <servlet-name>ImplicitObjectsJsp</servlet-name>
      <url-pattern>/implicitobjects.jsp</url-pattern>
    </servlet-mapping>
  </web-app>
```

Remember that a JSP gets compiled into a servlet at deployment time. As such, we can treat it as a servlet in the web.xml file. In order to be able to pass initialization parameters to a JSP, we must treat it like a servlet, as initialization parameters are placed between <init-param> and </init-param> XML tags. As shown in this web.xml file, the parameter name is placed between <param-name> and </param-name> tags, and the parameter value is placed between <param-value> and </param-value> tags. A servlet (and a JSP) can have multiple initialization parameters. Each initialization parameter must be declared inside a separate <init-param> tag.

Notice that in this web.xml file we declared a servlet mapping for our JSP. This was necessary to allow GlassFish's web container to pass the initialization parameters to the JSP. As we didn't want the URL of the JSP to change, we used the JSP's actual URL as the value for the <url-pattern> tag. Had we wanted to access the JSP via a different URL (not necessarily one ending in .jsp) we could have placed the desired URL inside the <url-pattern> tag.

At the bottom of implicitobjects.jsp, there is a hyperlink to a second JSP, called implicitobjects2.jsp. The markup and code for implicitobjects2.jsp looks like this:

```
<%@ page language="java" contentType="text/html; charset=UTF-8"
  pageEncoding="UTF-8"%>
<!DOCTYPE html PUBLIC "-//W3C//DTD HTML 4.01 Transitional//EN"
"http://www.w3.org/TR/html4/loose.dtd">
<%@page import="java.util.Enumeration"%>
<html>
<head>
<meta http-equiv="Content-Type" content="text/html; charset=UTF-8">
<title>Sanity Check</title>
</head>
<body>
<p>This page makes sure we can retrieve the application, session and
request attributes set in the previous page. <br />
```

```
</p>
<p>applicationAttribute value is:
<%=application.getAttribute("applicationAttribute")%>
<br />
sessionAttribute value is:
<%=session.getAttribute("sessionAttribute")%>
<br />
requestAttribute value is:
<%=request.getAttribute("requestAttribute")%>
<br />
</p>
<p>

The following attributes were found at the application scope:<br/
><br/>
<%
    Enumeration applicationAttributeNames = pageContext
        .getAttributeNamesInScope(pageContext.APPLICATION_SCOPE);

    while (applicationAttributeNames.hasMoreElements())
    {
      out.println(applicationAttributeNames.nextElement() +
      "<br/>");
    }
%>
</p>
<p><a href="buggy.jsp">This hyperlink points to a JSP that will throw
an exception.</a></p>
</body>
</html>
```

In this second JSP, we retrieve the objects that were attached to the application, session, and request objects. The attached objects are obtained by calling the appropriate implicit object's getAttribute() method. Notice how all calls to the getAttribute() method are nested between <%= and %> delimiters. Snippets of code between these delimiters are called **JSP expressions**. JSP expressions are evaluated and their return value is displayed in the browser without having to call the out.print() method.

This JSP also retrieves the names of all objects attached to the application scope and displays them in the browser window.

At the bottom of the above JSP there is a hyperlink to a third JSP; this third JSP is called buggy.jsp. Its only purpose in life is to demonstrate the errorPage attribute of the page directive, the error attribute of the page directive, and the exception implicit object; therefore it is not terribly complicated.

```jsp
<%@ page language="java" contentType="text/html; charset=UTF-8"
    pageEncoding="UTF-8" errorPage="error.jsp" %>
<!DOCTYPE html PUBLIC "-//W3C//DTD HTML 4.01 Transitional//EN"
"http://www.w3.org/TR/html4/loose.dtd">
<html>
<head>
<meta http-equiv="Content-Type" content="text/html; charset=UTF-8">
<title>Buggy JSP</title>
</head>
<body>
<p>
This text will never be seen in the browser since the exception will
be thrown before the page renders.
<%
Object o = null;
out.println(o.toString()); //NullPointerException thrown here.
%>
</p>
</body>
</html>
```

The only thing this JSP does is force a NullPointerException, which will result in GlassFish's servlet container directing the user to the page declared as the error page in the errorPage attribute of the page directive. This page is error.jsp; its markup and code is shown next:

```jsp
<%@ page language="java" contentType="text/html; charset=UTF-8"
  pageEncoding="UTF-8" isErrorPage="true"%>
<!DOCTYPE html PUBLIC "-//W3C//DTD HTML 4.01 Transitional//EN"
"http://www.w3.org/TR/html4/loose.dtd">
<%@page import="java.io.StringWriter"%>
<%@page import="java.io.PrintWriter"%>
<html>
<head>
<meta http-equiv="Content-Type" content="text/html; charset=UTF-8">
<title>There was an error in the application</title>
</head>
<body>
<h2>Exception caught</h2>
<p>Stack trace for the exception is:<br />
<%
    StringWriter stringWriter = new StringWriter();
    PrintWriter printWriter = new PrintWriter(stringWriter);
    exception.printStackTrace(printWriter);
    out.write(stringWriter.toString());
%>
</p>
</body>
</html>
```

Notice how this page declares itself to be an error page by setting the `isErrorPage` attribute of the `page` directive to true. As this page is an error page, it has access to the `exception` implicit object. This page simply calls the `printStackTrace()` method of the implicit exception object and sends its output to the browser via the `out` implicit object. In a real application, a user-friendly error message would probably be displayed.

As this application consists only of three JSPs, packaging it for deployment simply consists of putting all the JSPs in the root of the WAR file, and the `web.xml` file in its usual location (the `WEB-INF` subdirectory in the WAR file).

After deploying and pointing the browser to `http://localhost:8080/ jspimplicitobjects/implicitobjects.jsp`, we should see `implicitobjects. jsp` rendered in the browser.

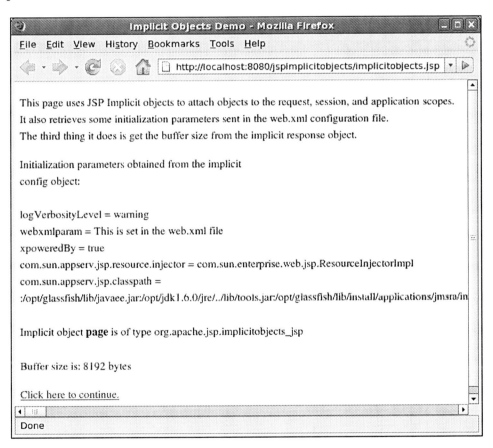

As you can see, the JSP has a number of "mysterious" initialization parameters, in addition to the one we set in the application's `web.xml` file. These additional initialization parameters are set automatically by GlassFish's web container.

Clicking on the hyperlink at the bottom of the page takes us to `implicitobjects2.jsp`.

Notice how the value for the request attribute shows up as **null**. The reason for this is that when we clicked on the hyperlink on the previous page, a new HTTP request was created, therefore any attributes attached to the previous request were lost. Had we forwarded the request to this JSP, we would have seen the expected value on the browser window.

Notice how, in addition to the attribute we attached to the application, GlassFish also attaches a number of other attributes to this implicit object.

Finally, clicking on the hyperlink at the bottom of the page takes us to the buggy JSP, which does not render; instead control is transferred to error.jsp.

Nothing surprising is displayed here; we see the exception's stack trace as expected.

JSPs and JavaBeans

It is very easy to set and retrieve JavaBean properties with JSPs. A JavaBean is a type of Java class. In order for a class to qualify as a JavaBean, it must have the following attributes:

1. It must have a public constructor taking no arguments.
2. All of its variables must be private.
3. Its variables must be accessed via getter and setter methods.

 Do not confuse JavaBeans with Enterprise JavaBeans, they are not the same thing. Enterprise JavaBeans are covered in detail in Chapter 9.

All the examples in this section will use the following JavaBean to illustrate JSP and JavaBean integration.

```
package net.ensode.glassfishbook.javabeanproperties;

public class CustomerBean
{
  public CustomerBean()
```

```
  {

  }

  String firstName;
  String lastName;

  public String getFirstName()
  {
    return firstName;
  }

  public void setFirstName(String firstName)
  {
    this.firstName = firstName;
  }

  public String getLastName()
  {
    return lastName;
  }

  public void setLastName(String lastName)
  {
    this.lastName = lastName;
  }
}
```

As you can see, the above class qualifies as a JavaBean because it meets all the requirements just listed. Notice how setter and getter method names follow naming conventions. Getter methods start with the word "get" followed by the property name, setter methods start with the word "set" followed by the property name. The only difference is that the property name is capitalized in the method names. It is important to follow these conventions for the JSP and JavaBean integration to work.

JSPs declare that they will use a JavaBean via the `<jsp:useBean>` tag. JavaBean properties are set via the `<jsp:setProperty>` tag, and retrieved via the `<jsp:getProperty>` tag.

 In JavaBean terminology, a property simply refers to one of the JavaBean's class variables.

The following example illustrates the use of these tags:

```
<%@ page language="java" contentType="text/html; charset=UTF-8"
  pageEncoding="UTF-8"%>
<jsp:useBean id="customer"
  class="net.ensode.glassfishbook.javabeanproperties.CustomerBean"
  scope="page"></jsp:useBean>
<jsp:setProperty name="customer" property="firstName" value="Albert"
/>
<jsp:setProperty name="customer" property="lastName" value="Chan" />
<!DOCTYPE html PUBLIC "-//W3C//DTD HTML 4.01 Transitional//EN"
"http://www.w3.org/TR/html4/loose.dtd">
<html>
<head>
<meta http-equiv="Content-Type" content="text/html; charset=UTF-8">
<title>JavaBean Properties</title>
</head>
<body>
<form>
<table cellpadding="0" cellspacing="0" border="0">
  <tr>
    <td align="right">First Name: </td>
    <td>
      <input type="text" name="firstName"
      value='<jsp:getProperty name="customer"
      property="firstName"/>'>
    </td>
  </tr>
  <tr>
    <td align="right">Last Name: </td>
    <td>
      <input type-"text" namc="lastName"
      value='<jsp:getProperty name="customer"
      property="lastName"/>'>
    </td>
  </tr>
  <tr>
    <td></td>
    <td><input type="submit" value="Submit"></td>
  </tr>
</table>
</form>
</body>
</html>
```

As can be seen in this example, the `<jsp:useBean>` tag is typically used with three attributes. The `id` attribute sets an identifier for the bean so that we can refer to it later. The `class` attribute specifies the fully qualified name of the bean, and the `scope` attribute specifies the scope of the bean. The bean in this example has a scope of `page`. This scope is specific to JSPs and cannot be used with servlets. Objects in this scope can only be accessed by the JSP that declares them. Other valid values for the scope attribute are `application`, `session`, and `request`. If an attribute other than `page` is specified, the JSP searches for an object attached to the specified scope with a name matching the specified ID. If it finds it, it uses it; otherwise it attaches the bean to the specified scope. If the attached object is not an instance of the expected class, a `ClassCastException` is thrown.

Bean properties can be set by using the `<jsp:setProperty>` tag. The `name` attribute of this tag identifies the bean we are setting the property for. Its value must match the value of the `id` attribute of the `<jsp:useBean>` tag. The `property` attribute value must match the name of one of the bean's properties. The `value` attribute determines the value to be assigned to the bean's property; behind the scenes, the property's setter method is called by the `<jsp:setProperty>` tag.

The `<jsp:getProperty>` tag has two attributes, a `name` attribute, and a `property` attribute. The name attribute identifies the bean we are obtaining the value from; its value must match the `id` attribute of the bean's `<jsp:useBean>` tag. The `property` attribute identifies what bean property we want; the `<jsp:getProperty>` invokes the getter method corresponding to the property specified in its property attribute.

After packaging and deploying this JSP and pointing the browser to `http://localhost:8080/javabeanproperties/beanproperties1.jsp`, we should see a page like the following:

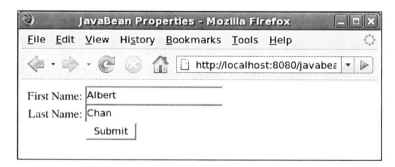

Notice how the form is pre-populated with the bean's properties, this happened because we embedded the `<jsp:getProperty>` tags inside the `value` attribute of the HTML `input` tag.

In this example, the JSP itself set the bean's properties from hard-coded values and later accessed them via the `<jsp:getProperty>` tag. More often than not, bean attributes are set from request parameters. If we take this JSP and replace the following code fragment:

```
<jsp:setProperty name="customer" property="firstName" value="Albert"
/>
<jsp:setProperty name="customer" property="lastName" value="Chan" />
```

with this one:

```
<jsp:setProperty name="customer" property="firstName"
  param="fNm" />
<jsp:setProperty name="customer" property="lastName"
  param="lNm" />
```

the JSP will populate the bean's attributes from request parameters. The only difference between the modified JSP and the original one is that the value attribute of the `<jsp:setProperty>` tag has been replaced with the `param` attribute. When the `<jsp:setProperty>` tag has a `param` attribute, it looks for a request parameter name matching its value. If it finds it, it sets the corresponding bean property to the value of the request parameter.

Redeploying the application and pointing the browser to `http://localhost:8080/javabeanproperties/beanproperties2.jsp?fNm=Albert&lNm=Chang` (assuming the modified JSP was saved as `beanproperties2.jsp`) should result in the display of a page identical to the previous screenshot.

If request parameter names match the bean property names, there is no need to explicitly set each property name to the corresponding request attribute. There is a shortcut that will set each bean attribute to its corresponding value in the request. If we modify the JSP once again, this time replacing this code fragment:

```
<jsp:setProperty name="customer" property="firstName"
  param="fNm" />
<jsp:setProperty name="customer" property="lastName"
  param="lNm" />
```

with this one:

```
<jsp:setProperty name="customer" property="*"/>
```

the `<jsp:setProperty>` tag will now look for request parameter names matching bean property names, and set the bean properties to the corresponding request parameters. Pointing the browser to `http://localhost:8080/javabeanproperties/beanproperties3.jsp?firstName=Albert&lastName=Chang` (assuming the modified JSP was saved as `beanproperties3.jsp`) we should once again see a page like the one in the previous screenshot displayed in the browser. Notice how in this case the request parameter names match the bean property names.

Even though the examples in this section dealt exclusively with `String` properties, the techniques demonstrated here work with numeric properties as well; property values from the request or in the `<jsp:setProperty>` tag are automatically converted to the appropriate type.

Reusing JSP Content

Most web applications' web pages contain certain areas that are identical across pages. For example, each page may display a company logo at the top, or a navigation menu. Copying and pasting the code to generate these common areas is not very maintainable, because if a change needs to be made to one of them, the change must be done on every page.

When using JSPs to develop a web application, it is possible to define each of these areas in a single JSP, then include this JSP as part of other JSPs. For example, we could have a JSP that renders the site's navigation menu, then have every other JSP include the navigation menu JSP to render the navigation menu. If the navigation menu needs to change, the change needs to be done only once; JSPs including the navigation menu JSP don't need to be changed.

There are two ways a JSP can be included in another JSP. It can be done via the `<jsp:include>` tag or via the `include` directive.

The following example illustrates the use of the `include` directive to include a JSP as part of a parent JSP:

```
<%@ page language="java" contentType="text/html; charset=UTF-8"
  pageEncoding="UTF-8"%>
 <%! String pageName = "Main"; %>
<!DOCTYPE html PUBLIC "-//W3C//DTD HTML 4.01 Transitional//EN"
"http://www.w3.org/TR/html4/loose.dtd">
<html>
<head>
<meta http-equiv="Content-Type" content="text/html; charset=UTF-8">
<title>Main Page</title>
</head>
<body>
<table cellpadding="0" cellspacing="0" border="1" width="100%"
height="100%">
```

```
  <tr>
    <td width="100">
      <%@ include file="navigation.jspf"%>
    </td>
    <td>This is the main page.</td>
  </tr>
</table>
</body>
</html>
```

As can be seen in the above example, the `include` directive is very straightforward to use. It takes a single attribute called `file`, the value of which is the file to include. Notice that the included file in the example has an extension of `jspf`. This is the recommended extension for JSP fragments, that is, JSPs that do not render into a proper HTML page.

Notice, near the top of the markup, the following line:

```
<%! String pageName = "Main"; %>
```

This line is a **JSP declaration**. Any variables (or methods) declared in a JSP declaration are available to the JSP declaring them and to any JSPs included via the `include` directive.

The code and markup for `navigation.jspf` is shown next.

```
<b>Application Menu</b>
<ul>
<li/> <a href="main.jsp">Main</a>
<li/> <a href="secondary.jsp">Secondary</a>
</ul>
Current page: <%= pageName %>
```

Notice how `navigation.jspf` accesses the `pageName` variable declared in the parent JSP (in order for this to work, any JSP including `navigation.jspf` must declare a variable called `pageName`).

There is a third file called `secondary.jsp`. This file is almost identical to `main.jsp` and is not shown; the only differences between `main.jsp` and `secondary.jsp` are the value of the `pageName` variable, the page title, and the text inside the second cell in the table.

After packaging and deploying this files into a WAR file and pointing the browser to `http://localhost:8080/jspcontentreuse/main.jsp`, we should see a page like this:

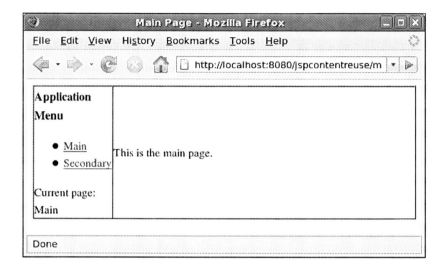

The menu at the left-hand side is rendered by `navigation.jspf`. The main area is rendered by `main.jsp`. Clicking on the hyperlink labeled **Secondary** will take us to the secondary page, which is virtually identical to the main page.

 We admit we are not using very fancy web design. The reason for this is that we want to keep the HTML as simple as possible, so that we can focus on the topic at hand.

JSP files included via a page directive are included at compile time, which is when our JSP is translated into a servlet. This is the reason included JSPs have access to variables declared in the parent JSP.

When using the `<jsp:include>` tag, the included JSP is added at run time, therefore it doesn't have access to any variable declared in the parent JSP.

The `<jsp:include>` tag has two attributes, a `page` attribute, which sets the page to include, and an optional `flush` attribute, which determines if any existing buffer should be flushed before reading in the included JSP. Valid values for the flush attribute are `true` and `false`; it defaults to `false`.

The preceding JSPs can be easily modified to use the `<jsp:include>` tag. All that needs to be done is replace the include directive with the equivalent `<jsp:include>` tag and of course, remove the JSP expression from `navigation.jspf`, as it will be included at run time and it will not have access to it.

JSP Custom Tags

JSP technology allows software developers to create custom tags. Custom tags can be used in JSP along with standard HTML tags. There are several ways of developing custom tags. In this section, we will discuss the two most popular ways, extending the `javax.servlet.jsp.tagext.SimpleTagSupport` class and creating a tag file.

Extending SimpleTagSupport

One way we can create custom JSP tags is by extending the `javax.servlet.jsp.tagext.SimpleTagSupport` class. This class provides default implementations of all methods in the `javax.servlet.jsp.tagext.SimpleTag` interface plus some methods not defined in this interface. In most cases, all that needs to be done to create a custom tag this way is override the `SimpleTagSupport.doTag()` method.

Let's illustrate this approach with an example. Most HTML forms have an embedded table containing several rows of labels and input fields. Let's create a JSP custom tag that will generate each of these rows (to keep things simple, our tag will only generate text fields):

```
package net.ensode.glassfishbook.customtags;

import java.io.IOException;
import javax.servlet.jsp.JspContext;
import javax.servlet.jsp.JspException;
import javax.servlet.jsp.JspWriter;
import javax.servlet.jsp.tagext.SimpleTagSupport;

public class LabeledTextField extends SimpleTagSupport
{
  private String label;
  private String value = "";
  private String name;

  @Override
  public void doTag() throws JspException, IOException
  {
    JspContext jspContext = getJspContext();
    JspWriter jspWriter = jspContext.getOut();

    jspWriter.print("<tr>");
    jspWriter.print("<td>");
    jspWriter.print("<b>");
    jspWriter.print(label);
    jspWriter.print("</b>");
    jspWriter.print("</td>");
```

```
      jspWriter.print("<td>");
      jspWriter.print("<input type=\"text\" name=\"");
      jspWriter.print(name);
      jspWriter.print("\" ");
      jspWriter.print("value=\"");
      jspWriter.print(value);
      jspWriter.print("\"");
      jspWriter.print("/>");
      jspWriter.print("</td>");
      jspWriter.println("</tr>");
   }

  public String getLabel()
  {
    return label;
  }

  public void setLabel(String label)
  {
    this.label = label;
  }

  public String getName()
  {
    return name;
  }

  public void setName(String name)
  {
    this.name = name;
  }

  public String getValue()
  {
    return value;
  }

  public void setValue(String value)
  {
    this.value = value;
  }
}
```

This class consists of an overriden version of the doTag() method and several attributes. Our doTag() method obtains a reference to an instance of javax.servlet.jsp.JspWriter by the getJSPContext() method. This method is defined in the tag's parent class and returns an instance of javax.servlet.jsp.JspContext. We then invoke the getOut() method of jspContext. This method returns an instance of javax.servlet.jsp.JspWriter that can be used to send output to the browser via its print() and println() methods. The rest of the doTag() method basically sends output to the browser via these two methods.

Notice how some of the calls to jspWriter.print() in the doTag() method take instance variables as their parameter. These attributes are set by the JSP containing the tag via the tag's **Tag Library Descriptor** file.

In order to be able to use custom tags in our JSPs, a Tag Library Descriptor (TLD) file must be created. The TLD tag for the above custom tag is shown next.

```xml
<taglib
  xsi:schemaLocation="http://java.sun.com/xml/ns/javaee web-jsptaglibrary_2_1.xsd"
  xmlns="http://java.sun.com/xml/ns/javaee"
  xmlns:xsi="http://www.w3.org/2001/XMLSchema-instance" version="2.1">

  <tlib-version>1.0</tlib-version>
  <uri>DemoTagLibrary</uri>

  <tag>
    <name>labeledTextField</name>
    <tag-class>
      net.ensode.glassfishbook.customtags.LabeledTextField
    </tag-class>
    <body-content>empty</body-content>
    <attribute>
      <name>label</name>
      <required>true</required>
      <rtexprvalue>true</rtexprvalue>
    </attribute>
    <attribute>
      <name>value</name>
      <rtexprvalue>true</rtexprvalue>
    </attribute>
    <attribute>
      <name>name</name>
      <required>true</required>
      <rtexprvalue>true</rtexprvalue>
    </attribute>
  </tag>
</taglib>
```

A TLD file must contain a `<tlib-version>` element, which indicates the tag library version; it must also contain a `<uri>` element. The `<uri>` element is used in the JSP containing the tag. It is used to uniquely identify the tag library. Finally, and most importantly, a TLD file must contain one or more `<tag>` elements. TLD files must be placed in the `WEB-INF` directory of the application's WAR file or one of its subdirectories. As is illustrated in the preceding example TLD file, the `<tag>` element contains several subelements:

 We are only covering the most commonly used elements of a TLD file. To see the complete list of TLD file elements, refer to the JSP 2.1 specification at `http://jcp.org/aboutJava/communityprocess/final/jsr245/index.html`.

- A `<name>` element that assigns a logical name to the custom tag
- A `<tag-class>` element that identifies the fully qualified name for the custom tag
- One or more `<attribute>` elements, which define attributes for the custom tag

The `<attribute>` element in turn can contain a number of subelements.

- A `<name>` element defining the name of the attribute. The value of this element must match the name of one of the tag's instance variables with a corresponding setter method.
- An optional `<required>` element indicating passing a value for the attribute if required. If this element is set to `true` and no value is sent to the attribute in the JSP, the page will fail to compile. The default value for this element is `false`.
- An optional `<rtexprvalue>` tag indicating if the attribute can contain a run-time expression as its value. If this element is set to `true`, then the tag will accept Unified Expression Language expressions as its value. The Unified Expression Language is discussed in detail in the next section.

Once we have the tag code and TLD, we are ready to use the tag in a JSP.

```
<%@ page language="java" contentType="text/html; charset=UTF-8"
  pageEncoding="UTF-8"%>
<%@taglib prefix="d" uri="DemoTagLibrary"%>
<!DOCTYPE html PUBLIC "-//W3C//DTD HTML 4.01 Transitional//EN"
"http://www.w3.org/TR/html4/loose.dtd">
<html>
<head>
<meta http-equiv="Content-Type" content="text/html; charset=UTF-8">
```

```
<title>Custom Tag Demo</title>
</head>
<body>
<form>
<table>
  <d:labeledTextField label="Line 1" name="line1" value="This is line
1"></d:labeledTextField>
  <d:labeledTextField label="Line 2" name="line2"></d:
labeledTextField>
  <d:labeledTextField label="City" name="city"></d:labeledTextField>
  <d:labeledTextField label="State" name="state"></d:labeledTextField>
  <d:labeledTextField label="Zip" name="zip"></d:labeledTextField>
  <tr>
    <td></td>
    <td><input type="submit" value="Submit"></td>
  </tr>
</table>
</form>
</body>
</html>
```

The above JSP uses our custom tag to generate a rudimentary address data entry form. The first thing we should notice about this JSP is the use of the `taglib` directive. This directive lets the JSP know that we will be using a custom tag library. The `uri` attribute of the `taglib` directive must match the value of the `<uri>` element in the tag library's TLD file. The value of the `prefix` attribute of the `taglib` is prepended before the name of any custom tag from the library we use. In the above example, all `<d:labeledField>` attributes are uses of the custom tag we have developed. The `d` before the `:` in each of those tags corresponds to the value of the prefix attribute.

The next thing that should catch our eye in the above example is the usage of the custom tag itself. Notice how every time we use the custom tag, we set a value for its `label` and `name` attributes. We must do this because these attributes were declared as `required` in the tag's TLD file. Only once did we set the value of the tag's `value` attribute; this is OK as this tag was not declared as required. The values we set for the tag's attributes are automatically used to set the values of the tag's Java class instance variables. The name of the attribute matches the corresponding instance variable. Behind the scenes, the tag's class setter method for the appropriate instance variable is called.

After we package and deploy the JSP, custom tag code, and TLD file in a WAR file and deploy it, we should see the JSP render in the browser as displayed in the following screenshot:

Notice how only the first text field has been prepopulated. This is because it was the only one we set the `value` attribute for.

If we look at the generated HTML markup from our JSP, we can see the markup that was actually generated from our custom tag.

```
<table>
  <tr><td><b>Line 1</b></td><td><input type="text" name="line1"
value="This is line 1"/></td></tr>

  <tr><td><b>Line 2</b></td><td><input type="text" name="line2"
value=""/></td></tr>

  <tr><td><b>City</b></td><td><input type="text" name="city"
value=""/></td></tr>

  <tr><td><b>State</b></td><td><input type="text" name="state"
value=""/></td></tr>

  <tr><td><b>Zip</b></td><td><input type="text" name="zip"
value=""/></td></tr>

  <tr>
    <td></td>

    <td><input type="submit" value="Submit"></td>
  </tr>
</table>
```

For simplicity and brevity, only a portion of the generated markup is shown. All highlighted lines were generated by the custom tag.

Using Tag Files to Create Custom JSP Tags

As was shown in the previous section, creating a custom tag by extending the `SimpleTagSupport` class involves writing some Java code to generate HTML markup; code to accomplish this is usually hard to write and hard to read. An alternative way of creating custom JSP tags is by using tag files. This alternative method does not involve writing any Java code.

A tag file is very similar to a JSP. Tag filenames must end with a `.tag` extension and tag files must be placed in a subdirectory called `tags` under the WAR file's `WEB-INF` directory. The following tag file generates a complete (and less rudimentary) address input field.

```
<%@ tag language="java"%>
<%@attribute name="addressType" required="true"%>
<jsp:useBean id="address" scope="request"
  class="net.ensode.glassfishbook.customtags.AddressBean" />
<table cellpadding="0" cellspacing="0" border="0">
  <tr>
    <td align="right" width="70"><b>Line 1</b> </td>
    <td><input type="text" name="${addressType}_line1" size="30"
      maxlength="100" value="${address.line1}"></td>
  </tr>
  <tr>
    <td align="right"><b>Line 2</b> </td>
    <td><input type="text" name="${addressType}_line2" size="30"
      maxlength="100" value="${address.line2}"></td>
  </tr>
  <tr>
    <td align="right"><b>City</b> </td>
    <td><input type="text" name="${addressType}_city" size="30"
      value="${address.city}"></td>
  </tr>
  <tr>
    <td align="right"><b>State</b> </td>
    <td><select name="${addressType}_state">
      <option value=""></option>
      <option value="AL"
        <% if(address.getState().equals("AL")) out.print (" selected
"); %>>Alabama</option>
      <option value="AK"
        <% if(address.getState().equals("AK")) out.print (" selected
"); %>>Alaska</option>
```

```
            <option value="AZ"
                <% if(address.getState().equals("AZ")) out.print (" selected
");  %>>Arizona</option>
            <option value="AR"
                <% if(address.getState().equals("AR")) out.print (" selected
");  %>>Arkansas</option>
            <option value="CA"
                <% if(address.getState().equals("CA")) out.print (" selected
");  %>>California</option>
            <option value="CO"
                <% if(address.getState().equals("CO")) out.print (" selected
");  %>>Colorado</option>
            <option value="CT"
                <% if(address.getState().equals("CT")) out.print (" selected
");  %>>Conneticut</option>
            <option value="DC"
                <% if(address.getState().equals("DC")) out.print (" selected
");  %>>District
        of Columbia</option>
            <option value="FL"
                <% if(address.getState().equals("FL")) out.print (" selected
");  %>>Florida</option>
          </select></td>
      </tr>
      <tr>
        <td align="right"><b>Zip</b> </td>
        <td><input type="text" name="${addressType}_zip" size="5"
          value="${address.zip}"></td>
      </tr>
    </table>
```

As can be seen in the example, a tag file is very similar to a JSP file. Just like a JSP, it can contain scriptlets and set and get JavaBean properties. One difference between tag files and JSPs is that tag files use a `tag` directive instead of the `page` directive. The most commonly used attribute of the `tag` directive is the `import` attribute, which, just like in the JSP `page` directive, is used to import individual classes or packages to be used in the tag file.

Tag files can have an `attribute` directive, which generates an attribute that can be set by the parent JSP file. The above example creates a required attribute called `addressType`.

Notice that the value for the `name` attribute of each input field in the example tag file contains text like the following: `${addressType}_line1`. The first part of this string (`${addressType}`) is a special notation to obtain the value of the `addressType` attribute. This notation can also be used to obtain values of JavaBean properties; the syntax to obtain JavaBean properties using this notation is `${<bean name>.<property name>}`. The `value` attribute of each `input` field in the example uses this notation to obtain the value of a property of the address bean. The address bean is a simple JavaBean declaring several attributes along with their corresponding setter and getter methods.

> The ${} notation is part of the Unified Expression Language, a new expression language for the JSP 2.1 specification. This notation is compatible with the JSP expression language introduced in JSP 2.0. However, the Unified Expression Language also supports the #{} notation; this new notation is not compatible with previous versions of the JSP specification. The #{} notation will be covered in detail in Chapter 6.

As can be seen in the example, tag files can contain scriptlets. The scriptlets in the example compare the value of the state attribute in the state bean to each option in the select element, then set the appropriate element to be selected (for simplicity and brevity, only a small subset of all states was used).

Using a custom tag defined in a tag file is almost identical to using a tag defined using Java code:

```
<%@ page language="java" contentType="text/html; charset=UTF-8"
    pageEncoding="UTF-8"%>
<%@ taglib prefix="ct" tagdir="/WEB-INF/tags"%>
<!DOCTYPE html PUBLIC "-//W3C//DTD HTML 4.01 Transitional//EN"
"http://www.w3.org/TR/html4/loose.dtd">
<html>
<head>
<meta http-equiv="Content-Type" content="text/html; charset=UTF-8">
<title>Custom Tag Demo</title>
</head>
<body>
<form>
<h3>Shipping Address</h3>
<ct:address addressType="shipping" />
</body>
</html>
```

Notice how the `taglib` directive is used to import the tag library into the JSP, but in this case, instead of using a `uri` attribute, a `tagdir` attribute is used to indicate the location of the tag library. All tag files in the same directory are implicitly part of a tag library; no TLD file is necessary. However, it is possible to add a TLD for a tag library composed of tag files. The TLD for such a tag library must be named `implicit.tld` and it must be placed in the same directory as the tag files (`WEB-INF/tags` in the preceding example; tag libraries must be placed in this directory or any subdirectory of the `tags` directory).

In order for this JSP to work properly, an instance of `net.ensode.glassfishbook.customtags.AddressBean` must be attached to the request. The following servlet will create an instance of this class, populate some of its fields, and forward the request to the JSP.

```java
package net.ensode.glassfishbook.customtags;

import java.io.IOException;
import java.io.PrintWriter;

import javax.servlet.ServletException;
import javax.servlet.http.HttpServlet;
import javax.servlet.http.HttpServletRequest;
import javax.servlet.http.HttpServletResponse;

public class CustomTagDemoServlet extends HttpServlet
{
  @Override
  protected void doGet(HttpServletRequest request, HttpServletResponse
response)
  {
    AddressBean addressBean = new AddressBean();

    addressBean.setLine1("43623 Park Ridge Ct");
    addressBean.setCity("Orlando");
    addressBean.setState("FL");
    addressBean.setZip("00303");

    request.setAttribute("address", addressBean);

    try
    {
      request.getRequestDispatcher(
          "customtagdemo2.jsp").forward(request,response);
    }
    catch (ServletException e)
    {
      e.printStackTrace();
```

```
    }
    catch (IOException e)
    {
      e.printStackTrace();
    }
  }
}
```

Of course, a real application would probably obtain this information from a database. This simple example just instantiates the bean and populates it with some arbitrary attributes.

After packaging the above JSP and tag file in a WAR file, deploying the WAR file, and pointing the browser to the servlet's URL (as defined in the `<servlet-mapping>` element of the application's `web.xml` file), we should see a page like the following:

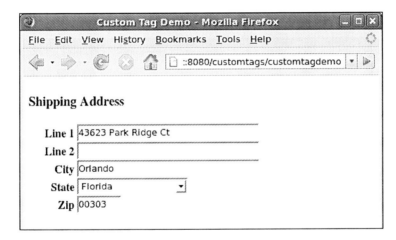

Unified Expression Language

In the previous section, we saw how the Unified Expression Language can be used to retrieve property values from JavaBeans. When JavaBeans' properties are accessed this way, GlassFish's web container looks for a JavaBean attached with the given name to the page , request, session, and application scopes, in that order. It uses the first one found invoke the getter method corresponding to the property we want to obtain.

If we know to what scope the bean we want is attached, we can obtain it from that scope directly as JSP expressions have access to the JSP implicit objects. In next example, we attach several instances of a JavaBean called `CustomerBean` to the different scopes. Before illustrating the JSP, let's take a look at the source code for this bean:

```
package net.ensode.glassfishbook.unifiedexprlang;

public class CustomerBean
{

  public CustomerBean()
  {

  }

  public CustomerBean(String firstName, String lastName)
  {
    this.firstName = firstName;
    this.lastName = lastName;
  }

  private String firstName;
  private String lastName;

  public String getFirstName()
  {
    return firstName;
  }

  public void setFirstName(String firstName)
  {
    this.firstName = firstName;
  }

  public String getLastName()
  {
    return lastName;
  }

  public void setLastName(String lastName)
  {
    this.lastName = lastName;
  }

  @Override
  public String toString()
  {
    StringBuffer fullNameBuffer = new StringBuffer();

    fullNameBuffer.append(firstName);
    fullNameBuffer.append(" ");
    fullNameBuffer.append(lastName);

    return fullNameBuffer.toString();
  }

}
```

This is a fairly simple JavaBean consisting of two properties and their corresponding setter and getter methods. In order for this class to qualify as a JavaBean, it must have a public constructor that takes no arguments. In addition to that constructor, we added a convenience constructor that takes two parameters to initialize the bean's properties. Additionally, the class overrides the `toString()` method so that its output is the customer's first and last names.

As we mentioned before, the following JSP obtains instances of `CustomerBean` from the different scopes through the Unified Expression Language and outputs the corresponding output to the browser window.

 Before this JSP is executed, all instances of `CustomerBean` must be attached to the corresponding scope. We wrote a servlet that does this and then forwards the request to the JSP. For brevity, this servlet is not shown but it is available as part of this book's code download.

```
<%@ page language="java" contentType="text/html; charset=UTF-8"
        pageEncoding="UTF-8"%>

<jsp:useBean scope="page" id="customer6"

class="net.ensode.glassfishbook.unifiedexprlang.CustomerBean" />

<jsp:setProperty name="customer6" property="firstName" value="David"
/>
<jsp:setProperty name="customer6" property="lastName"
        value="Heffelfinger" />

<!DOCTYPE html PUBLIC "-//W3C//DTD HTML 4.01 Transitional//EN"
"http://www.w3.org/TR/html4/loose.dtd">
<html>
<head>
<meta http-equiv="Content-Type" content="text/html; charset=UTF-8">
<title>Unified Expression Language Demo</title>
</head>
<body>
Customer attached to the application Scope:
${applicationScope.customer1}
<br />
<br />
Customer attached to the session scope:
${sessionScope.customer2.firstName} ${sessionScope.customer2.lastName}
<br />
<br />
Customer attached to the request scope:
${requestScope.customer3}
```

```
<br />
<br />
Customer attached to the page scope:
${pageScope.customer6}
<br />
<br />

List of customers attached to the session:
<br />
${sessionScope.customerList[0]}
<br />
${sessionScope.customerList[1].firstName}
${sessionScope.customerList[1].lastName}
<br />
<br />
</body>
</html>
```

The first highlighted line in this JSP looks for a bean attached to the application scope and with a name of customer1. As we aren't referencing any of the bean's properties, the bean's toString() method is invoked at that point.

The next two highlighted expressions look for a bean attached to the session scope with a name of customer2. In this case, we are accessing individual properties; the first expression accesses the firstName property, the second expression accesses the lastName property. Behind the scenes, Glassfish's web container invokes the corresponding getter method for each property.

The next two highlighted lines obtain instances of CustomerBean from the request and page scopes, respectively. Again as we aren't accessing individual properties, the bean's toString() method is invoked.

The last three highlighted lines illustrate a very nice feature of the Unified Expression Language. In this case, instances of CustomerBean were not attached to the session directly. Instead, an ArrayList containing instances of CustomerBean was attached to the session. This ArrayList was attached with a name of customerList. As can be seen in these three lines, we can access individual elements of the ArrayList by placing the element number in brackets, similar to what we would do with an array in regular Java code. This technique, by the way, also works with arrays, as well as any other class implementing the java.util.Collection interface.

After packaging this JSP into a WAR file, deploying it, and pointing the browser to the appropriate URL, we should see it rendered in the browser.

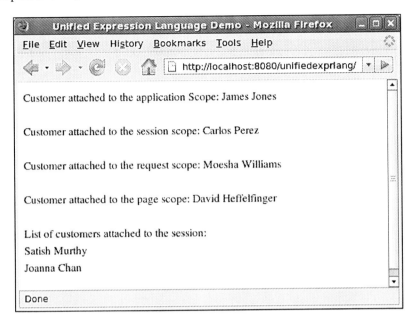

In this particular case, the `toString()` method outputs the customer's first and last names. Therefore the output is indistinguishable from displaying these two properties next to each other.

Of course, the techniques shown in the example work on every scope. We can access a bean attached to any scope by not specifying any properties. Similarly, we can access bean properties on any scope and, of course, we can access individual elements of a collection or array attached to any scope.

Summary

This chapter covered a lot of ground. We talked about how to develop and deploy simple JSPs. We also covered how to access implicit objects like `request`, `session`, etc. from JSPs. Additionally, we covered how to set and get the values of JavaBean properties via the `<jsp:useBean>` tag. In addition to that, we covered how to include a JSP into another JSP at run time via the `<jsp:include>` tag, and at compilation time via the JSP `include` directive. We also covered how to write custom JSP tags by extending `javax.servlet.jsp.tagext.SimpleTagSupport` or by writing tag files. Finally, we covered how to access JavaBeans and their properties via the Unified Expression Language.

4
Database Connectivity

Any non-trivial Java EE application will persist data to a relational database. In this chapter, we will cover how to connect to a database and perform CRUD operations (Create, Read, Update, Delete). There are two ways a Java EE application can interact with a relational database: through the Java Database Connectivity (JDBC) API or through the Java Persistence API (JPA). Both of these approaches will be discussed in this chapter.

The topics covered in this chapter include:

- Retrieving data from a database through JDBC
- Inserting data into a database through JDBC
- Updating data in a database through JDBC
- Deleting data in a database through JDBC
- Retrieving data from a database through JPA
- Inserting data into a database through JPA
- Updating data in a database through JPA
- Deleting data in a database through JPA

The CustomerDB Database

Examples in this chapter will use a database called CUSTOMERDB. This database contains tables to track customer and order information for a fictitious store. The database uses JavaDB for its RDBMS, as it comes bundled with GlassFish.

A script is included with this book's code download to create this database and pre-populate some of its tables. Instructions on how to execute the script and add a connection pool and datasource to access it are included in the download as well.

The schema for the CUSTOMERDB database is depicted in the following diagram.

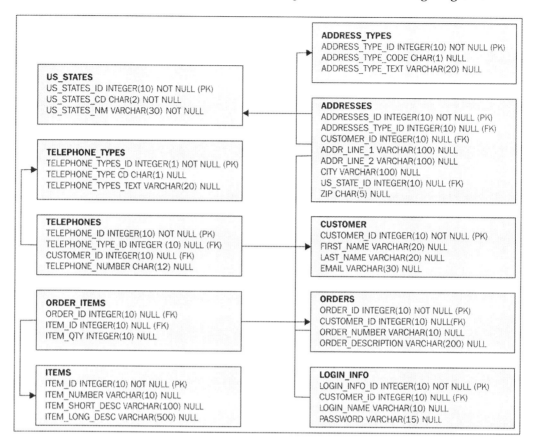

As can be seen in the diagram, the table contains tables to store customer information like name, address, and email address. It also contains tables to store order and item information.

The ADDRESS_TYPES table will store values like "Home", "Mailing", and "Shipping", to distinguish the type of address in the ADDRESSES table, similarly, the TELEPHONE_TYPES table stores the values "Cell", "Home", and "Work". These two tables are pre-populated when creating the database, as well as the US_STATES table.

 For simplicity's sake, our database only deals with U.S. Addresses.

JDBC

The Java Database Connectivity (JDBC) API is the standard API used for Java applications to interact with a database. Although JDBC is not part of the Java EE specification, it is used very frequently in Java EE applications.

JDBC allows us to send queries to a database to do selects, inserts, updates, and deletes. The most common way of interacting with a database through JDBC is through the `java.sql.PreparedStatement` interface. Using prepared statements through this interface offers a number of benefits over using standard JDBC statement objects. Some of the benefits of prepared statements are:

- Prepared statements are compiled into the RDBMS the first time they are executed, therefore increasing subsequent performance.
- Prepared statements are immune to SQL injection attacks.
- Prepared statements free us from explicitly having to add single quotes (') to our SQL statements to handle character values.

The `java.sql.PreparedStatement` interface has two methods that are very frequently used to send queries to the database. These two methods are `executeQuery()` and `executeUpdate()`. The `executeQuery()` method is used to issue `select` statements to the database and returns an instance of `java.sql.ResultSet` containing the rows returned from the query. The `executeUpdate()` method is used to issue `insert`, `update`, and `delete` statements to the database; it returns an `int` value corresponding to the number of rows affected by the query. In the following sections, we illustrate database interaction through the above two methods.

Retrieving Data from a Database

As we mentioned in the previous section, the `executeQuery()` method of the `java.sql.PreparedStatement` interface is used to send `select` statements to the database and retrieve data from it. The following example code illustrates this process.

```
package net.ensode.glassfishbook.jdbcselect;

import java.io.IOException;
import java.sql.Connection;
import java.sql.PreparedStatement;
import java.sql.ResultSet;
import java.sql.SQLException;
import java.util.ArrayList;

import javax.naming.InitialContext;
import javax.naming.NamingException;
```

```
import javax.servlet.ServletException;
import javax.servlet.http.HttpServlet;
import javax.servlet.http.HttpServletRequest;
import javax.servlet.http.HttpServletResponse;
import javax.sql.DataSource;
public class JDBCSelectServlet extends HttpServlet
{
  @Override
  protected void doGet(HttpServletRequest request,
                       HttpServletResponse response) throws
                       ServletException, IOException
  {
    String sql = "select us_state_nm, " +
        "us_state_cd from us_states order by us_state_nm";
    ArrayList<UsStateBean> stateList =
        new ArrayList<UsStateBean>();
    try
    {
      InitialContext initialContext = new InitialContext();
      DataSource dataSource = (DataSource) initialContext
          .lookup("jdbc/__CustomerDBPool");
      Connection connection = dataSource.getConnection();
      PreparedStatement preparedStatement =
          connection.prepareStatement(sql);
      ResultSet resultSet = preparedStatement.executeQuery();
      while (resultSet.next())
      {
        stateList.add(new
            UsStateBean(resultSet.getString("us_state_nm"),
            resultSet.getString("us_state_cd")));
      }

      resultSet.close();
      preparedStatement.close();
      connection.close();

      request.setAttribute("stateList", stateList);

      request.getRequestDispatcher("us_states.jsp").
          forward(request, response);
    }
    catch (NamingException namingException)
```

```
      {
        namingException.printStackTrace();
      }
      catch (SQLException sqlException)
      {
        sqlException.printStackTrace();
      }
    }
  }
```

In this servlet, we create a `String` containing the `select` statement we will be sending to the database.

We then create an instance of `javax.naming.InitialContext`; this instance is then used in a JNDI (Java Naming and Directory Interface) lookup for the `javax.sql.DataSource` corresponding to the database we wish to connect to. This is accomplished by calling the `InitialContext.lookup()` method; the String argument to this method must match the name of the datasource we set up in GlassFish (refer to Chapter 1). This method returns an instance of `java.lang.Object`; its return value must be cast to the appropriate type (`javax.sql.DataSource`, in this case).

Once we obtain a reference to the `DataSource` object by performing a JNDI lookup, we can obtain a connection from the connection pool by invoking the `getConnection()` method defined in the `javax.sql.DataSource` interface. This method returns an instance of `java.sql.Connection`.

Once we get a connection from a connection pool, we obtain an instance of a class implementing the `java.sql.PreparedStatement` interface by invoking the `prepareStatement()` method on the instance of `java.util.Connection` that we obtained in the previous step. The `preparedStatement()` method takes a String containing the SQL query as its sole argument.

Once we get an instance of a class implementing `java.sql.PreparedStatement`, we can finally query the database by invoking its `executeQuery()` method. The `PreparedStatement.executeQuery()` method returns an instance of a class implementing the `java.sql.ResultSet` interface; this instance contains the results of our query.

The servlet then iterates through the result set and populates an `ArrayList` with instances of a JavaBean of type `net.ensode.glassfishbook.jdbcselect.UsStateBean`.

Finally, we close the result set and the prepared statement by invoking their `close()` methods, and the connection is released back to the connection pool by calling the `close()` method in the `java.sql.Connection` instance that we were using.

Calling the `close()` method in the connection does not actually close the collection; it is released back to the connection pool so that other applications can use it.

The previously populated `ArrayList` is then attached to the request and the request is forwarded to a JSP called `us_states.jsp`.

 For brevity the sources for `UsStateBean.java` and `us_states.jsp` are not shown as these files don't illustrate anything we haven't seen before; both files are part of this book's code download.

After packaging the code in a WAR file, deploying, and pointing the browser to the appropriate URL, we should see the following page rendered in the browser:

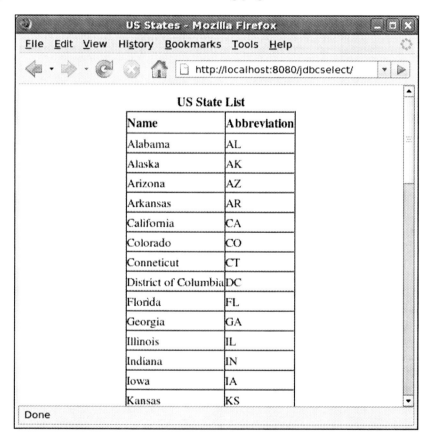

All the U.S. state data displayed in the page were retrieved from the database.

As can be seen in the example, the ResultSet interface has a next() method. This method returns a Boolean indicating if the result set has more rows. An instance of a class implementing ResultSet has a cursor pointing to the current row. Before any calls to the next() method, the cursor is positioned before the first row. When the next() method is called the first time, the cursor points to the first row in the result set. Subsequent calls to the next() method move the cursor to the next row. When the cursor is pointing to the last row in the ResultSet, a call to next() will return false, indicating that there are no more rows in the ResultSet.

The ResultSet.next() method is commonly used as the condition in a while loop. The loop will execute until this method returns false. Inside the loop operations can be done on the current row in the result set. The example uses this technique to populate a simple JavaBean with the values for the current row. As can be seen in the code, the ResultSet interface contains a method called getString(). The getString() method returns the value of the column indicated by it's sole parameter, which is a String corresponding to the column we would like to obtain the value for.

In addition to the getString() method, the ResultSet interface contains a series of methods for obtaining other types of data. The following table illustrates the most commonly used ones (for the complete list, refer to the JavaDoc documentation for the ResultSet interface at http://java.sun.com/javase/6/docs/api/index.html).

Method Name	Return Type
getBoolean()	boolean
getDate()	java.sql.Date
getDouble()	double
getFloat()	float
getInt()	int
getLong()	long
getShort()	short
getString()	java.lang.String
getTime()	java.sql.Time
getTimeStamp()	java.sql.Timestamp

There are two overloaded versions of each of the methods listed in the table. One version takes a String indicating the column name as a parameter; the other version takes an int indicating the position of the column in the query. For example, in the following query:

```
select column1, column2, column3 from table
```

The column called `column1` has a position of 1, `column2` has a position of 2, and `column3` has a position of 3. Using the version of this methods taking an int usually results in code that is harder to read and understand than using the version taking a String, therefore its usage is discouraged.

The `PreparedStatement` instance, obtained by calling `Connection.prepareStatement()`, contains not just an SQL statement but a precompiled SQL statement. An SQL statement is given to the `PreparedStatement` instance and this SQL statement is sent to the RDBMS for compilation. This means that when the `PreparedStatement` is executed, the RDBMS can run the `PreparedStatement` SQL statement without compiling it and the subsequent calls for execution are faster. Although this is nice for static queries like the one in this example, where it really shines is when queries are created dynamically by passing parameters to them. The following example is a modified version of the earlier servlet illustrating this concept:

```
package net.ensode.glassfishbook.jdbcselect;

import java.io.IOException;
import java.sql.Connection;
import java.sql.PreparedStatement;
import java.sql.ResultSet;
import java.sql.SQLException;
import java.util.ArrayList;

import javax.annotation.Resource;
import javax.servlet.ServletException;
import javax.servlet.http.HttpServlet;
import javax.servlet.http.HttpServletRequest;
import javax.servlet.http.HttpServletResponse;
public class JDBCSelectServlet2 extends HttpServlet
{
  @Resource(name = "jdbc/__CustomerDBPool")
  private javax.sql.DataSource dataSource;

  @Override
  protected void doGet(HttpServletRequest request, HttpServletResponse
  response)throws ServletException, IOException
  {
    String sql = "select us_state_nm, us_state_cd " +
        "from us_states where us_state_nm like ? " +
        "or us_state_nm like ? order by us_state_nm";
    ArrayList<UsStateBean> stateList =
        new ArrayList<UsStateBean>();
    try
    {
      Connection connection = dataSource.getConnection();
```

```
PreparedStatement preparedStatement =
    connection.prepareStatement(sql);
preparedStatement.setString(1, "North%");
preparedStatement.setString(2, "South%");
ResultSet resultSet = preparedStatement.executeQuery();
response.setContentType("text/html");
while (resultSet.next())
{
  stateList.add(new
      UsStateBean(resultSet.getString("us_state_nm"),
      resultSet.getString("us_state_cd")));
}
resultSet.close();
preparedStatement.close();
connection.close();
request.setAttribute("stateList", stateList);
request.getRequestDispatcher("
    us_states.jsp").forward(request, response);
}
catch (SQLException sqlException)
{
  sqlException.printStackTrace();
}
}
}
```

In this version of the servlet, we modified the SQL query to limit the result set according to some parameters. Notice the question marks in the SQL statement. These question marks are placeholders for query parameters and are not actually sent to the database.

In the above example, the setString() method of the PreparedStatement interface is used to substitute the query parameters with the actual values that will be sent to the database. This method takes two arguments; the first one is the parameter index for the substitution; the second one is the value to use as a substitute. After replacing the parameters with the values, the query in the above code will retrieve data for all states whose names start with the word "North" or start with the word "South".

 Notice that, unlike with arrays or collections, the index of the first parameter is 1, not 0.

After compiling the code, packaging in a WAR file, and deploying it, and pointing the browser to its URL, we should see a page displaying the following table in the browser:

US State List	
Name	**Abbreviation**
North Carolina	NC
North Dakota	ND
South Carolina	SC
South Carolina	SC
South Dakota	SD

In addition to the `setString()` method, the `PreparedStatement` interface contains many similar methods that allow us to set parameters of different types. The following table illustrates the most commonly used ones (for the complete list, refer to the JavaDoc documentation for the `PreparedStatement` interface at `http://java.sun.com/javase/6/docs/api/index.html`)

PreparedStatement Method Name
setBoolean(int parameterIndex, boolean b)
setDate(int parameterIndex, java.sql.Date d)
setDouble(int parameterIndex, double d)
setFloat(int parameterIndex, float f)
setInt(int parameterIndex, int i)
setLong(int parameterIndex, long l)
setShort(int parameterIndex, short s)
setString(int parameterIndex, String s)
setTime(int parameterIndex, java.sql.Time t)
setTimeStamp(int parameterIndex, java.sql.TimeStamp t)

In all of the above methods, the first argument defines the parameter index (starting with 1) and the second argument contains the value for the parameter.

In addition to modifying the query to accept parameters, we made an additional, unrelated change to the servlet. Instead of creating an instance of `javax.naming.InitialContext` and performing a JNDI lookup to obtain a reference to the `DataSource`, we used **dependency injection** to obtain this instance.

Dependency Injection is a design pattern in which an object's dependencies are injected at run time by a container. This design pattern was made popular in the Java world by the Spring framework. Java EE 5 uses the @Resource annotation to implement the pattern.

We accomplished this by moving the declaration of the dataSource object out of the doGet() method and making it a field. We then decorated it with the @Resource annotation. The @Resource annotation has an element called name; this element is used to indicate the JNDI name of the resource we want to obtain.

The @Resource annotation can be used to look up any kind of resources available through JNDI, not only DataSources.

Dependency injection is a new feature of Java EE 5, therefore applications taking advantage of this new feature cannot be deployed in application servers that don't support this version of the specification.

Modifying Database Data

In the previous section, we saw how we can use the executeQuery() method of the java.sql.PreparedStatement interface to read data from the database. In this section, we will see how we can use the executeUpdate() method of this interface to insert, update, or delete data in the database. The executeUpdate() method is illustrated in the following example:

```
package net.ensode.glassfishbook.jdbcupdate;

import java.io.IOException;
import java.sql.Connection;
import java.sql.PreparedStatement;
import java.sql.SQLException;

import javax.annotation.Resource;
import javax.servlet.ServletException;
import javax.servlet.http.HttpServlet;
import javax.servlet.http.HttpServletRequest;
import javax.servlet.http.HttpServletResponse;
import javax.sql.DataSource;
public class JdbcUpdateServlet extends HttpServlet
{
  @Resource(name = "jdbc/__CustomerDBPool")
  private DataSource dataSource;

  @Override
  protected void doGet(HttpServletRequest request,
```

```
      HttpServletResponse response)
      throws ServletException, IOException
{
  String insertCustomerSql = "insert into " +
      "customers  (customer_id, first_name, " +
      "last_name, email) values (?,?,?,?)";
  String updateCustomerLastNameSql = "update customers " +
      "set last_name = ? where customer_id = ?";
  String deleteCustomerSql = "delete from customers " +
      "where customer_id = ?";
  PreparedStatement insertCustomerStatement;
  PreparedStatement updateCustomerLastNameStatement;
  PreparedStatement deleteCustomerStatement;
  try
  {
    Connection connection = dataSource.getConnection();
    insertCustomerStatement = connection
        .prepareStatement(insertCustomerSql);
    updateCustomerLastNameStatement = connection
        .prepareStatement(updateCustomerLastNameSql);
    deleteCustomerStatement =
        connection.prepareStatement(deleteCustomerSql);
    insertCustomerStatement.setInt(1, 1);
    insertCustomerStatement.setString(2, "Leo");
    insertCustomerStatement.setString(3, "Smith");
    insertCustomerStatement.setString(4, "lsmith@fake.com");
    insertCustomerStatement.executeUpdate();

    insertCustomerStatement.setInt(1, 2);
    insertCustomerStatement.setString(2, "Jane");
    insertCustomerStatement.setString(3, "Davis");
    insertCustomerStatement.setString(4, null);
    insertCustomerStatement.executeUpdate();

    updateCustomerLastNameStatement.setString(1, "Jones");
    updateCustomerLastNameStatement.setInt(2, 2);
    updateCustomerLastNameStatement.executeUpdate();

    deleteCustomerStatement.setInt(1, 1);
    deleteCustomerStatement.executeUpdate();

    deleteCustomerStatement.close();
    updateCustomerLastNameStatement.close();
    insertCustomerStatement.close();
```

```
      connection.close();
      response.getWriter().println("Database Updated Successfully");
    }
    catch (SQLException e)
    {
      e.printStackTrace();
    }
  }
}
```

In this servlet, all SQL statements modify data in the database. Just as in the previous example, we obtain a reference to the data source by using dependency injection. We then obtain a connection from the connection pool by calling the `getConnection()` method defined in the `javax.sql.DataSource` interface.

We then obtain an instance of a class implementing the `javax.sql.PreparedStatement` interface for each SQL statement. We do this by calling the `prepareStatement()` method defined in the `java.sql.Connection` interface.

Just as before, we set the values for each parameter by calling the appropriate methods defined in the `PreparedStatement` interface (`setInt()` and `setString()` in the example). After each parameter is set, we call the `executeUpdate()` method. At this point, the statement is actually executed in the database.

After performing all four updates to the database, the servlet simply prints the message "Database Updated Successfully" in the browser.

The Java Persistence API

The Java Persistence API (JPA) is a new addition to Java EE. As its name implies, it is used to persist data to a Relational Database Management System. JPA replaces Entity Beans in Java EE 5 (of course, for backwards compatibility, Entity Beans are still supported). Java EE 5 Entities are regular Java classes; the Java EE container knows these classes are Entities because they are decorated with the `@Entity` annotation. Let's look at an Entity mapping to the CUSTOMER table in the CUSTOMERDB database.

```
package net.ensode.glassfishbook.jpa;

import java.io.Serializable;

import javax.persistence.Column;
import javax.persistence.Entity;
import javax.persistence.Id;
import javax.persistence.Table;

@Entity
```

```
@Table(name = "CUSTOMERS")
public class Customer implements Serializable
{
  @Id
  @Column(name = "CUSTOMER_ID")
  private Long customerId;

  @Column(name = "FIRST_NAME")
  private String firstName;

  @Column(name = "LAST_NAME")
  private String lastName;

  private String email;

  public Long getCustomerId()
  {
    return customerId;
  }
  public void setCustomerId(Long customerId)
  {
    this.customerId = customerId;
  }
  public String getEmail()
  {
    return email;
  }
  public void setEmail(String email)
  {
    this.email = email;
  }
  public String getFirstName()
  {
    return firstName;
  }
  public void setFirstName(String firstName)
  {
    this.firstName = firstName;
  }
  public String getLastName()
  {
    return lastName;
  }
  public void setLastName(String lastName)
  {
    this.lastName = lastName;
  }
}
```

In this code, the `@Entity` annotation lets GlassFish (or any other Java EE 5-compliant application server, for that matter) know that this class is an entity.

The `@Table(name = "CUSTOMERS")` annotation lets the application server know what table to map the entity to. The value of the `name` element contains the name of the database table that the entity maps to. This annotation is optional; if the name of the class maps the name of the database table, then it isn't necessary to specify what table the entity maps to.

The `@Id` annotation indicates that the `customerId` field maps to the primary key.

The `@Column` annotation maps each field to a column in the table. If the name of the field matches the name of the database column, then this annotation is not needed. This is the reason why the `email` field is not annotated.

That is pretty much all we need to do to create a Java EE 5 Entity. Compare this to Entity Beans, where the bean had to implement a number of life-cycle methods that were rarely used; we also had to write a local and/or remote interface, a local and/or remote home interface, plus a deployment descriptor in order to develop a single entity bean.

The `EntityManager` class is used to persist Entities to a database. The following example illustrates its usage:

```
package net.ensode.glassfishbook.jpa;

import java.io.IOException;

import javax.annotation.Resource;
import javax.persistence.EntityManager;
import javax.persistence.EntityManagerFactory;
import javax.persistence.PersistenceUnit;
import javax.servlet.ServletException;
import javax.servlet.http.HttpServlet;
import javax.servlet.http.HttpServletRequest;
import javax.servlet.http.HttpServletResponse;
import javax.transaction.HeuristicMixedException;
import javax.transaction.HeuristicRollbackException;
import javax.transaction.NotSupportedException;
import javax.transaction.RollbackException;
import javax.transaction.SystemException;
import javax.transaction.UserTransaction;

public class JpaDemoServlet extends HttpServlet
{
  @PersistenceUnit
  private EntityManagerFactory entityManagerFactory;
```

```
@Resource
private UserTransaction userTransaction;

@Override
protected void doGet(HttpServletRequest request,
    HttpServletResponse response)
    throws ServletException, IOException
{
  EntityManager entityManager =
      entityManagerFactory.createEntityManager();

  Customer customer = new Customer();
  Customer customer2 = new Customer();
  Customer customer3;

  customer.setCustomerId(3L);
  customer.setFirstName("James");
  customer.setLastName("McKenzie");
  customer.setEmail("jamesm@notreal.com");

  customer2.setCustomerId(4L);
  customer2.setFirstName("Charles");
  customer2.setLastName("Jonson");
  customer2.setEmail("cjohnson@phony.org");

  try
  {
    userTransaction.begin();
    entityManager.persist(customer);
    entityManager.persist(customer2);

    customer3 = entityManager.find(Customer.class, 4L);
    customer3.setLastName("Johnson");
    entityManager.persist(customer3);

    entityManager.remove(customer);

    userTransaction.commit();
  }
  catch (NotSupportedException e)
  {
    e.printStackTrace();
  }
  catch (SystemException e)
  {
    e.printStackTrace();
  }
  catch (SecurityException e)
  {
    e.printStackTrace();
```

```
    }
    catch (IllegalStateException e)
    {
      e.printStackTrace();
    }
    catch (RollbackException e)
    {
      e.printStackTrace();
    }
    catch (HeuristicMixedException e)
    {
      e.printStackTrace();
    }
    catch (HeuristicRollbackException e)
    {
      e.printStackTrace();
    }
    response.getWriter().println("Database Updated Successfully");
  }
}
```

This servlet obtains an instance of a class implementing the `javax.persistence.EntityManagerFactory` interface via dependency injection. This is done by decorating the `EntityManagerFactory` variable with the `@PersistenceUnit` annotation. The `EntityManagerFactory` instance is used to obtain a reference to an instance of a class implementing the `javax.persistence.EntityManager` interface.

An instance of a class implementing the `javax.transaction.UserTransaction` interface is then injected via the `@Resource` annotation. This object is necessary because without wrapping calls to persist Entities to the database, the code would throw a `javax.persistence.TransactionRequiredException`.

`EntityManagers` perform many of the duties that home interfaces performed for entity beans, like finding entities in the database, updating them, or deleting them. We obtain an instance of a class implementing `EntityManager` by invoking the `createEntityManager()` method on `EntityManagerFactory`.

As Java EE 5 Entities are plain old Java objects (POJOs), they can be instantiated via the `new` operator. We call methods on them directly, unlike with entity beans where methods on an instance of a class implementing their remote interface are used.

The call to the setCustomerId() method takes advantage of autoboxing, a feature added to the Java language in JDK 1.5. Notice that the method takes an instance of java.lang.Long as its parameter, but we are using long primitives. The code compiles and executes properly thanks to this feature.

Calls to the persist() method on EntityManager must be in a transaction, therefore it is necessary to start one by calling the begin() method on UserTransaction.

We then insert two new rows to the CUSTOMERS table by calling the persist() method on entityManager for the two instances of the Customer class we populated earlier in the code.

After persisting the data contained in the customer and customer2 objects, we search the database for a row in the CUSTOMERS table with a primary key of 4. We do this by invoking the find() method on entityManager. This method takes the class of the Entity we are searching for as its first parameter, and the primary key of the row corresponding to the object we want to obtain. This method is roughly equivalent to the findByPrimaryKey() method on an entity bean's home interface.

The primary key we set for the customer2 object was 4, therefore what we have now is a copy of this object. The last name for this customer was misspelled when we originally inserted his data into the database; we now correct Mr. Johnson's last name by invoking the setLastName() method on customer3, then update the information in the database by invoking entityManager.persist().

We then delete the information for the customer object by invoking entityManager.remove() and passing the customer object as a parameter.

Finally, we commit the changes to the database by invoking the commit() method on userTransaction.

In order for this code to work as expected, an XML configuration file named persistence.xml must be deployed in the WAR file containing this servlet. This file must be placed in the WEB-INF/classes/META-INF/ directory inside the WAR file. contents of this file for this code are shown next:

```xml
<?xml version="1.0" encoding="UTF-8"?>
<persistence version="1.0"
xmlns="http://java.sun.com/xml/ns/persistence"
xmlns:xsi="http://www.w3.org/2001/XMLSchema-instance"
xsi:schemaLocation="http://java.sun.com/xml/ns/persistence http://
java.sun.com/xml/ns/persistence/persistence_1_0.xsd">
  <persistence-unit name="customerPersistenceUnit">
    <jta-data-source>jdbc/__CustomerDBPool</jta-data-source>
  </persistence-unit>
</persistence>
```

The `persistence.xml` file must contain at least one `<persistence-unit>` element. Each `<persistence-unit>` element must provide a value for its `name` attribute and must contain a `<jta-data-source>` child element whose value is the JNDI name of the data source to be used for the persistence unit.

The reason more than one `<persistence-unit>` element is allowed is because an application may access more than one database. A `<persistence-unit>` element is required for each database the application will access. If the application defines more than one `<persistence-unit>` element, then the `@PersistenceUnit` annotation used to inject the `EntityManagerFactory` must provide a value for its `unitName` element; the value for this element must match the name attribute of the corresponding `<persistence-unit>` element in `persistence.xml`.

Cannot persist detached object Exception

Frequently, an application will retrieve a JPA entity via the `EntityManager.find()` method, then pass this entity to a business or user interface layer, where it will potentially be modified, and later the database data corresponding to the entity will be updated. In cases like this, invoking `EntityManager.persist()` will result in an exception. In order to update JPA entities this way we need to invoke `EntityManager.merge()`. This method takes an instance of the JPA entity as its single argument, and updates the corresponding row in the database with the data stored in it.

Entity Relationships

In the previous section, we saw how to retrieve, insert, update, and delete single entities in the database. Entities are rarely isolated; in the vast majority of cases they are related to other entities.

Entities can have one-to-one, one-to-many, many-to-one, and many-to-many relationships.

In the CustomerDB database, for example, there is a one-to-one relationship between the LOGIN_INFO and the CUSTOMERS tables. This means that each customer has exactly one corresponding row in the login info table. There is also a one-to-many relationship between the CUSTOMERS table and the ORDERS table. This is because a customer can place many orders. Additionally, there is a many-to-many relationship between the ORDERS table and the ITEMS table. This is because an order can contain many items and an item can be in many orders.

In the next few sections, we discuss how to establish relationships between JPA entities.

One-to-One Relationships

One-to-one relationships occur when an instance of an entity can have zero or one corresponding instance of another entity.

One-to-one entity relationships can be bi-directional (each entity is aware of the relationship) or uni-directional (only one of the entities is aware of the relationship). In the CUSTOMERDB database, the one-to-one mapping between the LOGIN_INFO and the CUSTOMERS tables is unidirectional, because the LOGIN_INFO table has a foreign key to the CUSTOMERS table, but not the other way around. As we will soon see, this fact does not stop us from creating a bi-directional one-to-one relationship between the Customer entity and the LoginInfo entity.

The source code for the LoginInfo entity, which maps to the LOGIN_INFO table, can be seen next:

```
package net.ensode.glassfishbook.entityrelationships;

import javax.persistence.Column;
import javax.persistence.Entity;
import javax.persistence.Id;
import javax.persistence.JoinColumn;
import javax.persistence.Table;

@Entity
@Table(name = "LOGIN_INFO")
public class LoginInfo
{
  @Id
  @Column(name = "LOGIN_INFO_ID")
  private Long loginInfoId;

  @Column(name = "LOGIN_NAME")
  private String loginName;

  private String password;

  @OneToOne
  @JoinColumn(name="CUSTOMER_ID")
  private Customer customer;

  public Long getLoginInfoId()
  {
    return loginInfoId;
  }

  public void setLoginInfoId(Long loginInfoId)
  {
    this.loginInfoId = loginInfoId;
  }
```

```
  public String getPassword()
  {
    return password;
  }
  public void setPassword(String password)
  {
    this.password = password;
  }
  public String getLoginName()
  {
    return loginName;
  }
  public void setLoginName(String userName)
  {
    this.loginName = userName;
  }
  public Customer getCustomer()
  {
    return customer;
  }
  public void setCustomer(Customer customer)
  {
    this.customer = customer;
  }
}
```

The code for this entity is very similar to the code for the Customer entity; it defines fields that map to database columns, each field whose name does not match the database column name is decorated with the @Column annotation, and in addition to that, the primary key is decorated with the @Id annotation.

Where this code gets interesting is in the declaration of the customer field. As can be seen in the code, the customer field is decorated with the @OneToOne annotation; this lets the application server (GlassFish) know that there is a one-to-one relationship between this entity and the Customer entity. The customer field is also decorated with the @JoinColumn annotation. This annotation lets the container know what column in the LOGIN_INFO table is the foreign key corresponding to the primary key on the CUSTOMER table. As LOGIN_INFO, the table that the LoginInfo entity maps to, has a foreign key to the CUSTOMER table, the LoginInfo entity owns the relationship. If the relationship was uni-directional, we wouldn't have to make any changes to the Customer entity. However, as we would like to have a bi-directional relationship between these two entities, we need to add a LoginInfo field to the Customer entity, along with the corresponding getter and setter methods.

As we mentioned before, in order to make the one-to-one relationship between the Customer and LoginInfo entities bi-directional, we need to make a few simple changes to the Customer entity:

```
package net.ensode.glassfishbook.entityrelationships;
import java.io.Serializable;
import java.util.Set;

import javax.persistence.CascadeType;
import javax.persistence.Column;
import javax.persistence.Entity;
import javax.persistence.Id;
import javax.persistence.OneToMany;
import javax.persistence.OneToOne;
import javax.persistence.Table;

@Entity
@Table(name = "CUSTOMERS")
public class Customer implements Serializable
{
  @Id
  @Column(name = "CUSTOMER_ID")
  private Long customerId;

  @Column(name = "FIRST_NAME")
  private String firstName;

  @Column(name = "LAST_NAME")
  private String lastName;

  private String email;

  @OneToOne(mappedBy = "customer")
  private LoginInfo loginInfo;

  public Long getCustomerId()
  {
    return customerId;
  }

  public void setCustomerId(Long customerId)
  {
    this.customerId = customerId;
  }

  public String getEmail()
  {
    return email;
  }

  public void setEmail(String email)
  {
```

```
      this.email = email;
    }
    public String getFirstName()
    {
      return firstName;
    }
    public void setFirstName(String firstName)
    {
      this.firstName = firstName;
    }
    public String getLastName()
    {
      return lastName;
    }
    public void setLastName(String lastName)
    {
      this.lastName = lastName;
    }
    public LoginInfo getLoginInfo()
    {
      return loginInfo;
    }
    public void setLoginInfo(LoginInfo loginInfo)
    {
      this.loginInfo = loginInfo;
    }
```

The only change we need to make to the Customer entity to make the one-to-one relationship bi-directional is to add a LoginInfo field to it, along with the corresponding setter and getter methods. The loginInfo field is decorated with the @OneToOne annotation. As the Customer entity does not own the relationship (the table it maps to does not have a foreign key to the corresponding table), the mappedBy element of the @OneToOne annotation needs to be added. This element specifies what field in the corresponding entity has the other end of the relationship. In this particular case, the customer field in the LoginInfo entity corresponds to the other end of this one-to-one relationship.

The following servlet illustrates the use of this entity:

```
package net.ensode.glassfishbook.entityrelationships;
import java.io.IOException;
import javax.annotation.Resource;
import javax.persistence.EntityManager;
```

```
import javax.persistence.EntityManagerFactory;
import javax.persistence.PersistenceUnit;
import javax.servlet.ServletException;
import javax.servlet.http.HttpServlet;
import javax.servlet.http.HttpServletRequest;
import javax.servlet.http.HttpServletResponse;
import javax.transaction.HeuristicMixedException;
import javax.transaction.HeuristicRollbackException;
import javax.transaction.NotSupportedException;
import javax.transaction.RollbackException;
import javax.transaction.SystemException;
import javax.transaction.UserTransaction;
public class OneToOneRelationshipDemoServlet extends HttpServlet
{
  @PersistenceUnit(unitName = "customerPersistenceUnit")
  private EntityManagerFactory entityManagerFactory;

  @Resource
  private UserTransaction userTransaction;

  @Override
  protected void doGet(HttpServletRequest request,
   HttpServletResponse response)
      throws ServletException, IOException
  {
    EntityManager entityManager = entityManagerFactory.
createEntityManager();

    Customer customer;

    LoginInfo loginInfo = new LoginInfo();

    loginInfo.setLoginInfoId(1L);
    loginInfo.setLoginName("charlesj");
    loginInfo.setPassword("iwonttellyou");

    try
    {
      userTransaction.begin();
      customer = entityManager.find(Customer.class, 4L);
      loginInfo.setCustomer(customer);

      entityManager.persist(loginInfo);
      userTransaction.commit();

      response.getWriter().println("Database updated successfully.");
    }
    catch (NotSupportedException e)
    {
      e.printStackTrace();
```

```
         }
      catch (SystemException e)
      {
         e.printStackTrace();
      }
      catch (SecurityException e)
      {
         e.printStackTrace();
      }
      catch (IllegalStateException e)
      {
         e.printStackTrace();
      }
      catch (RollbackException e)
      {
         e.printStackTrace();
      }
      catch (HeuristicMixedException e)
      {
         e.printStackTrace();
      }
      catch (HeuristicRollbackException e)
      {
         e.printStackTrace();
      }
   }
}
```

In this example, we first create an instance of the LoginInfo entity and populate it with some data. We then obtain an instance of the Customer entity from the database by invoking the `find()` method of EntityManager (data for this entity was inserted into the CUSTOMERS table in one of the JDBC examples). We then invoke the `setCustomer()` method on the LoginInfo entity, passing the customer object as a parameter. Finally, we invoke the `EntityManager.persist()` method to save the data in the database.

What happens behind the scenes is that the CUSTOMER_ID column of the LOGIN_INFO table gets populated with the primary key of the corresponding row in the CUSTOMERS table. This can be easily verified by querying the CUSTOMERDB database.

Notice how the call to `EntityManager.find()` to obtain the customer entity is inside the transaction in which we call `EntityManager.persist()`. This must be the case, otherwise the database will not be updated successfully.

One-to-Many Relationships

With JPA, one-to-many entity relationships can be bi-directional (one entity contains a many-to-one relationship with the corresponding entity that contains an inverse one-to-many relationship).

With SQL, one-to-many relationships are defined by foreign keys in one of the tables. The "many" part of the relationship is the one containing a foreign key to the "one" part of the relationship. One-to-many relationships defined in an RDBMS are typically uni-directional, as making them bi-directional usually results in denormalized data.

Just as when defining a uni-directional one-to-many relationship in an RDBMS, in JPA the "many" part of the relationship is the one that has a reference to the "one" part of the relationship; therefore the annotation used to decorate the appropriate setter method is `@ManyToOne`.

In the CUSTOMERDB database, there is an uni-directional one-to-many relationship between customers and orders. We define this relationship in the `Order` entity.

```
package net.ensode.glassfishbook.entityrelationships;

import javax.persistence.Column;
import javax.persistence.Entity;
import javax.persistence.Id;
import javax.persistence.JoinColumn;
import javax.persistence.ManyToOne;
import javax.persistence.Table;

@Entity
@Table(name = "ORDERS")
public class Order
{
  @Id
  @Column(name = "ORDER_ID")
  private Long orderId;

  @Column(name = "ORDER_NUMBER")
  private String orderNumber;

  @Column(name = "ORDER_DESCRIPTION")
  private String orderDescription;
```

```
@ManyToOne
@JoinColumn(name = "CUSTOMER_ID")
private Customer customer;
public Customer getCustomer()
{
  return customer;
}
public void setCustomer(Customer customer)
{
  this.customer = customer;
}
public String getOrderDescription()
{
  return orderDescription;
}
public void setOrderDescription(String orderDescription)
{
  this.orderDescription = orderDescription;
}
public Long getOrderId()
{
  return orderId;
}
public void setOrderId(Long orderId)
{
  this.orderId = orderId;
}
public String getOrderNumber()
{
  return orderNumber;
}
public void setOrderNumber(String orderNumber)
{
  this.orderNumber = orderNumber;
}
}
```

If we were to define a uni-directional many-to-one relationship between the Orders entity and the Customer entity, we wouldn't need to make any changes to the Customer entity. To define a bi-directional one-to-many relationship between the two entities, a new field decorated with the @OneToMany annotation needs to be added to the Customer entity.

```
package net.ensode.glassfishbook.entityrelationships;
import java.io.Serializable;
import java.util.Set;
import javax.persistence.Column;
import javax.persistence.Entity;
import javax.persistence.Id;
import javax.persistence.OneToMany;
import javax.persistence.Table;
@Entity
@Table(name = "CUSTOMERS")
public class Customer implements Serializable
{
  @Id
  @Column(name = "CUSTOMER_ID")
  private Long customerId;

  @Column(name = "FIRST_NAME")
  private String firstName;

  @Column(name = "LAST_NAME")
  private String lastName;

  private String email;

  @OneToOne(mappedBy = "customer")
  private LoginInfo loginInfo;

  @OneToMany(mappedBy="customer")
  private Set<Order> orders;

  public Long getCustomerId()
  {
    return customerId;
  }
  public void setCustomerId(Long customerId)
  {
    this.customerId = customerId;
  }
  public String getEmail()
  {
    return email;
  }
  public void setEmail(String email)
  {
    this.email = email;
  }
  public String getFirstName()
```

```
   {
      return firstName;
   }
   public void setFirstName(String firstName)
   {
      this.firstName = firstName;
   }
   public String getLastName()
   {
      return lastName;
   }
   public void setLastName(String lastName)
   {
      this.lastName = lastName;
   }
   public LoginInfo getLoginInfo()
   {
      return loginInfo;
   }
   public void setLoginInfo(LoginInfo loginInfo)
   {
      this.loginInfo = loginInfo;
   }
   public Set<Order> getOrders()
   {
      return orders;
   }
   public void setOrders(Set<Order> orders)
   {
      this.orders = orders;
   }
}
```

The only difference between this version of the Customer entity and the previous one is the addition of the orders field and related getter and setter methods. Of special interest is the @OneToMany annotation decorating this field. The mappedBy attribute must match the name of the corresponding field in the entity corresponding to the "many" part of the relationship. In simple terms, the value of the mappedBy attribute must match the name of the field decorated with the @ManyToOne annotation in the bean at the other side of the relationship.

The following servlet illustrates how to persist one-to-many relationships to the database.

```java
package net.ensode.glassfishbook.entityrelationships;

import java.io.IOException;

import javax.annotation.Resource;
import javax.persistence.EntityManager;
import javax.persistence.EntityManagerFactory;
import javax.persistence.PersistenceUnit;
import javax.servlet.ServletException;
import javax.servlet.http.HttpServlet;
import javax.servlet.http.HttpServletRequest;
import javax.servlet.http.HttpServletResponse;
import javax.transaction.HeuristicMixedException;
import javax.transaction.HeuristicRollbackException;
import javax.transaction.NotSupportedException;
import javax.transaction.RollbackException;
import javax.transaction.SystemException;
import javax.transaction.UserTransaction;

public class OneToManyRelationshipDemoServlet extends HttpServlet
{
  @PersistenceUnit(unitName = "customerPersistenceUnit")
  private EntityManagerFactory entityManagerFactory;

  @Resource
  private UserTransaction userTransaction;

  @Override
  protected void doGet(HttpServletRequest request, HttpServletResponse
  response) throws ServletException, IOException
  {
    EntityManager entityManager =
        entityManagerFactory.createEntityManager();

    Customer customer;
    Order order1;
    Order order2;

    order1 = new Order();
    order1.setOrderId(1L);
    order1.setOrderNumber("SFX12345");
    order1.setOrderDescription("Dummy order.");

    order2 = new Order();
    order2.setOrderId(2L);
    order2.setOrderNumber("SFX23456");
    order2.setOrderDescription("Another dummy order.");
```

```
    try
    {
      userTransaction.begin();
      customer = entityManager.find(Customer.class, 4L);

      order1.setCustomer(customer);
      order2.setCustomer(customer);

      entityManager.persist(order1);
      entityManager.persist(order2);

      userTransaction.commit();

      response.getWriter().
          println("Database updated successfully.");
    }
    catch (NotSupportedException e)
    {
      e.printStackTrace();
    }
    catch (SystemException e)
    {
      e.printStackTrace();
    }
    catch (SecurityException e)
    {
      e.printStackTrace();
    }
    catch (IllegalStateException e)
    {
      e.printStackTrace();
    }
    catch (RollbackException e)
    {
      e.printStackTrace();
    }
    catch (HeuristicMixedException e)
    {
      e.printStackTrace();
    }
    catch (HeuristicRollbackException e)
    {
      e.printStackTrace();
    }
  }
}
```

This code is pretty similar to the previous example. It instantiates two instances of the `Order` entity and populates them with some data; then in a transaction, an instance of the `Customer` entity is located, and used as the parameter of the `setCustomer()` method of both instances of the `Order` entity. We then persist both `Order` entities by invoking `EntityManager.persist()` for each one of them.

Just as when dealing with one-to-one relationships, what happens behind the scenes is that the `CUSTOMER_ID` column of the ORDERS table in the CUSTOMERDB database is populated with the primary key corresponding to the related row in the CUSTOMERS table.

As the relationship is bidirectional, we can obtain all orders related to a customer by invoking the `getOrders()` method on the Customer entity.

Many-to-Many Relationships

In the CUSTOMERDB database, there is a many-to-many relationship between the ORDERS table and the ITEMS table. We can map this relationship by adding a new `Collection<Item>` field to the Order entity and decorating it with the `@ManyToMany` annotation.

```
package net.ensode.glassfishbook.entityrelationships;

import java.util.Collection;
import javax.persistence.Column;
import javax.persistence.Entity;
import javax.persistence.Id;
import javax.persistence.JoinColumn;
import javax.persistence.JoinTable;
import javax.persistence.ManyToMany;
import javax.persistence.ManyToOne;
import javax.persistence.Table;

@Entity
@Table(name = "ORDERS")
public class Order
{
  @Id
  @Column(name = "ORDER_ID")
  private Long orderId;

  @Column(name = "ORDER_NUMBER")
  private String orderNumber;

  @Column(name = "ORDER_DESCRIPTION")
  private String orderDescription;

  @ManyToOne
```

```java
@JoinColumn(name = "CUSTOMER_ID")
private Customer customer;
@ManyToMany
@JoinTable(name = "ORDER_ITEMS",
    joinColumns = @JoinColumn(name = "ORDER_ID",
        referencedColumnName = "ORDER_ID"),
        inverseJoinColumns = @JoinColumn(name = "ITEM_ID",
            referencedColumnName = "ITEM_ID"))
private Collection<Item> items;
public Customer getCustomer()
{
  return customer;
}
public void setCustomer(Customer customer)
{
  this.customer = customer;
}
public String getOrderDescription()
{
  return orderDescription;
}
public void setOrderDescription(String orderDescription)
{
  this.orderDescription = orderDescription;
}
public Long getOrderId()
{
  return orderId;
}
public void setOrderId(Long orderId)
{
  this.orderId = orderId;
}
public String getOrderNumber()
{
  return orderNumber;
}
public void setOrderNumber(String orderNumber)
{
  this.orderNumber = orderNumber;
}
```

```
    public Collection<Item> getItems()
    {
      return items;
    }
    public void setItems(Collection<Item> items)
    {
      this.items = items;
    }
  }
```

As we can see in this code, in addition to being decorated with the `@ManyToMany` annotation, the `items` field is also decorated with the `@JoinTable` annotation. As its name suggests, this annotation lets the application server know what table is used as a join table to create the many-to-many relationship between the two entities. This annotation has three relevant elements: the name element, which defines the name of the join table, and the joinColumns and inverseJoinColumns elements, which define the columns that serve as foreign keys in the join table pointing to the entities' primary keys. Values for the joinColumns and inverseJoinColumns elements are yet another annotation, the `@JoinColumn` annotation. This annotation has two relevant elements, the name element, which defines the name of the column in the join table, and the referencedColumnName element, which defines the name of the column in the entity table.

The Item entity is a simple entity mapping to the ITEMS table in the CUSTOMERDB database.

```
package net.ensode.glassfishbook.entityrelationships;

import java.util.Collection;

import javax.persistence.Column;
import javax.persistence.Entity;
import javax.persistence.Id;
import javax.persistence.ManyToMany;
import javax.persistence.Table;

@Entity
@Table(name = "ITEMS")
public class Item
{
  @Id
  @Column(name = "ITEM_ID")
  private Long itemId;

  @Column(name = "ITEM_NUMBER")
  private String itemNumber;

  @Column(name = "ITEM_SHORT_DESC")
```

```java
private String itemShortDesc;
@Column(name = "ITEM_LONG_DESC")
private String itemLongDesc;
@ManyToMany(mappedBy="items")
private Collection<Order> orders;
public Long getItemId()
{
  return itemId;
}
public void setItemId(Long itemId)
{
  this.itemId = itemId;
}
public String getItemLongDesc()
{
  return itemLongDesc;
}
public void setItemLongDesc(String itemLongDesc)
{
  this.itemLongDesc = itemLongDesc;
}
public String getItemNumber()
{
  return itemNumber;
}
public void setItemNumber(String itemNumber)
{
  this.itemNumber = itemNumber;
}
public String getItemShortDesc()
{
  return itemShortDesc;
}
public void setItemShortDesc(String itemShortDesc)
{
  this.itemShortDesc = itemShortDesc;
}
public Collection<Order> getOrders()
{
  return orders;
}
```

```
  public void setOrders(Collection<Order> orders)
  {
    this.orders = orders;
  }
}
```

Just like one-to-one and one-to-many relationships, many-to-many relationships can be uni-directional or bi-directional. As we would like the many-to-many relationship between the Order and Item entities to be bi-directional, we added a `Collection<Order>` field and decorated it with the `@ManyToMany` annotation. As the corresponding field in the Order entity already has the join table defined, it is not necessary to do it again here. The entity containing the `@JoinTable` annotation is said to own the relationship; in a many-to-many relationship, either entity can own the relationship. In our example, the Order entity owns it, because its `Collection<Item>` field is decorated with the `@JoinTable` annotation.

Just as with the one-to-one and one-to-many relationships, the `@ManyToMany` annotation in the non-owning side of a bi-directional many-to-many relationship must contain a mappedBy element indicating what field in the owning entity corresponds to the relationship.

Now that we have seen the changes necessary to establish a bi-directional many-to-many relationship between the Order and Item entities, we can see the relationship in action in the following example:

```
package net.ensode.glassfishbook.entityrelationships;
import java.io.IOException;
import java.util.ArrayList;
import java.util.Collection;

import javax.annotation.Resource;
import javax.persistence.EntityManager;
import javax.persistence.EntityManagerFactory;
import javax.persistence.PersistenceUnit;
import javax.servlet.ServletException;
import javax.servlet.http.HttpServlet;
import javax.servlet.http.HttpServletRequest;
import javax.servlet.http.HttpServletResponse;
import javax.transaction.HeuristicMixedException;
import javax.transaction.HeuristicRollbackException;
import javax.transaction.NotSupportedException;
import javax.transaction.RollbackException;
import javax.transaction.SystemException;
import javax.transaction.UserTransaction;

public class ManyToManyRelationshipDemoServlet extends HttpServlet
```

```
{
  @PersistenceUnit(unitName = "customerPersistenceUnit")
  private EntityManagerFactory entityManagerFactory;

  @Resource
  private UserTransaction userTransaction;

  @Override
  protected void doGet(HttpServletRequest request,
                       HttpServletResponse response)
    throws ServletException, IOException
  {
    EntityManager entityManager =
        entityManagerFactory.createEntityManager();
    Order order;
    Collection<Item> items = new ArrayList<Item>();
    Item item1 = new Item();
    Item item2 = new Item();
    item1.setItemId(1L);
    item1.setItemNumber("BCD1234");
    item1.setItemShortDesc("Notebook Computer");
    item1.setItemLongDesc("64 bit Quad core CPU, 4GB memory");
    item2.setItemId(2L);
    item2.setItemNumber("CDF2345");
    item2.setItemShortDesc("Cordless Mouse");
    item2.setItemLongDesc("Three button, infrared, "
        + "vertical and horizontal scrollwheels");
    items.add(item1);
    items.add(item2);
    try
    {
      userTransaction.begin();
      entityManager.persist(item1);
      entityManager.persist(item2);

      order = entityManager.find(Order.class, 1L);
      order.setItems(items);

      entityManager.persist(order);
      userTransaction.commit();
      response.getWriter().println(
          "Database updated successfully");
    }
    catch (NotSupportedException e)
    {
```

```
        e.printStackTrace();
      }
      catch (SystemException e)
      {
        e.printStackTrace();
      }
      catch (SecurityException e)
      {
        e.printStackTrace();
      }
      catch (IllegalStateException e)
      {
        e.printStackTrace();
      }
      catch (RollbackException e)
      {
        e.printStackTrace();
      }
      catch (HeuristicMixedException e)
      {
        e.printStackTrace();
      }
      catch (HeuristicRollbackException e)
      {
        e.printStackTrace();
      }
    }
  }
```

This code creates two instances of the Item entity and populates them with some data. It then adds these two instances to a collection. A transaction is then started, and the two Item instances are persisted to the database. Then an instance of the Order entity is retrieved from the database. The setItems() method of the Order entity instance is then invoked, passing the collection containing the two Item instances as a parameter. The Customer instance is then persisted into the database. At this point, to rows are created behind the scenes to the ORDER_ITEMS table, which is the join table between the ORDERS and ITEMS tables.

Composite Primary Keys

Most tables in the CUSTOMERDB database have a column with the sole purpose of serving as a primary key (this type of primary key is sometimes referred to as a surrogate primary key or as an artificial primary key). However, some databases are not designed this way; instead a column in the database that is known to be unique across rows is used as the primary key, or if there is no column whose value is guaranteed to be unique across rows, then a combination of two or more rows is used as the table's primary key. It is possible to map this kind of primary key to JPA entities by using a primary key class.

There is one table in the CUSTOMERDB database that does not have a surrogate primary key; this table is the ORDER_ITEMS table. This table serves as a join table between the ORDERS and the ITEMS tables; in addition to having foreign keys for these two tables, this table has an additional column called ITEM_QTY, which stores the quantity of each item in an order. As this table does not have a surrogate primary key, the JPA entity mapping to it must have a custom primary key class. In this table, the combination of the ORDER_ID and the ITEM_ID columns must be unique, therefore this is a good combination for a composite primary key.

```
package net.ensode.glassfishbook.compositekeys;

import java.io.Serializable;

public class OrderItemPK implements Serializable
{
  public Long orderId;
  public Long itemId;

  public OrderItemPK()
  {

  }

  public OrderItemPK(Long orderId, Long itemId)
  {
    this.orderId = orderId;
    this.itemId = itemId;
  }

  @Override
  public boolean equals(Object obj)
  {
    boolean returnVal = false;

    if (obj == null)
    {
      returnVal = false;
    }
    else if (!obj.getClass().equals(this.getClass()))
    {
      returnVal = false;
    }
    else
    {
      OrderItemPK other = (OrderItemPK) obj;
```

```
        if (this == other)
        {
          returnVal = true;
        }
        else if (orderId != null && other.orderId != null
            && this.orderId.equals(other.orderId))
        {
          if (itemId != null && other.itemId != null
              && itemId.equals(other.itemId))
          {
            returnVal = true;
          }
        }
        else
        {
          returnVal = false;
        }
      }
      return returnVal;
    }
    @Override
    public int hashCode()
    {
      if (orderId == null || itemId == null)
      {
        return 0;
      }
      else
      {
        return orderId.hashCode() ^ itemId.hashCode();
      }
    }
}
```

A custom primary key class must satisfy the following requirements:

1. The class must be public.
2. It must implement `java.io.Serializable`.
3. It must have a public constructor that takes no arguments.
4. Its fields must be public or protected.
5. Its field names and types must match those of the entity.
6. It must override the default `hashCode()` and `equals()` methods defined in the `java.lang.Object` class.

The OrderPK class shown earlier, meets all of these requirements. It also has a convenience constructor that takes two Long objects meant to initialize its orderId and itemId fields. This constructor was added for convenience; this is not a requirement for the class to be used as a primary key class.

When an entity uses a custom primary key class, it must be decorated with the @IdClass annotation. The OrderItem class uses OrderItemPK as its custom primary key class, so it must be decorated with this annotation.

```
package net.ensode.glassfishbook.compositekeys;

import javax.persistence.Column;
import javax.persistence.Entity;
import javax.persistence.Id;
import javax.persistence.IdClass;
import javax.persistence.Table;

@Entity
@Table(name = "ORDER_ITEMS")
@IdClass(value = OrderItemPK.class)
public class OrderItem
{
  @Id
  @Column(name = "ORDER_ID")
  private Long orderId;

  @Id
  @Column(name = "ITEM_ID")
  private Long itemId;

  @Column(name = "ITEM_QTY")
  private Long itemQty;

  public Long getItemId()
  {
    return itemId;
  }
  public void setItemId(Long itemId)
  {
    this.itemId = itemId;
  }
  public Long getItemQty()
  {
    return itemQty;
  }
  public void setItemQty(Long itemQty)
  {
```

```
      this.itemQty = itemQty;
  }
  public Long getOrderId()
  {
    return orderId;
  }
  public void setOrderId(Long orderId)
  {
    this.orderId = orderId;
  }
}
```

There are two differences between this entity and previous entities we have seen. The first difference is that this entity is decorated with the @IdClass annotation, indicating the primary key class corresponding to it. The second difference is that this entity has more than one field decorated with the @Id annotation. As this entity has a composite primary key, each field that is part of the primary key must be decorated with this annotation.

Obtaining a reference of an entity with a composite primary key is not much different than obtaining a reference to an entity with a primary key consisting of a single field. The following example demonstrates how to do this.

```
package net.ensode.glassfishbook.compositekeys;

import java.io.IOException;
import java.io.PrintWriter;

import javax.persistence.EntityManager;
import javax.persistence.EntityManagerFactory;
import javax.persistence.PersistenceUnit;
import javax.servlet.ServletException;
import javax.servlet.http.HttpServlet;
import javax.servlet.http.HttpServletRequest;
import javax.servlet.http.HttpServletResponse;

public class CompositeKeyDemoServlet extends HttpServlet
{
  @PersistenceUnit(unitName = "customerPersistenceUnit")
  private EntityManagerFactory entityManagerFactory;

  @Override
  protected void doGet(HttpServletRequest request, HttpServletResponse
  response) throws ServletException, IOException
  {
    PrintWriter printWriter = response.getWriter();
    EntityManager entityManager =
                        entityManagerFactory.createEntityManager();
```

```
      OrderItem orderItem;
      orderItem = entityManager.find(OrderItem.class,
                          new OrderItemPK(1L, 2L));
      response.setContentType("text/html");
      if (orderItem != null)
      {
        printWriter
            .println("Found an instance of Order Item for the supplied
            primary key:<br/>");
        printWriter.println("OrderItem order id: " +
        orderItem.getOrderId()
            + "<br/>");
        printWriter.println("OrderItem item id: " +
        orderItem.getItemId()
            + "<br/>");
      }
      else
      {
        printWriter
            .println("No instance of OrderItem found for the supplied
                    primary key.");
      }
    }
  }
}
```

As can be seen in this example, the only difference between locating an entity with a composite primary key and an entity with a primary key consisting of a single field is that an instance of the custom primary key class must be passed as the second argument of the EntityManager.find() method; fields for this instance must be populated with the appropriate values for each field that is part of the primary key.

Java Persistence Query Language

All of our examples that obtain entities from the database so far have conveniently assumed that the primary key for the entity is known ahead of time. We all know that frequently this is not the case. Whenever we need to search for an entity by a field other than the entity's primary key we must use the Java Persistence Query Language (JPQL).

JPQL is an SQL-like language used for retrieving, updating, and deleting entities in a database. The following example illustrates how to use JPQL to retrieve a subset of states from the US_STATES table in the CUSTOMERDB database:

```
package net.ensode.glassfishbook.jpaquerylang;
import java.io.IOException;
import java.io.PrintWriter;
import java.util.List;
```

```
import javax.persistence.EntityManager;
import javax.persistence.EntityManagerFactory;
import javax.persistence.PersistenceUnit;
import javax.persistence.Query;
import javax.servlet.ServletException;
import javax.servlet.http.HttpServlet;
import javax.servlet.http.HttpServletRequest;
import javax.servlet.http.HttpServletResponse;
public class SelectQueryDemoServlet extends HttpServlet
{
  @PersistenceUnit(unitName = "customerPersistenceUnit")
  private EntityManagerFactory entityManagerFactory;
  @Override
  protected void doGet(HttpServletRequest request,
      HttpServletResponse response)
      throws ServletException, IOException
  {
    PrintWriter printWriter = response.getWriter();
    List<UsState> matchingStatesList;
    EntityManager entityManager =
        entityManagerFactory.createEntityManager();
    Query query = entityManager.createQuery(
        "SELECT s FROM UsState s WHERE s.usStateNm " +
        "LIKE :name");
    query.setParameter("name", "New%");
    matchingStatesList = query.getResultList();
    response.setContentType("text/html");
    printWriter.println("The following states match " +
        "the criteria:<br/>");
    for (UsState state : matchingStatesList)
    {
      printWriter.println(state.getUsStateNm() + "<br/>");
    }
  }
}
```

The above code invokes the `EntityManager.createQuery()` method, passing a String containing a JPQL query as a parameter. This method returns an instance of `javax.persistence.Query`. The query retrieves all UsState entities whose names start with the word "New".

As can be seen in the above code, JPQL is similar to SQL; however, there are some differences that may confuse readers with SQL knowledge. The equivalent SQL code for the query in the code would be:

```
SELECT * from US_STATES s where s.US_STATE_NM like 'New%'
```

The first difference between JPQL and SQL is that in JPQL, we always retrieve all properties of an entity, where in SQL individual columns may be retrieved. The "s" after the entity name in the JPQL query is an alias for the entity. Table aliases are optional in SQL, but entity aliases are required in JPQL. Keeping these differences in mind, the JPQL query should now be a lot less confusing.

The `:name` in the query is a named parameter; named parameters are meant to be substituted with actual values. This is done by invoking the `setParameter()` method in the instance of `javax.persistence.Query` returned by the call to `EntityManager.createQuery()`. A JPQL query can have multiple named parameters.

To actually run the query and retrieve the entities from the database, the `getResultList()` method must be invoked in the instance of `javax.persistence.Query` obtained from `EntityManager.createQuery()`. This method returns an instance of a class implementing the `java.util.List` interface; this list contains the entities matching the query criteria. If no entities match the criteria, then an empty list is returned.

If we are certain that the query will return a single entity, then the `getSingleResult()` method may be alternatively called on `Query`; this method returns an `Object` that must be cast to the appropriate entity.

The earlier example uses the LIKE operator to find entities whose names start with the word "New". This is accomplished by substituting the query's named parameter with the value "New%". The percent sign at the end of the parameter value means that any number of characters after the word "New" will match the expression. The percent sign can be used anywhere in the parameter value, for example, a value of "%Dakota" would match any entities whose names end in "Dakota", a value of "A%a" would match any states whose names start with a capital "A" and end with a lowercase "a". There can be more than one percent sign in a parameter value. The underscore sign (_) can be used to match a single character; all the rules for the percent sign apply to the underscore as well.

In addition to the `LIKE` operator, there are other operators that can be used to retrieve entities from the database.

- The = operator will retrieve entities whose field at the left of the operator exactly matches the value to the right of the operator.

- The > operator will retrieve entities whose field at the left of the operator is greater than the value to the right of the operator.

- The < operator will retrieve entities whose field at the left of the operator is less than the value to the right of the operator.

- The >= operator will retrieve entities whose field at the left of the operator is greater than or equal to the value to the right of the operator.

- The <= operator will retrieve entities whose field at the left of the operator is less than or equal to the value to the right of the operator.

All of these operators work the same way as the equivalent operators in SQL. Just as in SQL, these operators can be combined with the "AND" and "OR" operators. Conditions combined with the "AND" operator match if both conditions are true, conditions combined with the "OR" operator match if at least one of the conditions is true.

If we intend to use a query many times, it can be stored in a **named query**. Named queries can be defined by decorating the relevant entity class with the @NamedQuery annotation. This annotation has two elements, a name element used to set the name of the query, and a query element defining the query itself. To execute a named query, the createNamedQuery() method must be invoked in an instance of EntityManager. This method takes a String containing the query name as its sole parameter, and returns an instance of javax.persistence.Query.

In addition to retrieving entities, JPQL can be used to modify or delete entities. However, entity modification and deletion can be done programmatically via the EntityManager interface; doing so results in code that tends to be more readable than that when using JPQL. Because of this, we will not cover entity modification and deletion via JPQL. Readers interested in writing JPQL queries to modify and delete entities, as well as readers wishing to know more about JPQL are encouraged to read Chapter 4 of the JSR 220: Enterprise JavaBeans,Version 3.0 specification. This specification can be downloaded at http://jcp.org/aboutJava/communityprocess/final/jsr220/index.html.

Final Notes

In the examples of this chapter, we showed database access done directly from servlets. We did this to get the point across without bogging ourselves down with details; however, in general, this is not a good practice. Database access code should be encapsulated in Data Access Objects (DAOs).

 For more information on the DAO design pattern, see
http://java.sun.com/blueprints/corej2eepatterns/
Patterns/DataAccessObject.html

Also, our examples showed servlets that did pretty much nothing but database access. Servlets typically serve as controllers when following the Model View Controller (MVC) design pattern. We chose not to add any user interface code to our examples because it is irrelevant to the topic at hand, but for real applications we would of course have entities populated from user interface components, most likely input fields in a JSP. These fields would be in an HTML form that when submitted would pass control to a servlet, which would then populate Entities from the data entered by the user and pass the entities to a DAO, which would then persist the data to the database.

 For more information about the MVC design pattern, see `http://java.sun.com/blueprints/patterns/MVC.html`.

Summary

This chapter covered how to access data in a database both via the Java Database Connectivity (JDBC) API and through the Java Persistence API (JPA).

We covered how to obtain data from the database by using JDBC via the `executeQuery()` method defined in the `java.sql.PreparedStatement` interface. We also covered how to insert, update, and delete database data via the `executeUpdate()` method defined in the same interface. Additionally, we covered using dependency injection to inject a Data Source into an object.

We also covered setting a Java class as an entity by decorating it with the `@Entity` annotation. Additionally, we covered how to map an entity to a database table via the `@Table` annotation. We also covered how to map entity fields to database columns via the `@Column` annotation, as well as declaring an entity's primary key via the `@Id` annotation.

We covered using the `javax.persistence.EntityManager` interface to find, persist, and update JPA entities.

We covered defining both unidirectional and bidirectional one-to-one, one-to-many, and many-to-many relationships between JPA entities as well.

Additionally, we covered how to use JPA composite primary keys by developing custom primary key classes.

Lastly, we covered how to retrieve entities from a database by using the Java Persistence Query Language (JPQL).

5

JSP Standard Tag Library

The JSP Standard Tag Library (JSTL) is a collection of standard JSP tags that perform several common tasks. This frees us from having to develop custom tags for these tasks, or from using a mix of tags from several organizations to do our work. JSTL contains core tags that perform, among other things, conditional logic and iteration through collections; format tags that do String formatting and internationalization; SQL tags that interact with a database; XML tags for XML processing. Additionally, JSTL contains a number of functions that perform several tasks, most of which are for String manipulation.

In this chapter, we will cover each of the JSTL tag libraries, providing examples for the most commonly used tags and functions. Topics we will cover in this chapter include:

- Core JSTL tag library
- Formatting JSTL tag library
- SQL JSTL tag library
- XML JSTL tag library
- JSTL functions

Core JSTL Tag Library

Core JSTL tags perform tasks like writing output to the browser, conditional display of segments in a page, and iterating through collections. Much of what the core JSTL tags do can be accomplished with scriptlets; however, the page is much easier to read and therefore more maintainable if core JSTL tags are used, instead of scriptlets.

The following example shows a JSP using some of the most common JSTL core tags:

```jsp
<%@ page language="java" contentType="text/html; charset=UTF-8"
  pageEncoding="UTF-8"%>
<%@taglib uri="http://java.sun.com/jsp/jstl/core" prefix="c"%>
<!DOCTYPE html PUBLIC "-//W3C//DTD HTML 4.01 Transitional//EN"
"http://www.w3.org/TR/html4/loose.dtd">
<%@page import="java.util.ArrayList"%>
<html>
<%
      ArrayList<String> nameList = new ArrayList<String>(4);

      nameList.add("David");

      nameList.add("Raymond");

      nameList.add("Beth");

      nameList.add("Joyce");

      request.setAttribute("nameList", nameList);
%>
<head>
<meta http-equiv="Content-Type" content="text/html; charset=UTF-8">
<title>Core Tag Demo</title>
</head>
<body>
<c:set var="name" scope="page" value="${param.name}"></c:set>
<c:out value="Hello"></c:out>
<c:choose>
  <c:when test="${!empty name}">
    <c:out value="${name}"></c:out>
  </c:when>
  <c:otherwise>
    <c:out value="stranger"></c:out>
    <br />
    <c:out value="Need a name? Here are a few options:" />
    <br />
    <ul>
      <c:forEach var="nameOption"
                items="${requestScope.nameList}">
        <li /><c:out value="${nameOption}"></c:out>
      </c:forEach>
    </ul>
  </c:otherwise>
</c:choose>
<c:remove var="name" scope="page" />
</body>
</html>
```

In a nutshell, the previous code segment looks for a request parameter called name; if it finds it, it displays the message "Hello ${name}" in the browser (${name} is actually replaced with the value of the parameter). If the parameter is not found, it prints the message "Hello stranger" and gets a little smart with the user, suggesting a few names.

The page employs the taglib directive to declare that it uses the JSTL core tag library. Though any prefix can be used for this library, using the prefix "c" is standard practice.

Before doing anything with JSTL, the page has a scriptlet that initializes an instance of `java.util.ArrayList` with some Strings containing names, and attaches the `ArrayList` to the request (this would typically be done in a servlet or some other class, not in the JSP itself; it was done this way in the example for simplicity).

The first JSTL tag used in the page is the `<c:set>` tag. This tag sets the result of the expression defined in its `variable` attribute and stores it in a variable in the specified scope. The name of the variable is defined in the tag's `var` attribute. The scope of the variable is defined in the tag's `scope` attribute, if no scope is specified, the page scope is used by default. The expression to be evaluated is defined in the tag's `value` attribute.

Page scope is always the default

A number of JSTL tags contain a `var` attribute to define a variable in a scope specified by a `scope` attribute. In all cases, if no scope is specified, the page scope is used by default.

In the preceding example, the expression is looking for the value of a request parameter with a name of "name"; `param` is an implicit variable that resolves to a map using request parameter names as keys and request parameter values as values. This implicit variable is equivalent to calling the `getParameterMap()` method on the request. The value after the dot (`name` in the example) corresponds to the key we want to get from the parameter map (which in turn corresponds to the request parameter name).

The next core JSTL tag we see in the example is the `<c:out>` tag. This tag simply displays in the browser the value of the expression defined in its `value` attribute. In this particular case, the expression defined in the `value` attribute is a constant, therefore it is displayed verbatim in the browser output.

Next, we see the `<c:choose>` tag. This tag allows us to do if/then/else-like conditions in the page. The `<c:choose>` tag must contain one or more `<c:when>` tags and optionally a `<c:otherwise>` tag. The `<c:when>` tag contains a `test` attribute that must contain an Boolean expression. Once the expression in one of the `<c:when>` tags nested in a `<c:choose>` tag evaluates to true, the body of the tag is executed and the `test` attributes of other `<c:when>` tags nested inside the same `<c:choose>` tag are not evaluated.

The next new tag we see in the example is the `<c:otherwise>` tag. The body of this optional tag is executed if none of the expressions in any `<c:when>` tag evaluates to true. In the example, the body of the tag is executed when no request parameter with a name of "name" exists in the request, or if the value of the parameter is an empty String.

In this example, the `<c:when>` tag contains the ! operator that, just as in Java, negates a Boolean expression. The tag also contains the `empty` operator, this operator checks to see if a string is null or has a length of zero. The `test` attribute of the `<c:when>` tag can have several logical and/or relational operators that can be combined to build more complex expressions. All relational operators that can be used in the test attribute (or any other Unified Expression Language expression, for that matter) are listed in the following table:

Relational Operator	Description
`==` or `eq`	Equals: evaluates to true if the expression to the left of the operator equals the expression to the right of the operator.
`>` or `gt`	Greater than: evaluates to true if the expression to the left of the operator is greater than the expression to the right of the operator.
`<` or `lt`	Less than: evaluates to true if the expression to the left of the operator is less than the expression to the right of the operator.

Relational Operator	Description
>= or ge	Greater than or equal: evaluates to true if the expression to the left of the operator is greater than or equal to the expression to the right of the operator.
<= or le	Less than or equal: evaluates to true if the expression to the left of the operator is less than or equal to the expression to the right of the operator.
!= or ne	Not equal: evaluates to true if the expression to the left of the operator is not equal to the expression to the right of the operator.

All of the above symbolic operators work the same way as their equivalent Java operators, therefore their use should be natural to any Java developer. In addition to allowing us to use the symbolic operators, in the unified expression language, all symbolic operators have a textual equivalent. These textual equivalents are used if we need our page to be valid XML, as using the symbolic operators typically results in invalid XML markup.

In addition to relational operators, logical operators can be used in Unified Expression Language expressions. Valid logical operators are listed in the following table:

Logical Operator	Description
&& or and	Evaluates to true if both the expression to the left of the operator and the one to the right of the operator are true.
|| or or	Evaluates to true if either the expression to the left of the operator or the one to the right of the operator is true (or both).
! or not	Negates the expression to the right of the operator, if the expression evaluates to true, this operator makes it evaluate to false, and vice versa.
empty	Evaluates to true if the value to the right of the operator is null or empty. The value to the right of the operator must be a String or a Collection.
$E_1 ? E_2 : E_3$	Conditional expression: if E_1 is true, it evaluates to E_2, otherwise it evaluates to E_3.

Just as with relational operators, logical operators work the same way as their Java equivalents; and each one has a symbolic and textual variant.

The Unified Expression Language also contains arithmetic operators, listed in the following table.

Arithmetic Operator	Description
+	Addition: adds the values to the left and right of the operator.
- (binary)	Subtraction: subtracts the value to the right of the operator from the value to the left of the operator.
*	Multiplication: multiplies the values to the left and right of the operator.
/ or div	Division: divides the values to the left (dividend) and right (divisor) of the operator.
% or mod	Modulo: divides the values to the left (dividend) and right (divisor) of the operator and returns the reminder.
- (unary)	Minus: multiplies the value to the right of the operator by -1.

All arithmetic operators must be used with numerical values.

After our brief discussion of the Unified Expression Language operators, we can now get back to discussing the example. The next new tag we see in the example is the `<c:forEach>` tag. This tag iterates through a Collection, array, or Map. In the example, it iterates through the instance of `java.util.ArrayList` attached to the request in the scriptlet defined earlier in the page.

The `var` attribute of the `<c:forEach>` tag defines a variable to be used to access the current element in the collection; this variable is only visible inside the body of the tag.

The `items` attribute of the `<c:forEach>` tag indicates the array, Collection, or Map to iterate through.

The `<c:forEach>` tag has additional attributes not shown in the example; the `begin` attribute indicates the index of the first item to iterate from and the `end` attribute indicates the last item to iterate to. If the `begin` attribute is not set, iteration begins at the first item in the Collection, array, or Map; if the `end` attribute is not set, iteration ends at the last element of the Collection, array, or Map. An additional attribute of the `<c:forEach>` tag is the `step` attribute; it indicates the increment from one index to the next, and defaults to 1. In addition to iterating through a Collection, array, or Map, the `<c:forEach>` tag can be used to execute its body a number of times. To use the `<c:forEach>` tag this way, its `items` attribute is omitted, and its `begin` and `end` attributes are required.

The next new tag we see in the example is the `<c:remove>` tag. This tag is used to remove a variable attached to the scope specified in its `scope` attribute. If no scope is specified, the `<c:remove>` tag uses a default scope of page.

There are some additional core JSTL tags not shown in the example. These remaining tags are explained next.

The `<c:if>` tag is similar to the `<c:when>` tag; its body is executed if the expression defined by its `test` attribute is true. The `<c:if>` tag has two optional attributes, a `var` attribute that defines the name of a Boolean variable storing the results of the tag's `test` attribute, and a `scope` attribute defining the scope of the `var` attribute. The `<c:if>` tag should not be nested in a `<c:choose>` tag. Unlike that of the `<c:when>` tag, the expression defined in the `test` attribute of multiple `<c:if>` tags is evaluated, regardless of if a previous `<c:if>` expression resolved to `true` or not.

The `<c:forTokens>` tag iterates over a delimiter-separated string. The `<c:forTokens>` tag has two required attributes: `items` and `delims`. The `items` attribute value must be an expression resolving to a String, or a String constant. The value of the `delims` attribute must be an expression or a String constant indicating the characters to be used as delimiters. Each individual character in the `delims` attribute will be used as a delimiter for the value of the item, similar to the way the `java.util.StringTokenizer` class works. Additionally, the `<c:forTokens>` tag has a `var` attribute that works essentially the same way as the `var` attribute of the `<c:forEach>` tag. That is, it defines a name for the current item in its `items` attribute, allowing it to be accessed in the body of the `<c:forTokens>` tag.

The `<c:import>` tag is similar to `<jsp:include>`, it includes the contents of a relative or absolute URL into the rendered JSP; optionally, this tag can store the contents of the included URL in a String or in an instance of `java.io.Reader`.

The `<c:import>` tag has one required attribute called `url`; the value for this attribute is a String expression containing the URL to be imported. If we wish to store the contents of the included URL in a String, then the `var` attribute must be used. The value of this attribute is the name of the string that will hold the contents of the included URL. If we wish to include the contents of the included URL in an instance of `java.io.Reader`, then the `varReader` attribute must be used. The value of this attribute is the name of the variable that will hold the contents of the included URL. The `<c:import>` tag has an optional scope attribute that defines the scope of the variable defined by the `var` or `varReader` attributes. If this attribute is not used, the `var` or `varReader` variable will have a default scope of page.

The `<c:redirect>` tag redirects the browser to the URL specified in its `url` attribute It is equivalent to calling the `sendRedirect()` method of an instance of `javax.servlet.http.HttpServletResponse`.

The `<c:url>` tag constructs a URL from the value of its `url` attribute and stores it in a string whose name is defined in the tag's `var` attribute. The default scope of the variable defined by the `var` attribute is page. This can be changed by using the tag's `scope` attribute.

It is possible to pass parameters to the URL defined in the url attribute of the <c:import>, <c:redirect>, or <c:url> tags. This is done by using the <c:param> tag. This tag must be nested inside one of the above three tags. The <c:param> tag has two attributes: a required name attribute defining the parameter name and a value attribute defining the parameter value.

The last core JSTL tag is the <c:catch> tag. This tag catches any java.lang.Throwable thrown inside its body.

> java.lang.Throwable is the parent class of java.lang.Exception and java.lang.Error; therefore any Exception or Error thrown inside the body of the <c:catch> tag is also caught.

If a Throwable is thrown inside the body of the <c:catch> tag, control goes to the line immediately following the closing </c:catch> tag. Any lines inside the body of the <c:catch> tag that were processed before the Throwable is thrown, are processed. The <c:catch> tag has a single optional attribute named var. This attribute defines a variable to hold the Throwable that was thrown inside the body of the <c:catch> tag. This variable always has a scope of page.

The following table lists all of the JSTL core tag libraries

Tag	Description	Example

<c:catch>	Catches any Exception, Error or Throwable thrown inside its body.	```<c:catch var="e">```
		``` <c:out value="1/0"/>```
		``` <c:if test="e!=null">```
		``` <c:out value=```
		``` "e.message"/>```
		``` </c:if>```
		```</c:catch>```

<c:choose>	Used to wrap <c:when> and (optionally) <c:otherwise> tags. The body of the first <c:when> tag containing a test expression that evaluates to true is executed. If none of the <c:when> tags contain a test expression that evaluates to true, then the body of the <c:otherwise> tag is executed.	```<c:choose>```
		``` <c:when test="empty o">```
		``` <c:out value=```
		``` "o is empty"/>```
		``` </c:when>```
		``` <c:otherwise>```
		``` <c:out value=```
		``` "o is not empty"/>```
		``` </c:otherwise>```
		```</c:choose>```

Tag	Description	Example
`<c:forEach>`	Iterates over an array, `Collection`, or Map.	`<c:forEach items="${session.arrayOrCollection}" var="item">` `<c:out value="item = ${item}> ` `</c:forEach>`
`<c:if>`	Its body gets executed if the test expression evaluates to `true`.	`<c:if test="${a>b}">` `<c:out value="a is greater than b"/>` `</c:if>`
`<c:import>`	Imports content from the URL indicated in the `url` attribute into the rendered page.	`<c:import url="http://foo.com/somePage.jsp">` `<c:param name="someName" value="some val"/>` `</c:import>`
`<c:out>`	Outputs the value of the `value` expression.	`<c:out value="> is the greater than symbol" escapeXml="true"/>`.
`<c:otherwise>`	Its body gets executed if none of the test expressions in the `<c:when>` tags nested in the same `<c:choose>` tag evaluates to `true`.	See example for `<c:choose>`
`<c:param>`	Sets a parameter for a URL defined in the `<c:url>` or `<c:import>` tag.	See example for `<c:import>`.
`<c:redirect>`	Redirects to the specified URL.	`<c:redirect url="http://ensode.net"/>`
`<c:remove>`	Removes a variable from the page scope or the specified scope.	`<c:remove var="varName" scope="session"/>`
`<c:set>`	Sets a variable in the page scope or the specified scope.	`<c:set var="varName" value="foo" scope-"scssion"/>`
`<c:url>`	Creates a URL variable.	`<c:url value="http://foo.com" var="fooUrl"/>`
`<c:when>`	Its body gets executed when its test expression evaluates to `true`.	See example for `<c:choose>`.

Formatting JSTL Tag Library

The formatting JSTL tag library provides tags that ease internationalization and localization of web applications. This tag library allows displaying a page in different languages, based on the user's locale, it also allows locale-specific formatting of dates and currency.

The following example illustrates the use of the Formatting JSTL tag library.

```
<%@ page language="java" contentType="text/html; charset=UTF-8"
  pageEncoding="UTF-8"%>
<%@ taglib uri="http://java.sun.com/jsp/jstl/fmt" prefix="fmt"%>

<!DOCTYPE html PUBLIC "-//W3C//DTD HTML 4.01 Transitional//EN"
"http://www.w3.org/TR/html4/loose.dtd">
<html>
<head>
<meta http-equiv="Content-Type" content="text/html; charset=UTF-8">
<title>Format Tag Demo</title>
</head>
<body>
<jsp:useBean id="today" class="java.util.Date" />
<fmt:setLocale value="en_US" />
<fmt:bundle basename="ApplicationResources">
  <fmt:message key="greeting" />,<br />
  <fmt:message key="proposal" />
  <fmt:formatNumber type="currency" value="42000" />.<br />
  <fmt:message key="offer_ends" />
  <fmt:formatDate value="${today}" type="date" dateStyle="full" />.
  </fmt:bundle>
<br />
<br />
<fmt:setLocale value="es_ES" />
<fmt:bundle basename="ApplicationResources">
  <fmt:message key="greeting" />,<br />
  <fmt:message key="proposal" />
  <fmt:formatNumber type="currency" value="42000" />.<br />
  <fmt:message key="offer_ends" />
  <fmt:formatDate value="${today}" type="date" dateStyle="full" />
</fmt:bundle>
</body>
</html>
```

This page's display basically greets the user, then proceeds to make a proposal (sales pitch) followed by a price and an offer end date.

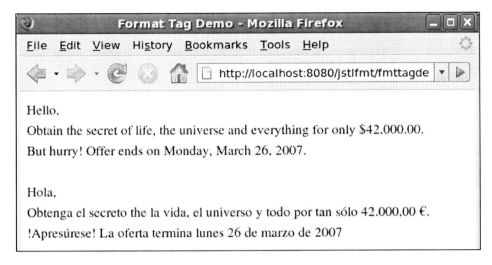

As this page is internationalized, the actual text of the page is stored in a property file called a resource bundle. The resource bundle for the page is called `ApplicationResources.properties`; this is set in the page via the `<fmt:bundle>` tag.

The page displays the same message in English and Spanish; therefore two resource bundles are needed, one for each locale. The locale to use is defined in the `value` attribute of the `<fmt:setLocale>` tag.

A real application would not simultaneously display the same messages in two languages; instead, it would detect the user's locale from the request and use the appropriate resource bundle. If the user's locale doesn't match any of the available resource bundles, then the default one would be used.

The English (and default) version of `ApplicationResources.properties` looks like this:

```
greeting=Hello
proposal=Obtain the secret of life, the universe and everything for
only
offer_ends=But hurry! Offer ends on
```

The Spanish version of the resource bundle is called
`ApplicationResources_es.properties`.

```
greeting=Hola
proposal=Obtenga el secreto the la vida, el universo y todo por tan
sólo
offer_ends=!Apresúrese! La oferta termina
```

As we can see, a resource bundle is nothing but a property file with keys and values. The keys in each localized resource bundle must be the same; the value should vary according to the locale.

In order to be accessible to JSP pages and Java code, resource bundles need to be placed in any directory in the `WEB-INF/classes` directory folder or any of its subdirectories in the WAR file where the application is deployed. If they are placed in a subdirectory of the `WEB-INF/classes` directory, then the `basename` attribute of the `<fmt:bundle>` tag must include each directory under this directory separated by dots. For example, if the `ApplicationResources.properties` and `ApplicationResources_es.properties` were placed under `WEB-INF/classes/net/ensode`, the `<fmt:bundle>` tag would look like this:

```
<fmt:bundle basename="net.ensode.ApplicationResources">
```

As we can see, this looks like a fully qualified class name, but in reality we are pointing to the resource bundle.

Resource bundle names for each locale must have the same base name as the base resource bundle (`ApplicationProperties`, in this case), followed by an underscore, and followed by the appropriate locale (es in this case). The locale can specify a language only (en or es, for example) , or a language and country (en_US or es_ES, for example). If no country is specified in the locale, any country whose primary language matches the locale will use the resource bundle for that language.

 The above example uses es_ES as the locale, assuming every page that is in Spanish comes from Spain; obviously this wouldn't work in a real application and was done this way for simplicity.

The `<fmt:message>` tag looks for a key in the resource bundle matching its `key` attribute and displays its value on the page. Though not illustrated in the example, sometimes resource bundle values can have parameters; these parameters are substituted at run time with appropriate values. Parameters are designated by an integer between curly braces, as in the following example:

```
personalGreeting=Hello {0}
```

The {0} in this property is a parameter. Parameters can be substituted by the appropriate values at run time by using the `<fmt:param>` tag. This tag must be nested inside an `<fmt:message>` tag. The `<fmt:message>` tag has an attribute named `value`, the value of which can be a String constant or Unified Expression Language expression; it is used to substitute the parameter with this value.

The next formatting tag we see in the example is the `<fmt:formatNumber>` tag. This tag formats a number according to the locale; some locales use a comma to separate thousands and a dot as a decimal separator, while for others is the other way around; as can be seen in the previous screenshot, the `<fmt:formatNumber>` tag will take care of this for us. Another useful attribute of the `<fmt:formatNumber>` tag is the `type` attribute, which has three valid values: `number`, `percent`, or `currency`. As can be seen in the example, if the `type` attribute is set to `currency`, then the appropriate currency symbol for the locale is automatically added to the number.

The next new formatting tag we see in the example is the `<fmt:formatDate>`; this tag will take a `Date` object specified by its `value` attribute and format it appropriately for the given locale. In addition to translating the date into the appropriate language, this tag will place the day of the week, the day of the month, the month and the year in the appropriate order for the corresponding locale. It will also use the correct capitalization for the first letter of the month. The `dateStyle` attribute of the `<fmt:formatDate>` tag has the following valid values: `full`, `long`, `medium`, `short`, and `default`; if no value is specified, `default` is used.

The Format tag library tags we have covered so far are the most commonly used; the following table lists all the JSTL formatting library tags:

Tag	Description	Example
`<fmt:bundle>`	Load a resource bundle to be used inside its body.	`<fmt:bundle basename="resbund"> <fmt:message key="greeting"> </fmt:bundle>`
`<fmt:formatDate>`	Formats the date specified by its `value` attribute, optionally using a specified value and pattern.	`<fmt:formatDate value="${today}" pattern= "MM/dd/yyyy"/>`
`<fmt:formatNumber>`	Formats the number specified by its `value` attribute according to the current locale. Can be used to format the number as currency or percentage, depending on the value of its optional `type` attribute.	`<fmt:formatNumber value="42000" />`

Tag	Description	Example
`<fmt:message>`	Displays a localized message corresponding to the key defined in its `key` attribute.	`<fmt:message key="offer_ends" />`
`<fmt:param>`	Substitutes a parameter in the enclosing `<fmt:message>` tag.	`<fmt:param value="someVal"/>`
`<fmt:parseDate>`	Parses a String containing a date into a `Date` object.	`<fmt:parseDate value="03/31/2007" pattern= "MM/dd/yyyy" var="parsedDate"/>`
`<fmt:parseNumber>`	Parses a numeric String into a `Long` or `Double` object.	`<fmt:parseNumber value="42,000.00" var="parsedNumber"/>`
`<fmt: requestEncoding>`	Used to set the request's character encoding.	`<fmt:requestEncoding key="ISO-8859-1"/>`
`<fmt:setBundle>`	Sets the resource bundle to use in the specified scope. Default scope is `page`.	`<fmt:setBundle baseName="resbund" var="bundle" scope="session"/>`
`<fmt:setLocale>`	Sets the locale to use in the specified scope. Default scope is `page`.	`<fmt:setLocale value="en_US" />`
`<fmt:setTimeZone>`	Sets the time zone to use in the specified scope. Default scope is `page`.	`<fmt:setTimeZone value="EST" var= "sessionTimeZone" scope="session"/>`
`<fmt:timeZone>`	Sets the time zone to use inside its body.	`<fmt:timeZone value="EST"> <fmt:formatDate value="${today}"/> </fmt:timeZone>`

SQL JSTL Tag Library

The SQL JSTL tag library allows us to execute SQL queries from JSP pages. As this tag library mixes presentation and database access code, it should only be used for prototyping and for writing simple "throwaway" applications. For more complex applications, it is always a good idea to follow the DAO and MVC design patterns.

The following example illustrates the most commonly used tags in the SQL JSTL Tag Library.

```
<%@ page language="java" contentType="text/html; charset=UTF-8"
  pageEncoding="UTF-8"%>
<%@ taglib uri="http://java.sun.com/jsp/jstl/sql" prefix="sql"%>
<%@taglib uri="http://java.sun.com/jsp/jstl/core" prefix="c"%>
<!DOCTYPE html PUBLIC "-//W3C//DTD HTML 4.01 Transitional//EN"
"http://www.w3.org/TR/html4/loose.dtd">
<html>
<head>
<meta http-equiv="Content-Type" content="text/html; charset=UTF-8">
<title>SQL Tag Demo</title>
</head>
<body>
<sql:setDataSource dataSource="jdbc/__CustomerDBPool" />
<sql:transaction>
  <sql:update>
    insert into CUSTOMERS (CUSTOMER_ID, FIRST_NAME, LAST_NAME) values
(((select max(CUSTOMER_ID) from customers) + 1), ?, ?)
    <sql:param value="${param.firstName}" />
    <sql:param value="${param.lastName}" />
  </sql:update>
</sql:transaction>
<p>Successfully inserted the following row into the CUSTOMERS table:</
p>
<sql:query var="selectedRows"
  sql="select FIRST_NAME, LAST_NAME from customers where FIRST_NAME =
? and LAST_NAME = ?">
  <sql:param value="${param.firstName}" />
  <sql:param value="${param.lastName}" />
</sql:query>
<table border="1" cellpadding="0" cellspacing="0">
  <tr>
    <td>First Name</td>
    <td>Last Name</td>
  </tr>
  <c:forEach var="currentRow" items="${selectedRows.rows}">
    <tr>
      <td><c:out value="${currentRow.FIRST_NAME}" /></td>
      <td><c:out value="${currentRow.LAST_NAME}" /></td>
    </tr>
  </c:forEach>
</table>
</body>
</html>
```

After packaging this JSP in a WAR file, deploying the WAR file, and pointing the browser to the JSP's URL, we should see a page like the following:

Like most of our examples, the above page is pretty simplistic, and does not necessarily represent what would be done in an actual application. The page inserts a row into the CUSTOMERS table and then queries the table for rows matching the values inserted. A real application (keeping in mind that the SQL tag library should only be used for very simple applications) would typically insert values obtained from request parameters into the database. It would be unlikely for the same page to query the database for the data just inserted; this would probably be done in a separate page.

The first JSTL SQL tag we see in the example is the `<sql:setDataSource>` tag. This tag sets the data source to be used for database access. The data source can either be obtained via JNDI by using its JNDI name as the value of this tags `datasource` attribute or by specifying a JDBC URL, user name, and password via the `url`, `user`, and `password` attributes. This example uses the first approach. In order for this approach to work correctly, a `<resource-ref>` element must be added to the application's `web.xml` file.

```
<web-app xmlns="http://java.sun.com/xml/ns/javaee" version="2.5"
  xmlns:xsi="http://www.w3.org/2001/XMLSchema-instance"
  xsi:schemaLocation="http://java.sun.com/xml/ns/javaee http://java.
sun.com/xml/ns/javaee/web-app_2_5.xsd">
  <resource-ref>
    <res-ref-name>jdbc/__CustomerDBPool</res-ref-name>
    <res-type>javax.sql.DataSource</res-type>
    <res-auth>Container</res-auth>
  </resource-ref>
</web-app>
```

The `<res-ref-name>` subelement of the `<resource-ref>` element contains the JNDI name of the data source. This needs to be set up in the application server. The example uses the data source we used in Chapter 4 (refer to the `readme.txt` file for Chapter 4 for instructions on setting up this data source).

The `<res-type>` subelement of the `<resource-ref>` element contains the fully qualified name of the resource to be obtained via JNDI; for data sources, this will always be `javax.sql.DataSource`.

The `<res-auth>` subelement of the `<resource-ref>` element should have a value of `Container` when using the `<resource-ref>` element to define a data source as a resource. This allows the application server to use the credentials set up in the connection pool corresponding to the data source to log into the database.

No Suitable Driver SQL Exception

Sometimes the `<sql:setDataSource>` tag will result in a `java.sql.SQLException: No suitable driver` exception when using its `datasource` attribute to locate the data source via JNDI. This typically means that we forgot to modify the application's `web.xml` as described above.

As we mentioned before, an alternative way of using the `<sql:setDataSource>` tag is to specify the database connection URL and credentials. Had we used this approach in the example, the `<sql:setDataSource>` tag would have looked like this:

```
<sql:setDataSource url="jdbc:derby://localhost:1527/customerdb"
    user="dev" password="dev" />
```

The attributes used are self-explanatory. The `url` attribute should contain the JDBC URL for the connection. The `user` and `password` attributes should contain the user name and password used to log in to the database, respectively.

The next JSTL SQL tag we see in the example is the `<sql:transaction>` tag; this tag, unsurprisingly, wraps any `<sql:query>` and `<sql:update>` tags it contains in a transaction.

Next, we see the `<sql:update>` tag, which is used to execute any queries that modify data in the database. It can be used for INSERT, UPDATE, or DELETE SQL statements. As can be seen in the example, queries inside this tag can have one or more parameters. Just as when using JDBC Prepared Statements, question marks are used as placeholders for parameters. The `<sql:param>` tag is used to set the values of any parameters in a query defined in an `<sql:update>` or an `<sql:query>` tag. The `<sql:param>` tag sets the value for its containing tag via its `value` attribute, which may contain a String constant or a Unified Expression Language expression.

The <sql:query> tag is used to query data from the database via a SELECT statement. The query's result set is stored in a variable defined by this tag's var attribute. By default, the var attribute has a scope of page; this can be changed by using the <sql:query> scope attribute and setting its value to the appropriate scope (page, request, session, or application). As can be seen in the example, we can iterate through the variable defined by this tag's var attribute by using a <c:forEach> tag.

The following table lists all the JSTL SQL tags:

Tag	Description	Example
<sql:dateParam>	Sets the value for a date parameter in an <sql:query> or <sql:update> tag.	See example for <sql:query>.
<sql:param>	Sets the value for a text or numeric parameter in an <sql:query> or <sql:update> tag.	See example for <sql:update>.

<sql:query>	Executes the SQL query defined in its sql attribute and optionally attaches the resulting result set into the specified scope using the specified variable name.	<sql:query
		  sql=
		  "select * from table
		  where last_update
		  < ?"
		  var="selectedRows">
		<sql:dateParam
		
		  value=
		    "${someDate}"/>
		</sql:query>

<sql:setDataSource>	Defines the data source to be used at the specified scope. If no scope is specified, the default scope is page. The data source can be obtained via a JNDI lookup or by specifying a JDBC URL through the url, user, and password attributes.	<sql:setDataSource dataSource="jdbc/__ CustomerDBPool" />

Tag	Description	Example

`<sql:transaction>`	Wraps any `<sql:query>` and `<sql:update>` tags inside its body in a transaction.	`<sql:transaction>`
		`  <sql:update`
		`    sql="update table`
		`set some_col = ?">`
		`    <sql:param`
		`value="someValue"/>`
		`  </sql:update>`
		`  <sql:update`
		`    sql="update table2`
		`set some_col = ?">`
		`    <sql:param`
		`value="someValue"/>`
		`  </sql:update>`
		`</sql:transaction>`

`<sql:update>`	Executes an SQL INSERT, UPDATE, or DELETE statement.	`<sql:update`
		`  sql="update table`
		`set some_col = ?">`
		`  <sql:param`
		`value="someValue"/>`
		`</sql:update>`

XML JSTL Tag Library

The XML JSTL tag library provides an easy way to parse XML documents and to do Extensible Stylesheet Language transformations (XSLT). This tag library uses XPath expressions navigate through elements in an XML document.

XPath is an expression language used for finding information in an XML document, or for making calculations based on the content of an XML document. For more information about XPath, see `http://www.w3.org/TR/xpath`.

The following example illustrates the most commonly used tags in the XML JSTL Tag Library.

```
<%@ page language="java" contentType="text/html; charset=UTF-8"
  pageEncoding="UTF-8"%>
<%@ taglib uri="http://java.sun.com/jsp/jstl/xml" prefix="x"%>
<%@ taglib uri="http://java.sun.com/jsp/jstl/core" prefix="c"%>

<c:import url="customers.xml" var="xml" />
<x:parse doc="${xml}" var="doc" />
<!DOCTYPE html PUBLIC "-//W3C//DTD HTML 4.01 Transitional//EN"
"http://www.w3.org/TR/html4/loose.dtd">
```

```
<html>
<head>
<meta http-equiv="Content-Type" content="text/html; charset=UTF-8">
<title>XML Tag Demo</title>
</head>
<body>
<table cellpadding="0" cellspacing="0" border="1">
  <tr>
    <td>First Name</td>
    <td>Last Name</td>
    <td>Email</td>
  </tr>
  <x:forEach select="$doc/customers/customer">
    <tr>
      <td>
        <x:out select="firstName" />
      </td>
      <td>
        <x:out select="lastName" /></td>
      <td>
        <x:choose>
          <x:when select="email">
            <x:out select="email" />
          </x:when>
          <x:otherwise>
            <c:out value="N/A" />
          </x:otherwise>
        </x:choose>
      </td>
    </tr>
  </x:forEach>
</table>
</body>
</html>
```

The first thing we should notice in this example is the use of the core JSTL tag `<c:import>` to import an XML file from a URL. The value of the `url` attribute defines the URL where the XML file can be located; it can be a relative or absolute URL. In the example, the `customers.xml` file is in the same directory as the JSP, therefore a relative path is used to obtain it. The `customers.xml` has customer information including first name, last name, and email address it is shown next.

```
<?xml version="1.0" encoding="UTF-8"?>
<customers>
  <customer>
    <firstName>Karl</firstName>
    <lastName>Smith</lastName>
    <email>karls@nonexistent.org</email>
  </customer>
```

```
<customer>
  <firstName>Jenny</firstName>
  <lastName>Conte</lastName>
  <email>jenny@notreal.com</email>
</customer>
<customer>
  <firstName>Rhonda</firstName>
  <lastName>Benedict</lastName>
</customer>
</customers>
```

After packaging these two files in a WAR file and visiting the JSP's URL, we should see a page like the following:

The first JSTL XML tag that we see in the example is the `<x:parse>` tag. This tag parses an XML document and stores it in the variable defined by its `var` attribute. The XML document to parse is defined in its `doc` attribute.

The XML JSTL tag library contains several tags that are analogous to similar tags in the Core JSTL tag libraries; these tags include: `<x:if>`, `<x:choose>`, `<x:when>`, `<x:otherwise>`, `<x:forEach>`, `<x:param>`, and `<x:set>`. Usage of these tags is very similar to their core tag counterparts. The main difference is that these tags contain a `select` attribute containing an XPath expression to evaluate, instead of the `value` attribute that the corresponding core tags contain. The example illustrates the usage of most of these tags.

The next JSTL XML tag we see in the example is the `<x:forEach>` tag. This tag iterates over the elements of an XML document. Elements to iterate over are specified as an XPath expression through the `select` attribute.

The next JSTL XML tag we see in the example is the `<x:out>` tag, which outputs the value of the XPath expression defined in its `select` attribute.

Next, we see the `<x:choose>` tag, which is the parent tag of the `<x:when>` and (optionally) `<x:otherwise>` tags. The body of the first nested `<x:when>` tag containing an XPath expression evaluating to true as its `select` attribute is executed;

`select` expressions for subsequent `<x:when>` attributes are not evaluated after one of them evaluates to true. If no `select` attributes for any of the `<x:when>` tags evaluate to true, the body of the optional `<x:otherwise>` tag is executed.

An additional XML JSTL tag is the `<x:transform>` tag, which is used to do XSLT transformations on XML documents. This tag is typically used with two attributes. The `xml` attribute indicates the location of the XML document to transform; it can be imported via the `<c:import>` tag as illustrated in the example. The `xslt` attribute indicates the XSL stylesheet used to transform the document. This stylesheet can also be imported via the `<c:import>` tag.

The following table lists all of the JSTL XML tags.

Tag	Description	Example
`<x:choose>`	Used to wrap `<x:when>` and (optionally) `<x:otherwise>` tags. The body of the first `<x:when>` tag containing a select expression that evaluates to `true` is executed. If none of the `<x:when>` tags contain a test expression that evaluates to `true`, then the body of the `<x:otherwise>` tag is executed.	See example for `<x:forEach>`.

`<x:forEach>`	Iterates over the elements of an XML document. Elements to iterate over are specified through the `select` attribute.	`<x:forEach select="$doc/customers/customer">`
		`<tr>`
		`  <td>`
		`  <x:out select="firstName" />`
		`  </td>`
		`  <td>`
		`  <x:out select="lastName" />`
		`  </td>`
		`  <td>`
		`  <x:choose>`
		`    <x:when select="email">`
		`      <x:out select="email" />`
		`    </x:when>`
		`    <x:otherwise>`
		`      <c:out value="N/A" />`
		`    </x:otherwise>`
		`  </x:choose>`
		`  </td>`
		`  </tr>`
		`</x:forEach>`

Tag	Description	Example
`<x:otherwise>`	Its body gets executed if none of the test expressions in the `<x:when>` tags nested in the same `<x:choose>` tag evaluates to `true`.	See example for `<x:forEach>`.
`<x:out>`	Outputs an XPath expression defined by the `select` attribute.	See example for `<x:forEach>`.
`<x:param>`	Adds a parameter to the containing `<x:transform>` tag.	See example for `<x:transform>`.
`<x:parse>`	Parses an XML document and stores it in the variable defined by its `var` attribute.	`<x:parse doc="${xml}" var="doc" />`
`<x:set>`	Saves the result of the XPath expression defined in its `select` attribute into a variable in the specified scope. If no scope is defined, a default scope of `page` is used.	`<x:set var="custEmail" select="email"/>`
`<x:transform>`	Transforms the XML document defined by the `xml` attribute using the XSL stylesheet defined by the `xslt` attribute.	`<x:transform xml="${someXmlDoc}" xslt="${xslt}"> <x:param name="paramName" value="${paramValue}"/> </x:transform>`
`<x:when>`	Its body gets executed when its select expression evaluates to `true`.	See example for `<x:forEach>`.

JSTL Functions

JSTL contains a number of functions that take Unified Expression Language expressions as parameters. All JSTL functions except one are used exclusively for String manipulation. The exception is the `fn:length()` function, which can take a String, Collection, or array as a parameter; it returns the length of the `String`, the size of the Collection, or the length of the array, depending on what parameter is passed to it. The following JSP illustrates the use of JSTL functions.

```
<%@ page language="java" contentType="text/html; charset=UTF-8"
    pageEncoding="UTF-8"%>
<%@ taglib uri="http://java.sun.com/jsp/jstl/functions" prefix="fn"%>
<%@ taglib uri="http://java.sun.com/jsp/jstl/core" prefix="c"%>
```

```
<!DOCTYPE html PUBLIC "-//W3C//DTD HTML 4.01 Transitional//EN"
"http://www.w3.org/TR/html4/loose.dtd">
<html>
<head>
<meta http-equiv="Content-Type" content="text/html; charset=UTF-8">
<title>Function Tag Demo</title>
</head>
<body>
<c:set var="nameArr"
  value="${fn:split('Kevin,Danielle,Alex,Beatrice',',')}" />
We have a list of ${fn:length(nameArr)} names, here they are:
<br />
<ol>
  <c:forEach var="currentName" items="${nameArr}">
    <li />
      ${fn:toUpperCase(currentName)}
    <br />
  </c:forEach>
</ol>
</body>
</html>
```

After packaging the above JSP in a WAR file, deploying it, and pointing the browser to its URL, we should see a page like the following:

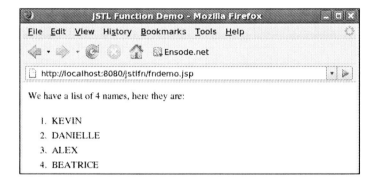

The above JSP illustrates the use of some of the JSTL functions. The `fn:split()` function splits a String into an array of Strings, using the character specified by its second parameter as a delimiter.

> Notice that the Strings inside the `fn:split()` function are enclosed inside single quotes. JSTL allows this since using double quotes for the Strings would have resulted in illegal syntax because the `fn:split()` function is already inside double quotes.

In the example, the `fn:length()` function returns the number of elements in the array we created when the `fn:split()` function was executed. As we mentioned earlier, the `fn:split()` can also take a `Collection` or a `String` as a parameter. When applied to a Collection, the function returns the number of elements in it; when applied to a String, the function returns the number of characters in the String.

The next function illustrated in the example is `fn:toUpperCase()`, which simply makes every alphabetical character in the `String` it takes as a parameter upper case. There are many other JSTL functions, all of them are very intuitive to use. The following table lists all the JSTL functions.

Function	Description	Example
`fn:contains(String, String)`	Returns a Boolean indicating if the second parameter is contained in the first one.	`${fn:contains("environment", "iron")}`
`fn:containsIgnoreCase(String, String)`	Case insensitive version of `fn:contains()`.	`${fn:containsIgnoreCase("environment", "Iron")}`
`fn:endsWith(String, String)`	Returns a Boolean indicating if the first parameter ends with a String equal to the second parameter.	`${fn:endsWith("GlassFish", "Fish")}`
`fn:escapeXml(String)`	Returns a String with all XML characters in the parameter escaped into their respective XML character entity code.	`${fn:escapeXml("<html>")}`
`fn:indexOf(String, String)`	Returns an int indicating the index of the second parameter in the first parameter. Returns -1 if the second parameter is not a substring of the first parameter.	`${fn:indexOf("GlassFish", "Fish")}`
`fn:join(String[], String)`	Returns a String composed of the elements in the first parameter, using the second parameter as a delimiter.	`${fn:join(arrayVar, ", ")}`

Function	Description	Example
`fn:length(Object)`	Returns the length of an array, the size of a Collection, or the length of a String, depending on the type of the parameter.	`${fn:length("String, Collection or Array")}`
`fn:replace(String, String, String)`	Returns a String replacing every instance of the second parameter in the first parameter with the third parameter.	`${fn: replace("CrystalFish", "Glass")}`
`fn:startsWith(String, String)`	Returns a Boolean indicating if the first parameter starts with the second parameter.	`${fn: startsWith("GlassFish", "Glass")}`
`fn:split(String, String)`	Returns an array of Strings containing elements in the first parameter as delimited by the second parameter.	`${fn:split("Eeny, meeny",",")}`
`fn:substring(String, int, int)`	Returns a String containing the substring in the first parameter, starting at the index indicated by the second parameter and ending just before the index indicated by the third parameter.	`${fn:substring( "0123456789",3, 6) }`
`fn: substringAfter(String, String)`	Returns a String containing the substring in the first parameter starting after the first occurrence of the second parameter until the end of the first parameter.	`${fn:substringAfter( "GlassFish", "Glass")}`
`fn: substringBefore(String, String)`	Returns a String containing the substring in the first parameter starting from the start of the first parameter and ending just before the first occurrence of the second parameter.	`${fn:substringBefore( "GlassFish", "Fish")}`

Function	Description	Example
fn:toLowerCase(String)	Returns a String containing a version of the parameters with all alphabetical characters as lower case.	${fn:toLowerCase("GlassFish")}
fn:toUpperCase(String)	Returns a String containing a version of the parameters with all alphabetical characters as upper case.	${fn:toUppserCase("GlassFish")}
fn:trim(String)	Returns a String containing a modified version of the parameter with all whitespace at the beginning and end of the parameter removed.	${fn:trim(" GlassFish ")}

Summary

This chapter covered all JSP Standard Tag Library tags, including the core, formatting, SQL, and XML tags, and also covered JSTL functions, with examples illustrating the most common JSTL tags and functions.

6

JavaServer Faces

In this chapter, we will cover JavaServer Faces (JSF), the standard component framework of the Java EE platform. JSF applications consist of a number of JSPs for the user interface (other view technologies are supported, but JSP is the default), a series of managed beans that can serve to hold data entered in the JSPs and can also serve as controllers, and a configuration file declaring all the managed beans and page navigation for the application.

 Please note that JSF is a component framework that can use several different view technologies to generate the user interface. When using JSP as its view technology, tag libraries are used to render JSF components as HTML input fields. This chapter uses the terms "tag" and "component" interchangeably.

Developing Our First JSF Application

To illustrate basic JSF concepts, we will develop a simple application consisting of two JSPs and a single managed bean.

As we mentioned in this chapter's introduction, the default view technology for JSF is JSP. A "JSF-enabled" JSP is nothing but a standard JSP using a number of JSF-specific tags. The following example shows what a typical JSF JSP looks like:

```
<%@ page language="java" contentType="text/html; charset=UTF-8"
  pageEncoding="UTF-8"%>
<%@ taglib uri="http://java.sun.com/jsf/core" prefix="f"%>
<%@ taglib uri="http://java.sun.com/jsf/html" prefix="h"%>
<!DOCTYPE html PUBLIC "-//W3C//DTD HTML 4.01 Transitional//EN"
"http://www.w3.org/TR/html4/loose.dtd">
<html>
<head>
<meta http-equiv="Content-Type" content="text/html; charset=UTF-8">
```

```
<style type="text/css">
.leftAlign { text-align: left;}
.rightAlign { text-align: right;}
</style>
<title>Enter Customer Data</title>
</head>
<body>
<f:view>
  <h:form>
    <h:messages></h:messages>
    <h:panelGrid columns="2"
      columnClasses="rightAlign,leftAlign">
      <h:outputText value="First Name:">
      </h:outputText>
      <h:inputText label="First Name"
        value="#{Customer.firstName}"
        required="true">
        <f:validateLength minimum="2"
          maximum="30"></f:validateLength>
      </h:inputText>
      <h:outputText value="Last Name:"></h:outputText>
      <h:inputText label="Last Name"
        value="#{Customer.lastName}"
        required="true">
        <f:validateLength minimum="2"
          maximum="30"></f:validateLength>
      </h:inputText>
      <h:outputText value="Email:">
      </h:outputText>
      <h:inputText label="Email" value="#{Customer.email}">
        <f:validateLength minimum="3"
          maximum="30"></f:validateLength>
      </h:inputText>
      <h:panelGroup></h:panelGroup>
      <h:commandButton action="save"
        value="Save"></h:commandButton>
    </h:panelGrid>
  </h:form>
</f:view>
</body>
</html>
```

The following screenshot illustrates how this JSP renders in the browser.

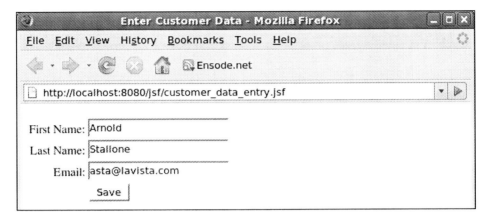

The above screenshot, of course, was taken after entering some data in every text field; originally, each text field was blank.

Pretty much any JSF-enabled JSP will include the two tag libraries illustrated in the example. The first tag library (`<%@ taglib uri="http://java.sun.com/jsf/core" prefix="f"%>`) is the core JSF tag library, by convention, the prefix "f" (for "faces") is used when using this tag library.

The second tag library (`<%@ taglib uri="http://java.sun.com/jsf/html" prefix="h"%>`) is for tags that render HTML components; by convention, the prefix "h" (for "HTML") is used when using this tag library.

The example opposite contains some of the most frequently used JSF tags. The first tag we see in the example is the `<f:view>` tag, which tells the container that JSF is used to manage the components inside of it. Any JSF tags (core, HTML, or custom) must be placed inside the `<f:view>` tag.

The next tag we see is the `<h:form>` tag. This tag generates an HTML form when the JSP is rendered. As can be seen in the example, there is no need to specify an `action` or a `method` attribute for this tag; as a matter of fact, there is no `action` attribute nor `method` attribute for this tag. The `action` attribute for the rendered HTML form will be generated automatically, and the `method` attribute will always be `"post"`.

The next tag we see is the `<h:messages>` tag. As its name implies, this tag is used to display any messages. As we will see shortly, JSF can automatically generate validation messages; these will be displayed inside this tag. Additionally, arbitrary messages can be added programmatically via the `addMessage()` method defined in `javax.faces.context.FacesContext`.

The next JSF tag we see is `<h:panelGrid>`. This tag is roughly equivalent to an HTML table, but it works a bit differently. Instead of declaring rows and columns, the `<h:panelGrid>` tag has a `columns` attribute; the value of this attribute indicates the number of columns in the table rendered by this tag. As we place components inside this tag, they will be placed in a row until the number of columns defined in the `columns` attribute is reached, and then the next component will be placed in the next row. In the example, the value of the columns attribute is two, therefore the first two tags will be placed in the first row, the next two will be placed in the second row, and so forth.

Another interesting attribute of `<h:panelGrid>` is the `columnClasses` attribute. This attribute assigns a CSS class to each column in the rendered table. In the example, two CSS classes (separated by a comma) are used as the value for this attribute. This has the effect of assigning the first CSS class to the first column, and the second one to the second column. Had there been three or more columns, the third one would have gotten the first CSS class, the fourth one the second one, and so on, alternating between the first one and the second one. To clarify how this works, the next code snippet illustrates a portion of the source of the HTML markup generated by our sample JSP.

```
<table>
  <tbody>
    <tr>
      <td class="rightAlign">
        First Name:
      </td>
      <td class="leftAlign">
        <input type="text" name="j_id_id18:j_id_id27" /></td>
    </tr>
    <tr>
      <td class="rightAlign">
        Last Name:
      </td>
      <td class="leftAlign">
        <input type="text"
          name="j_id_id18:j_id_id34" />
      </td>
    </tr>
    <tr>
      <td class="rightAlign">Email:</td>
      <td class="leftAlign">
        <input type="text" name="j_id_id18:j_id_id42" />
      </td>
    </tr>
    <tr>
```

```
      <td class="rightAlign"></td>
      <td class="leftAlign">
        <input type="submit"
          name="j_id_id18:j_id_id49" value="Save" />
      </td>
    </tr>
  </tbody>
</table>
```

Notice how each `<td>` tag has an alternating CSS tag of `"rightAlign"` or `"leftAlign"`; we achieved this by assigning the value `"rightAlign,leftAlign"` to the `columnClasses` attribute of `<h:panelGrid>`.

At this point in the example, we start adding components inside `<h:panelGrid>`. These components will be rendered inside the table rendered by `<h:panelGrid>`. As we mentioned before, the number of columns in the rendered table is defined by the columns attribute of `<h:panelGrid>`. Therefore, we don't need to worry about columns (or rows); we just start adding components and they will be placed in the right place.

The next tag we see is the `<h:outputText>` tag. This tag is similar to the core JSTL `<c:out>` tag. It outputs the text or expression in its `value` attribute to the rendered page.

Next, we see the `<h:inputText>` tag. This tag generates a text field in the rendered page; its label attribute is used for any validation messages. It lets the user know what field the message refers to.

> Although it is not required for the value of the `label` attribute of `<h:inputText>` to match the label displayed on the page, it is highly recommended to use this value. This will let the user know exactly what field the message is referring to.

Of particular interest is the tag's `value` attribute. What we see as the value for this attribute is a **value binding expression**. What this means is that this value is tied to a property of one of the application's managed beans. In the example, this particular text field is tied to a property called `firstName` in a managed bean called `Customer`. When a user enters a value for this text field and submits the form, the corresponding property in the managed bean is updated with this value. The tag's `required` attribute is optional and valid values for it are `true` and `false`. If this attribute is set to `true`, the container will not let the user submit the form until the user enters some data for the text field.

If the user attempts to submit the form without entering a required value, the page will be reloaded and an error message will be displayed inside the `<h:messages>` tag.

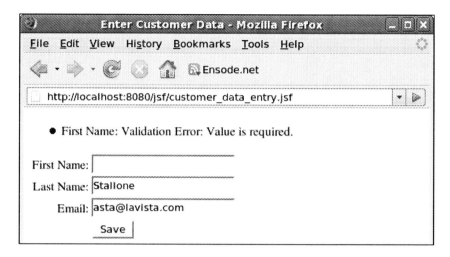

The above screenshot illustrates the default error message shown when the user attempts to save the form in the example without entering a value for the customer's first name. The first part of the message ("First Name") is taken from the value of the `label` attribute of the corresponding `<h:inputTextField>` tag. The text of the message can be customized, as well as its style (font, color, etc.). We will cover how to do this later in this chapter.

 Having an `<h:messages>` tag on every JSF page is a good idea; without it, the user might not see validation messages and will have no idea of why the form submission is not going through.

Each `<h:inputField>` tag in our example has a nested `<f:validateLength>` tag. As its name implies, this tag validates that the entered value for the text field is between a minimum and maximum length. Minimum and maximum values are defined by the tag's `minimum` and `maximum` attributes. `<f:validateLength>` is one of the standard validators included with JSF. Just as with the `required` attribute of `<h:inputText>`, JSF will automatically display a default error message when a user attempts to submit a form with a value that does not validate.

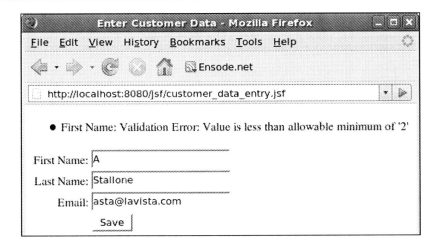

Again, the default message and style can be overridden; we will cover how to do this in the next section.

In addition to `<f:validateLength>` JSF includes two other standard validators: `<f:validateDoubleRange>` validates that the value is a valid `Double` value between the two values specified by the tag's `minimum` and `maximum` attributes, inclusive. `<f:validateLongRange>` validates that the value is a valid `Long` value between the values specified by the tag's `minimum` and `maximum` attributes.

`<h:panelGroup>` is the next new tag in the example. Typically, `<h:panelGroup>` is used to group several components together so that they occupy a single cell in an `<h:panelGrid>`. This can be accomplished by adding components inside `<h:panelGroup>` and adding `<h:panelGroup>` to `<h:panelGrid>`. As can be seen in the example, this particular instance of `<h:panelGroup>` has no child components. In this particular case, the purpose of `<h:panelGroup>` is to have an "empty" cell and have the next component, `<h:commandButton>`, align with all other input fields in the form.

`<h:commandButton>` renders an HTML input field in the browser, just as with standard HTML and JSPs; its purpose is to submit the form. Its `value` attribute simply sets the button's label. This tag's `action` attribute is used for navigation; the next JSP to show is based on the value of this attribute. The `action` attribute can have a String constant or Unified Expression Language as its value; additionally it can have a **method binding expression**, meaning that it can point to a method in a managed bean that returns a String. We will see an example of a `<h:commandButton>` tag whose action attribute is a method-binding expression later in this chapter.

Even though the label for the button reads **Save**, clicking on the button won't actually save any data. Later in this chapter, we will see a more advanced version of this application that will actually implement this functionality.

Navigation rules and managed beans are defined in a configuration file called `faces-config.xml`. This file must be placed in the `WEB-INF` folder of the application's WAR file. The `faces-config.xml` file for our example application looks like this:

```
<faces-config xmlns="http://java.sun.com/xml/ns/javaee"
    xmlns:xsi="http://www.w3.org/2001/XMLSchema-instance"
    xsi:schemaLocation="http://java.sun.com/xml/ns/javaee http://
                        java.sun.com/xml/ns/javaee/web-facesconfig_1_2.xsd"
    version="1.2">
    <managed-bean>
      <managed-bean-name>Customer</managed-bean-name>
      <managed-bean-class>
        net.ensode.glassfishbook.jsf.Customer
      </managed-bean-class>
      <managed-bean-scope>request</managed-bean-scope>
    </managed-bean>
    <navigation-rule>
      <from-view-id>/customer_data_entry.jsp</from-view-id>
      <navigation-case>
        <from-outcome>save</from-outcome>
        <to-view-id>/confirmation.jsp</to-view-id>
      </navigation-case>
    </navigation-rule>
</faces-config>
```

The `<managed-bean>` element defines a managed bean that can be used for value-binding and method binding expressions. Its nested `<managed-bean-name>` element defines a logical name for this managed bean. The `<managed-bean-class>` element must contain the fully qualified name of the managed bean's class. The `<managed-bean-scope>` element indicates the scope of the bean. Valid values for this element include `request`, `session`, `application`, and `none`. The managed bean will be attached as an attribute of the specified scope. Several managed beans can be declared in this manner. In our example application, there is only one managed bean. Its source code is shown in the following code listing:

```
package net.ensode.glassfishbook.jsf;
public class Customer
{
```

```
private String firstName;
private String lastName;
private String email;
public String getEmail()
{
   return email;
}
public void setEmail(String email)
{
   this.email = email;
}
public String getFirstName()
{
   return firstName;
}
public void setFirstName(String firstName)
{
   this.firstName = firstName;
}
public String getLastName()
{
   return lastName;
}
public void setLastName(String lastName)
{
   this.lastName = lastName;
}
}
```

Notice that there is nothing special about this bean. It is a standard JavaBean with private properties and corresponding getter and setter methods.

The next tag we see in `faces-config.xml` is the `<navigation-rule>` tag. This tag defines where a page will navigate after a certain outcome. In this example, this navigation rule ties to the `<h:commandButton>` tag that had a value for its `action` attribute of "save". When the form is submitted, the container will look for an action of "save", as defined in the `<from-outcome>` element in the above `faces-config. xml`, and navigate to the JSP defined in the `<to-view-id>` element (`/confirmation. jsp` in this case). Each `<navigation-rule>` element must have only one `<from-view-id>` child element, but it can have several `<navigation-case>` elements, one for each outcome.

Same page reloading when clicking on a button or link that should navigate to another page?

When JSF does not recognize the value of a `<to-view-id>` element in `faces-config.xml`, it will by default navigate to the same page that was displayed in the browser when the user clicked on a button or link that is meant to navigate to another page.

Notice that the values for `<from-view-id>` and `<to-view-id>` start with a slash and match the exact name and location of a JSP in the application. If there is a typo in the value for one or both of these elements, navigation will not work correctly. A common mistake is to forget to add the slash at the beginning of these values.

As can be seen in `faces-config.xml`, when the user clicks on the "save" button from the `customer_data_entry.jsp`, our application will navigate to a JSP called `confirmation.jsp`. The source for this JSP looks like this:

```
<%@ page language="java" contentType="text/html; charset=UTF-8"
  pageEncoding="UTF-8"%>
<%@ taglib uri="http://java.sun.com/jsf/core" prefix="f"%>
<%@ taglib uri="http://java.sun.com/jsf/html" prefix="h"%>
<!DOCTYPE html PUBLIC "-//W3C//DTD HTML 4.01 Transitional//EN"
"http://www.w3.org/TR/html4/loose.dtd">
<html>
<head>
<meta http-equiv="Content-Type" content="text/html; charset=UTF-8">
<title>Customer Data Entered</title>
</head>
<body>
<p>The following data was entered:</p>
<f:view>
  <h:panelGrid columns="2">
    <h:outputText value="First Name:"></h:outputText>
    <h:outputText value="#{Customer.firstName}"></h:outputText>
    <h:outputText value="Last Name:"></h:outputText>
    <h:outputText value="#{Customer.lastName}"></h:outputText>
    <h:outputText value="Email:"></h:outputText>
    <h:outputText value="#{Customer.email}"></h:outputText>
  </h:panelGrid>
</f:view>
</body>
</html>
```

There are no tags we haven't seen before in this JSP. One thing to notice about it is that it is using value-binding expressions as the value for all of its `<h:outputText>` tags. As these value-binding expressions are the same expressions used in the previous page for the `<h:inputText>` tags, their values will correspond to the data the user entered.

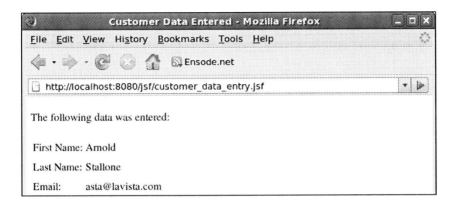

The last piece of the puzzle is the application's `web.xml` file.

```
<web-app xmlns="http://java.sun.com/xml/ns/javaee" version="2.5"
  xmlns:xsi="http://www.w3.org/2001/XMLSchema-instance"
  xsi:schemaLocation="http://java.sun.com/xml/ns/javaee http://
                      java.sun.com/xml/ns/javaee/web-app_2_5.xsd">
  <display-name>Archetype Created Web Application</display-name>
  <servlet>
    <display-name>FacesServlet</display-name>
    <servlet-name>FacesServlet</servlet-name>
    <servlet-class>javax.faces.webapp.FacesServlet</servlet-class>
    <load-on-startup>1</load-on-startup>
  </servlet>
  <servlet-mapping>
    <servlet-name>FacesServlet</servlet-name>
    <url-pattern>*.jsf</url-pattern>
  </servlet-mapping>
  <servlet-mapping>
    <servlet-name>FacesServlet</servlet-name>
    <url-pattern>/faces/*</url-pattern>
  </servlet-mapping>
</web-app>
```

A JSF application is a standard web application; therefore a standard `web.xml` file is needed. As can be seen in the example, a single servlet is added to the `web.xml` configuration file; this servlet is included in the JSF libraries.

It is customary to use a suffix mapping of `.jsf` or a prefix mapping of `/faces/` to access the FacesServlet. This example declares both mappings.

Custom Data Validation

In addition to providing standard validators for our use, JSF allows us to create custom validators. This can be done in one of two ways: by creating a custom validator class or by adding validation methods to our managed beans.

Creating Custom Validators

In addition to the standard validators, JSF allows us to create custom validators by creating a Java class implementing the `javax.faces.validator.Validator` interface.

The following class implements an email address validator, which we will use to validate the email text input field in our customer data entry screen.

```java
package net.ensode.glassfishbook.jsfcustomval;
import javax.faces.application.FacesMessage;
import javax.faces.component.UIComponent;
import javax.faces.component.html.HtmlInputText;
import javax.faces.context.FacesContext;
import javax.faces.validator.Validator;
import javax.faces.validator.ValidatorException;
public class EmailValidator implements Validator
{
  public void validate(FacesContext facesContext,
      UIComponent uiComponent,
      Object value) throws ValidatorException
  {
    org.apache.commons.validator.EmailValidator emailValidator
      = org.apache.commons.validator.EmailValidator
        .getInstance();
    HtmlInputText htmlInputText = (HtmlInputText) uiComponent;
    if (!emailValidator.isValid((String) value))
    {
      FacesMessage facesMessage = new
          FacesMessage(htmlInputText.getLabel()
          + ": email format is not valid");
      throw new ValidatorException(facesMessage);
    }
  }
}
```

As can be seen in the example, the only method we need to implement when implementing the `Validator` interface is a method called `validate()`. This method takes three parameters, an instance of `javax.faces.context.FacesContext`, an instance of `javax.faces.component.UIComponent`, and an object. Typically, application developers only need to be concerned with the last two. The second parameter is the component whose data we are validating; the third parameter is the actual value. In the example, we cast `uiComponent` to `javax.faces.component.html.HtmlInputText`; this way we get access to its `getLabel()` method, which we can use as part of the error message.

If the entered value is not a valid email address format, a new instance of `javax.faces.application.FacesMessage` is created, passing the error message to be displayed in the browser as its constructor parameter. We then throw a new `javax.faces.validator.ValidatorException`. The error message is then displayed in the browser; how it gets there is done behind the scenes by the JSF API. The next screenshot illustrates the above validator in action.

Apache Commons Validator

The validator opposite uses Apache Commons Validator to do the actual validation. This library includes many common validations like dates, credit card numbers, ISBN numbers, and emails. When implementing a custom validator, it is worth investigating if this library already has a validator that we can use.

In order to use our validator in our page, we need to use the `<f:validator>` JSF tag. The following JSP is a modified version of the customer data entry screen. This version uses the `<f:validator>` tag to validate email addresses.

```
<%@ page language="java" contentType="text/html; charset=UTF-8"
  pageEncoding="UTF-8"%>
<%@ taglib uri="http://java.sun.com/jsf/core" prefix="f"%>
<%@ taglib uri="http://java.sun.com/jsf/html" prefix="h"%>
<!DOCTYPE html PUBLIC "-//W3C//DTD HTML 4.01 Transitional//EN"
"http://www.w3.org/TR/html4/loose.dtd">
<html>
<head>
<meta http-equiv="Content-Type" content="text/html; charset=UTF-8">
<style type="text/css">
.leftAlign { text-align: left;}
.rightAlign { text-align: right;}
</style>
<title>Enter Customer Data</title>
</head>
<body>
```

```
<f:view>
  <h:form>
    <h:messages></h:messages>
    <h:panelGrid columns="2" columnClasses="rightAlign,leftAlign">
      <h:outputText value="First Name:">
      </h:outputText>
      <h:inputText label="First Name" value="#{Customer.firstName}"
        required="true">
        <f:validateLength minimum="2" maximum="30"></f:validateLength>
      </h:inputText>
      <h:outputText value="Last Name:"></h:outputText>
      <h:inputText label="Last Name" value="#{Customer.lastName}"
        required="true">
        <f:validateLength minimum="2" maximum="30"></f:validateLength>
      </h:inputText>
      <h:outputText value="Email:">
      </h:outputText>
      <h:inputText label="Email" value="#{Customer.email}">
        <f:validator validatorId="emailValidator" />
      </h:inputText>
      <h:panelGroup></h:panelGroup>
      <h:commandButton action="save" value="Save"></h:commandButton>
    </h:panelGrid>
  </h:form>
</f:view>
</body>
</html>
```

In addition to creating the `Validator` class and using the `<f:validator>` tag, the custom validator class must be declared in the application's `faces-config.xml` file.

```
<faces-config xmlns="http://java.sun.com/xml/ns/javaee"
  xmlns:xsi="http://www.w3.org/2001/XMLSchema-instance"
  xsi:schemaLocation="http://java.sun.com/xml/ns/javaee http://
                  java.sun.com/xml/ns/javaee/web-facesconfig_1_2.xsd"
  version="1.2">
  <managed-bean>
    <managed-bean-name>Customer</managed-bean-name>
    <managed-bean-class>
      net.ensode.glassfishbook.jsfcustomval.Customer
    </managed-bean-class>
    <managed-bean-scope>request</managed-bean-scope>
  </managed-bean>
  <navigation-rule>
    <from-view-id>/customer_data_entry.jsp</from-view-id>
```

```
    <navigation-case>
      <from-outcome>save</from-outcome>
      <to-view-id>/confirmation.jsp</to-view-id>
    </navigation-case>
  </navigation-rule>
  <validator>
    <validator-id>emailValidator</validator-id>
    <validator-class>
      net.ensode.glassfishbook.jsfcustomval.EmailValidator
    </validator-class>
  </validator>
</faces-config>
```

The `<validator-id>` element contains an application-unique identifier for the validator. The `<validator-class>` contains the fully qualified name for the validator.

After performing all of these steps for our application, redeploying it, and pointing the browser to the appropriate URL, we can see our validator in action.

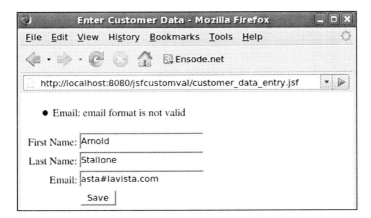

Validator Methods

The second way we can implement custom validation is by adding validation methods to one or more of the application's managed beans. The following Java class illustrates the use of validator methods for JSF validation:

```
package net.ensode.glassfishbook.jsfcustomval;

import javax.faces.application.FacesMessage;
import javax.faces.component.UIComponent;
import javax.faces.component.html.HtmlInputText;
import javax.faces.context.FacesContext;
```

```
import javax.faces.validator.ValidatorException;
import org.apache.commons.lang.StringUtils;
public class AlphaValidator
{
  public void validateAlpha(FacesContext facesContext,
      UIComponent uiComponent,
      Object value) throws ValidatorException
  {
    if (!StringUtils.isAlphaSpace((String) value))
    {
      HtmlInputText htmlInputText = (HtmlInputText)
          uiComponent;
      FacesMessage facesMessage = new
          FacesMessage(htmlInputText.getLabel()
          + ": only alphabetic characters are allowed.");
      throw new ValidatorException(facesMessage);
    }
  }
}
```

In this example, the class contains only the validator method. We can give our validator method any name we want; however, its return value must be void, and it must take the three parameters illustrated in the example, in that order. In other words, except for the method name, the signature of a validator method must be identical to the signature of the validate() method defined in the javax.faces. validator.Validator interface.

As we can see, the body of the above validator method is nearly identical to the body of our custom validator's validate() method. We check the value entered by the user to make sure it contains only alphabetic characters and/or spaces, if it does not, then we throw a ValidatorException passing an instance of FacesMessage containing an appropriate error message String.

StringUtils

In the example, we used org.apache.commons.lang.StringUtils to perform the actual validation logic. In addition to the method used in the example, this class contains several methods for verifying that a String is numeric or alphanumeric. This class, part of the Jakarta commons-lang library, is very useful when writing custom validators.

As every validator method must be in a managed bean, we need to declare the bean containing the validator method(s) in the application's `faces-config.xml` file.

```xml
<faces-config xmlns="http://java.sun.com/xml/ns/javaee"
  xmlns:xsi="http://www.w3.org/2001/XMLSchema-instance"
  xsi:schemaLocation="http://java.sun.com/xml/ns/javaee http://
                    java.sun.com/xml/ns/javaee/web-facesconfig_1_2.xsd"
  version="1.2">

  <managed-bean>
    <managed-bean-name>Customer</managed-bean-name>
    <managed-bean-class>
      net.ensode.glassfishbook.jsfcustomval.Customer
    </managed-bean-class>
    <managed-bean-scope>request</managed-bean-scope>
  </managed-bean>

  <managed-bean>
    <managed-bean-name>AlphaValidator</managed-bean-name>
    <managed-bean-class>
      net.ensode.glassfishbook.jsfcustomval.AlphaValidator
    </managed-bean-class>
    <managed-bean-scope>application</managed-bean-scope>
  </managed-bean>

  <navigation-rule>
    <from-view-id>/customer_data_entry.jsp</from-view-id>
    <navigation-case>
      <from-outcome>save</from-outcome>
      <to-view-id>/confirmation.jsp</to-view-id>
    </navigation-case>
  </navigation-rule>

  <validator>
    <validator-id>emailValidator</validator-id>
    <validator-class>
      net.ensode.glassfishbook.jsfcustomval.EmailValidator
    </validator-class>
  </validator>
</faces-config>
```

The last thing we need to do to use our validator method is to bind it to our component via the tag's `validator` attribute.

```jsp
<%@ page language="java" contentType="text/html; charset=UTF-8"
  pageEncoding="UTF-8"%>
<%@ taglib uri="http://java.sun.com/jsf/core" prefix="f"%>
<%@ taglib uri="http://java.sun.com/jsf/html" prefix="h"%>
<!DOCTYPE html PUBLIC "-//W3C//DTD HTML 4.01 Transitional//EN"
```

```
   "http://www.w3.org/TR/html4/loose.dtd">
<html>
<head>
<meta http-equiv="Content-Type" content="text/html; charset=UTF-8">
<style type="text/css">
.leftAlign { text-align: left;}
.rightAlign { text-align: right;}
</style>
<title>Enter Customer Data</title>
</head>
<body>
<f:view>
  <h:form>
    <h:messages></h:messages>
    <h:panelGrid columns="2"
      columnClasses="rightAlign,leftAlign">
      <h:outputText value="First Name:">
      </h:outputText>
      <h:inputText label="First Name"
        value="#{Customer.firstName}"
        required="true"
        validator="#{AlphaValidator.validateAlpha}">
        <f:validateLength minimum="2"
            maximum="30"></f:validateLength>
      </h:inputText>
      <h:outputText value="Last Name:"></h:outputText>
      <h:inputText label="Last Name"
        value="#{Customer.lastName}"
        required="true"
        validator="#{AlphaValidator.validateAlpha}">
        <f:validateLength minimum="2"
          maximum="30"></f:validateLength>
      </h:inputText>
      <h:outputText value="Email:">
      </h:outputText>
      <h:inputText label="Email" value="#{Customer.email}">
        <f:validator validatorId="emailValidator" />
      </h:inputText>
      <h:panelGroup></h:panelGroup>
      <h:commandButton action="save"
        value="Save"></h:commandButton>
    </h:panelGrid>
  </h:form>
</f:view>
</body>
</html>
```

Because neither the first name nor the last name fields should accept anything other than alphabetic characters or spaces, we added our custom validator method to both of these fields.

After following all of the previous steps, we can now see our validator method in action.

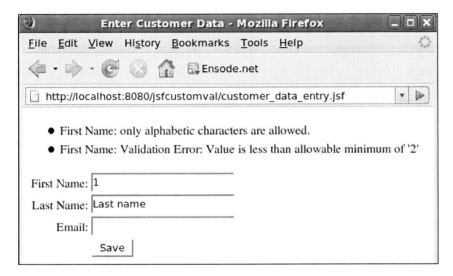

Notice how for the **First Name** field, both our custom validator message and the standard length validator were executed.

Implementing validator methods has the advantage of not having the overhead of creating a whole class just for a single validator method (our example does just that, but in many cases validator methods are added to an existing managed bean containing other methods); however, the disadvantage is that each component can only be validated by a single validator method. When using validator classes, several `<f:validator>` tags can be nested inside the tag to be validated; therefore multiple validations, both custom and standard, can be done on the field.

Customizing JSF's Default Messages

As we mentioned in the previous section, it is possible to customize the style (font, color, text, etc.) of JSF's default validation messages.

Customizing Message Styles

Customizing message styles can be done via Cascading Style Sheets (CSS). This can be accomplished by using the `<h:message>` style or `styleClass` attributes. The `style` attribute is used when we want to declare the CSS style inline. The `styleClass` attribute is used when we want to use a predefined style in a CSS style sheet or inside a `<style>` tag in our JSP.

The following JSP illustrates using the `style` attribute to alter the style of error messages; it is a modified version of the JSP we saw in the previous section.

```
<%@ page language="java" contentType="text/html; charset=UTF-8"
  pageEncoding="UTF-8"%>
<%@ taglib uri="http://java.sun.com/jsf/core" prefix="f"%>
<%@ taglib uri="http://java.sun.com/jsf/html" prefix="h"%>
<!DOCTYPE html PUBLIC "-//W3C//DTD HTML 4.01 Transitional//EN"
"http://www.w3.org/TR/html4/loose.dtd">
<html>
<head>
<meta http-equiv="Content-Type" content="text/html; charset=UTF-8">
<style type="text/css">
.leftAlign { text-align: left;}
.rightAlign { text-align: right;}
</style>
<title>Enter Customer Data</title>
</head>
<body>
<f:view>
  <h:form>
    <h:messages style="color: red;"></h:messages>
    <h:panelGrid columns="2" columnClasses="rightAlign,leftAlign">
      <h:outputText value="First Name:">
      </h:outputText>
      <h:inputText label="First Name" value="#{Customer.firstName}"
        required="true">
        <f:validateLength minimum="2" maximum="30"></f:validateLength>
      </h:inputText>
      <h:outputText value="Last Name:"></h:outputText>
      <h:inputText label="Last Name" value="#{Customer.lastName}"
        required="true">
        <f:validateLength minimum="2" maximum="30"></f:validateLength>
      </h:inputText>
      <h:outputText value="Email:">
      </h:outputText>
      <h:inputText label="Email" value="#{Customer.email}">
```

```
        <f:validator validatorId="emailValidator" />
      </h:inputText>
      <h:panelGroup></h:panelGroup>
      <h:commandButton action="save" value="Save"></h:commandButton>
    </h:panelGrid>
  </h:form>
</f:view>
</body>
</html>
```

As we can see, the only difference between this page and the previous one is the use of the `style` attribute of the `<h:messages>` tag. The following screenshot illustrates how the validation error messages look after implementing this change:

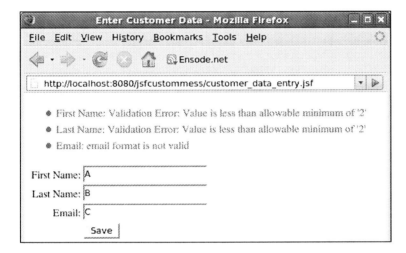

In this particular case, we just set the color of the error message text to red, but we are only limited by CSS capabilities in setting the style of the error messages.

 Pretty much any standard JSF component has both a `style` and a `styleClass` attribute that can be used to alter its style. The former is used for predefined CSS styles, the latter is used for inline CSS.

Customizing Message Text

Some times it is desirable to override JSF's default validation errors. Default validation errors are defined in a resource bundle called `Messages.properties`. This file can be found inside the `jsf-impl.jar` file under `[glassfish installation directory]/glassfish/lib`. It can be found under the `javax.faces` folder inside the JAR file. The file contains several messages; we are only interested in validation errors at this point.

The default validation error messages are defined as follows:

```
javax.faces.validator.NOT_IN_RANGE=Validation Error: Specified
attribute is not between the expected values of {0} and {1}.
javax.faces.validator.DoubleRangeValidator.MAXIMUM={1}: Validation
Error: Value is greater than allowable maximum of "{0}"
javax.faces.validator.DoubleRangeValidator.MINIMUM={1}: Validation
Error: Value is less than allowable minimum of ''{0}''
javax.faces.validator.DoubleRangeValidator.NOT_IN_RANGE={2}:
Validation Error: Specified attribute is not between the expected
values of {0} and {1}.
javax.faces.validator.DoubleRangeValidator.TYPE={0}: Validation Error:
Value is not of the correct type
javax.faces.validator.LengthValidator.MAXIMUM={1}: Validation Error:
Value is greater than allowable maximum of ''{0}''
javax.faces.validator.LengthValidator.MINIMUM={1}: Validation Error:
Value is less than allowable minimum of ''{0}''
javax.faces.validator.LongRangeValidator.MAXIMUM={1}: Validation
Error: Value is greater than allowable maximum of ''{0}''
javax.faces.validator.LongRangeValidator.MINIMUM={1}: Validation
Error: Value is less than allowable minimum of ''{0}''
javax.faces.validator.LongRangeValidator.NOT_IN_RANGE={2}: Validation
Error: Specified attribute is not between the expected values of {0}
and {1}.
javax.faces.validator.LongRangeValidator.TYPE={0}: Validation Error:
Value is not of the correct type.
```

In order to override the default error messages, we need to create our own resource bundle, using the same keys used in the default one, but altering the values to suit our needs. Here is a very simple customized resource bundle for our application:

```
javax.faces.validator.LengthValidator.MINIMUM={1}: minimum allowed
length is ''{0}''
```

In this resource bundle, we override the error message for when the value entered for a field validated by the `<f:validateLength>` tag is less than the allowed minimum. In order to let our application know that we have a custom resource bundle for message properties, we need to modify the application's `faces-config.xml` file.

```
<faces-config xmlns="http://java.sun.com/xml/ns/javaee"
   xmlns:xsi="http://www.w3.org/2001/XMLSchema-instance"
   xsi:schemaLocation="http://java.sun.com/xml/ns/javaee http://
                   java.sun.com/xml/ns/javaee/web-facesconfig_1_2.xsd"
   version="1.2">
   <application>
     <message-bundle>net.ensode.Messages</message-bundle>
   </application>
   <managed-bean>
```

```
    <managed-bean-name>Customer</managed-bean-name>
    <managed-bean-class>
      net.ensode.glassfishbook.jsfcustommess.Customer
    </managed-bean-class>
    <managed-bean-scope>request</managed-bean-scope>
  </managed-bean>
  <navigation-rule>
    <from-view-id>/customer_data_entry.jsp</from-view-id>
    <navigation-case>
      <from-outcome>save</from-outcome>
      <to-view-id>/confirmation.jsp</to-view-id>
    </navigation-case>
  </navigation-rule>
  <validator>
    <validator-id>emailValidator</validator-id>
    <validator-class>
      net.ensode.glassfishbook.jsfcustommess.EmailValidator
    </validator-class>
  </validator>
</faces-config>
```

As we can see, the only thing we need to do to the application's `faces-config.xml` file is to add a `<message-bundle>` element indicating the name and location of the resource bundle containing our custom messages.

After adding our custom message resource bundle and modifying the application's `faces-config.xml` file, we can see our custom validation message in action.

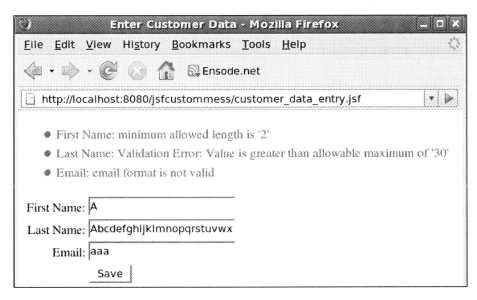

As we can see, if we haven't overridden a validation message, the default will still be displayed. In our resource bundle, we only overrode the minimum length validation error message, therefore our custom error message is shown for the **First Name** text field. As we didn't override the error message for data entry going over the maximum allowed length, the default error message is shown. The email validator is the custom validator we developed previously in this chapter; as it is a custom validator, its error message is not affected.

Integrating JSF and JPA

So far we have covered most of the features of JSF; however, our example application does not actually save any data yet. In this section, we will cover how JavaServer Faces and the Java Persistence API can be easily integrated to save user input to a database.

As we have seen in this chapter, JSF managed beans are nothing but standard JavaBeans. In Chapter 4, we saw that JPA uses standard JavaBeans for object-relational mapping. As both JSF managed beans and JPA beans are standard JavaBeans, there is nothing stopping us from using JPA beans as JSF managed beans.

As we covered earlier, JSF tags can contain value-binding expressions, which are used to automatically populate managed beans when the form is submitted. If we use a JPA bean as a managed bean, the bean's properties are populated in this way. We can then simply call the `EntityManager.persist()` method to save the data into the database.

The first thing we need to do is use a JPA bean as the managed bean to be used for value-binding expressions.

```
package net.ensode.glassfishbook.jsfjpa;
import java.io.Serializable;
import javax.persistence.Column;
import javax.persistence.Entity;
import javax.persistence.Id;
import javax.persistence.Table;
@Entity
@Table(name = "CUSTOMERS")
public class Customer implements Serializable
{
  @Id
  @Column(name = "CUSTOMER_ID")
  private Long customerId;
  @Column(name = "FIRST_NAME")
```

```java
    private String firstName;
    @Column(name = "LAST_NAME")
    private String lastName;
    private String email;
    public Long getCustomerId()
    {
      return customerId;
    }
    public void setCustomerId(Long customerId)
    {
      this.customerId = customerId;
    }
    public String getEmail()
    {
      return email;
    }
    public void setEmail(String email)
    {
      this.email = email;
    }
    public String getFirstName()
    {
      return firstName;
    }
    public void setFirstName(String firstName)
    {
      this.firstName = firstName;
    }
    public String getLastName()
    {
      return lastName;
    }
    public void setLastName(String lastName)
    {
      this.lastName = lastName;
    }
}
```

The above class is an exact copy of the Customer bean we saw in Chapter 4, the only difference being the package it belongs to.

We then need to add an additional managed bean to be used as a controller, because it is always a good practice to follow the Model-View-Controller design pattern.

```
package net.ensode.glassfishbook.jsfjpa;

import java.sql.Connection;
import java.sql.PreparedStatement;
import java.sql.ResultSet;
import java.sql.SQLException;

import javax.annotation.Resource;
import javax.persistence.EntityManager;
import javax.persistence.EntityManagerFactory;
import javax.persistence.PersistenceUnit;
import javax.sql.DataSource;
import javax.transaction.UserTransaction;

public class CustomerController
{
  @Resource(name = "jdbc/__CustomerDBPool")
  private DataSource dataSource;

  @PersistenceUnit(unitName = "customerPersistenceUnit")
  private EntityManagerFactory entityManagerFactory;

  @Resource
  private UserTransaction userTransaction;

  private Customer customer;

  public String saveCustomer()
  {
    String returnValue = "success";
    EntityManager entityManager =
        entityManagerFactory.createEntityManager();

    try
    {
      userTransaction.begin();

      Long customerId = getNewCustomerId();
      customer.setCustomerId(customerId);
      entityManager.persist(customer);

      userTransaction.commit();
    }
    catch (Exception e)
    {
      e.printStackTrace();
      returnValue = "failure";
    }

    return returnValue;
```

```
    }
    private Long getNewCustomerId()
    {
      Connection connection;
      Long newCustomerId = null;
      try
      {
        connection = dataSource.getConnection();
        PreparedStatement preparedStatement = connection
            .prepareStatement(
            "select max(customer_id)+1 as new_customer_id " +
            "from customers");
        ResultSet resultSet = preparedStatement.executeQuery();
        if (resultSet != null && resultSet.next())
        {
          newCustomerId = resultSet.getLong("new_customer_id");
        }
        connection.close();
      }
      catch (SQLException e)
      {
        e.printStackTrace();
      }
      return newCustomerId;
    }
    public Customer getCustomer()
    {
      return customer;
    }
    public void setCustomer(Customer customer)
    {
      this.customer = customer;
    }
  }
```

The saveCustomer() method in the above class will be called whenever a user clicks on the "Save" button on the HTML form; a slight modification needs to be made to the JSP containing the form, which we will cover shortly. This method simply saves the data contained in the Customer bean to the database. Refer to Chapter 4 for details.

Of special interest here are the `setCustomer()` and `getCustomer()` methods. These methods are not meant to be invoked directly by an application developer instead they should be invoked by GlassFish's JSF implementation with the appropriate instance of the Customer bean. We need to declare the `customer` property of this controller as a **managed property**. This can be accomplished by modifying the application's `faces-config.xml` file.

```
<faces-config xmlns="http://java.sun.com/xml/ns/javaee"
  xmlns:xsi="http://www.w3.org/2001/XMLSchema-instance"
  xsi:schemaLocation="http://java.sun.com/xml/ns/javaee http://
                    java.sun.com/xml/ns/javaee/web-facesconfig_1_2.xsd"
  version="1.2">

  <managed-bean>
    <managed-bean-name>CustomerController</managed-bean-name>
    <managed-bean-class>
      net.ensode.glassfishbook.jsfjpa.CustomerController
    </managed-bean-class>
    <managed-bean-scope>request</managed-bean-scope>
    <managed-property>
      <property-name>customer</property-name>
      <property-class>
        net.ensode.glassfishbook.jsfjpa.Customer
      </property-class>
      <value>#{Customer}</value>
    </managed-property>
  </managed-bean>

  <managed-bean>
    <managed-bean-name>Customer</managed-bean-name>
    <managed-bean-class>
      net.ensode.glassfishbook.jsfjpa.Customer
    </managed-bean-class>
    <managed-bean-scope>request</managed-bean-scope>
  </managed-bean>

  <navigation-rule>
    <from-view-id>/save_customer.jsp</from-view-id>
    <navigation-case>
      <from-outcome>success</from-outcome>
      <to-view-id>/customer_saved.jsp</to-view-id>
    </navigation-case>
    <navigation-case>
      <from-outcome>failure</from-outcome>
      <to-view-id>/error_saving_customer.jsp</to-view-id>
    </navigation-case>
  </navigation-rule>
</faces-config>
```

As can be seen in the example opposite, the `<managed-property>` tag contains a nested `<property-name>` tag that contains the name of the property to manage. Its value must match the bean's property name as declared in its Java code. The `<property-class>` element contains the fully qualified class name of the property, and the `<property-value>` element contains a value-binding expression matching the `<managed-bean-name>` element for the bean corresponding to the property.

After we set up our `faces-config.xml` file in this way, the `setCustomer()` method of our controller class will automatically be called with the appropriate instance of the `Customer` bean.

Finally, in order for the `saveCustomer()` method to be called whenever the user submits the form and all fields validate correctly, we need to make a slight modification to the customer data-entry JSP.

```
<%@ page language="java" contentType="text/html; charset=UTF-8"
  pageEncoding="UTF-8"%>
<%@ taglib uri="http://java.sun.com/jsf/core" prefix="f"%>
<%@ taglib uri="http://java.sun.com/jsf/html" prefix="h"%>
<!DOCTYPE html PUBLIC "-//W3C//DTD HTML 4.01 Transitional//EN"
"http://www.w3.org/TR/html4/loose.dtd">
<html>
<head>
<meta http-equiv="Content-Type" content="text/html; charset=UTF-8">
<title>Save Customer</title>
</head>
<body>
<f:view>
  <h:form>
    <h:messages></h:messages>
    <table cellpadding="0" cellspacing="0" border="0">
      <tr>
        <td align="right">First Name:</td>
        <td align="left">
          <h:inputText label="First Name"
          value="#{Customer.firstName}" required="true">
          <f:validateLength minimum="2" maximum="30">
          </f:validateLength>
        </h:inputText></td>
      </tr>
      <tr>
        <td align="right">Last Name:</td>
        <td align="left"><h:inputText label="Last Name"
          value="#{Customer.lastName}" required="true">
          <f:validateLength minimum="2" maximum="30">
```

```
      </f:validateLength>
      </h:inputText></td>
    </tr>
    <tr>
      <td align="right">Email:</td>
      <td align="left"><h:inputText label="Email"
        value="#{Customer.email}">
        <f:validateLength minimum="2" maximum="30">
        </f:validateLength>
      </h:inputText></td>
    </tr>
    <tr>
      <td></td>
      <td align="left">
        <h:commandButton
          action="#{CustomerController.saveCustomer}"
          value="Save"></h:commandButton>
      </td>
    </tr>
    </table>
  </h:form>
</f:view>
</body>
</html>
```

The only significant difference between this version of the JSP and previous versions is that the action attribute of the `<h:commandButton>` tag was changed to point to the `saveCustomer()` method of the `CustomerController` managed bean. As can be seen in the source code for this bean (shown earlier in this section), this method returns the `String` "success" if the data was saved successfully, or "failure" if there was any problem saving the data. These two values are used in the application's `faces-config.xml` file to decide what page to navigate to after this method ends: a confirmation page if everything went well, or an error page if there was a problem. These navigation rules can be seen inside the `<navigation-rule>` element of the `faces-config.xml` file, which was also shown earlier in this section.

There are a few more changes made to this version of the data entry JSP, which are unrelated to the task at hand. First, for simplicity, we removed some of the features we covered earlier in the chapter (custom validators, error message styling, etc.). Additionally, and slightly more interestingly, we replaced the `<h:panelGrid>` component with a standard HTML table. Most JSP developers are very familiar with HTML, therefore using standard HTML components whenever possible leverages this knowledge and potentially makes the page markup more readable. In previous versions of the JSF specification, it wasn't recommended to mix standard HTML and

JSF tags inside the `<f:view>` tag, because doing so sometimes resulted in unexpected results. This restriction has been lifted in the latest version of the JSF specification (JSF 1.2), which, of course, is part of the Java EE 5 specification and is supported by GlassFish.

JSF Standard Components include several standard components; we have only covered a subset of these components so far. The following sections cover all available JSF components.

JSF Core Components

JSF core components are components that are not tied to HTML rendering or any other rendering mechanism. They provide functionality like type conversion and validation, among others. In this section, we will cover all core JSF components.

<f:actionListener>

This tag executes the `processAction()` method of the action listener defined by the tag's type attribute. The value of the type attribute must be the fully qualified name of a class implementing the `javax.faces.event.ActionListener` interface. This tag is typically a child tag of `<h:commandButton>` or `<h:commandLink>`; when the user clicks on the parent component, the `processAction()` method of the declared `ActionListener` implementation is automatically executed. The following markup segment illustrates how this tag is typically used:

```
<h:commandButton action="save" value="Save">
  <f:actionListener type="net.ensode.CustomActionListener"/>
</h:commandButton>
```

<f:attribute>

This tag sets an attribute on the parent component, with a key defined by the tag's name attribute and a value defined by the tag's value attribute. All component attributes can later be programmatically retrieved as a Map by invoking the `getAttributes()` method of the appropriate instance of `javax.faces.component.UIComponent`. This tag is frequently used in conjunction with the `<f:actionListener>` class to pass parameters to the action listener.

The following markup segment illustrates typical use of this tag:

```
<h:commandButton action="save" value="Save">
  <f:actionListener type="net.ensode.CustomActionListener"/>
  <f:attribute name="someAttribute" value="someValue"/>
</h:commandButton>
```

The `processAction()` method of our `CustomActionListener` class would look something like this:

```
public void processAction(ActionEvent actionEvent)
{
  String attribute = (String)
      actionEevent.getComponent().getAttributes().
      get("attrname1");
  //processing continues...
}
```

`<f:convertDateTime>`

This tag converts the value of the parent component into an instance of `java.util. Date`. This tag allows a correctly formatted user-entered string to be assigned to a date field in a managed bean. The following segment of markup illustrates typical usage for this tag:

```
<h:inputText value="#{Customer.birthDate}">
  <f:convertDateTime dateStyle="short"/>
</h:inputText>
```

`<f:convertNumber>`

This tag converts the value of the parent component into an instance of `java.lang. Number`. This tag allows a correctly formatted user-entered string to be assigned to a numeric field in a managed bean. As `java.lang.Number` is the parent class of `java.lang.Integer`, `java.lang.Long`, `java.lang.Float`, and `java.lang.Double` (among other numeric types), this tag can be used to convert pretty much any type of numeric data entry field into the appropriate type.

The following markup segment illustrates typical usage for this tag:

```
<h:inputText value="#{Customer.age}">
  <f:convertNumber/>
</h:inputText>
```

`<f:converter>`

This tag registers the custom converter specified by the tag's `converterId` attribute with the parent tag. The specified converter must be a class implementing the `javax.faces.convert.Converter` interface and it must be registered in the application's `faces-config.xml` file via the `<converter>` tag.

Suppose we have created a custom class named `TelephoneNumber` to store telephone numbers, and that a managed bean named `Customer` has a field called `telephone` of type `TelephoneNumber`, we could create a custom validator to convert a user-entered telephone number into an instance of the `TelephoneNumber` class.

```
<h:inputText value="#{Customer.telephone}">
  <f:converter converterId="TelephoneConverter"/>
</h:inputText>
```

As we explained, our custom converter would have to be registered in the application's `faces-config.xml` file.

```
<converter>
    <converter-id>TelephoneConverter</converter-id>
    <converter-class>
      net.ensode.TelephoneConverter
    </converter-class>
  </converter>
```

The `TelephoneConverter` class would have to implement `javax.faces.convert.Converter`.

<f:facet>

This tag registers a facet on the parent component. A facet is a special child component that can be accessed via the `UIComponent.getFacet()` method. This method can be overridden for custom components; it allows components inside a facet to be treated differently. For example, the standard `<h:dataTable>` tag can have a facet named "header" that is used to render all components in the `<f:facet>` tag as the header of the rendered HTML table.

The following markup segment illustrates typical usage of this tag:

```
<h:dataTable value="{Order.items}" var="item">
  <h:column>
    <f:facet name="header">
      <h:outputText value="Item Number" />
    </f:facet>
    <h:outputText value="#{item.itemNumber}" />
  </h:column>
  <h:column>
    <f:facet name="header">
      <h:outputText value="Item Description" />
    </f:facet>
    <h:outputText value="#{item.itemShortDesc}" />
  </h:column>
</h:dataTable>
```

<f:loadBundle>

This tag loads a resource bundle into the request scope. The resource bundle name is specified by the tag's `basename` attribute. The variable to use to access the resource bundle properties is defined by the tag's `var` attribute.

The following markup segment illustrates typical usage of this tag:

```
<f:view
    locale="#{facesContext.externalContext.request.locale}">
  <f:loadBundle basename="net.ensode.Messages" var="mess"/>
  <h:outputText value="#{mess.greeting}"/>
</f:view>
```

<f:param>

When this tag is a child of `<h:commandLInk>`, it generates a request parameter defined by its name and value attributes. When this tag is a child of `<h:outputFormat>`, it substitutes a parameter in the string defined by the `value` attribute of `<h:outpufFormat>`.

The following markup segment illustrates typical usage of this tag:

```
<h:outputFormat value="Hello, {0}">
  <f:param value="#{Customer.firstName}"/>
</h:outputFormat>
```

<f:phaseListener>

This tag registers a phase listener to the current page. The phase listener must be an instance of a class implementing `javax.faces.event.PhaseListener`; this class is defined by the tag's `type` attribute.

The following markup segment illustrates typical usage of this tag:

```
<f:view>
  <f:phaseListener type="net.ensode.CustomPhaseListener"/>
</f:view>
```

<f:selectItem>

This tag adds a selectable item belonging to the parent component. The way this component is rendered depends on the parent component. It can be used as a child component of `<h:selectManyCheckBox>`, `<h:selectManuListBox>`, `<h:selectManyMenu>`, `<h:selectOneListbox>`, `<h:selectOneMenu>`, `<h:selectOneRadio>`.

The following markup segment illustrates typical usage of this tag.

```
<h:selectManyCheckBox value="#{Order.items}">
  <f:selectItem itemValue="#{Item1}"
    itemLabel="Wireless keyboard"/>
  <f:selectItem itemValue="#{Item1}"
    itemLabel="Wireless mouse"/>
</h:selectManyCheckBox>
```

<f:selectItems>

This tag adds a series to of selectable items belonging to the parent tag. This tag's `value` attribute must be a deferred-value expression resolving to an array or a List of `javax.faces.model.SelectItem` objects.

The following markup segment illustrates typical usage of this tag.

```
<h:selectManyCheckBox value="#{Order.items}">
  <f:selectItems value="#{ValueContainer.allItems} "/>
</h:selectManyCheckBox>
```

<f:setPropertyActionListener>

This tag can be a child tag of `<h:commandLink>` or `<h:commandButton>`. When the button or linked is clicked, this tag sets an attribute in a managed bean defined by the tag's `target` attribute with the value of the tag's `value` attribute.

The following markup segment illustrates typical usage of this tag.

```
<h:commandButton value="Save"
    action="#{Controller.save}">
  <f:setPropertyActionListener
      target="#{Order.lastUpdUserId}" value="#{User.userId}"/>
</h:commandButton>
```

<f:subview>

Any JSPs included via a `<jsp:include>` tag or JSTL's `<c:import>` tag must be inside an `<f:subview>` tag.

The following markup segment illustrates typical usage of this tag.

```
<f:view>
  <table>
    <tr>
      <td width="30%">
```

```
      <f:subview>
        <jsp:include page="menu.jsp">
      </f:subview>
    </td>
    <td>
      Additional content here.
    </td>
  </tr>
  </table>
</f:view>
```

<f:validateDoubleRange>

This tag validates that the value for the parent component is an instance of `java.lang.Double` that is between the values defined by the tag's `minimum` and `maximum` attributes.

The following markup segment illustrates typical usage of this tag.

```
<h:inputText value="#{Item.price}">
  <f:validateDoubleRange minimum="1.0" maximum="100.0"/>
</h:inputText>
```

<f:validateLength>

This tag validates that the value for the parent component is a string whose length is between the values defined by the tag's `minimum` and `maximum` attributes, inclusive.

The following markup segment illustrates typical usage of this tag.

```
<h:inputText label="First Name"
    value="#{Customer.firstName}"
    required="true">
  <f:validateLength minimum="2"
      maximum="30"></f:validateLength>
</h:inputText>
```

<f:validateLongRange>

This tag validates that the value for the parent component is an instance of `java.lang.Long` that is between the values defined by the tag's `minimum` and `maximum` attributes.

The following markup segment illustrates typical usage of this tag.

```
<h:inputText value="#{OrderItem.quantity}">
  <f:validateDoubleRange minimum="1" maximum="100"/>
</h:inputText>
```

<f:validator>

This tag validates the value of the parent component against a custom validator implementing the `javax.faces.validator.Validator` interface. The custom validator must be declared in the application's `faces-config.xml` file.

The following markup segment illustrates typical usage of this tag.

```
<h:inputText label="Email" value="#{Customer.email}">
  <f:validator validatorId="emailValidator" />
</h:inputText>
```

<f:valueChangeListener>

This tag registers an instance of a class implementing the `javax.faces.event.ValueChangeListener` interface with the parent component. The `ValueChangeListener` implementation will implement a `processValueChange()` method that can perform an action if the value of the parent component changes.

The following markup segment illustrates typical usage of this tag:

```
<h:inputText value="#{OrderItem.quantity}">
  <f:valueChangeListener
    type="net.ensode.CustomValueChangeListener"/>
</h:inputText>
```

<f:verbatim>

The content of this tag is passed "as-is" to the rendered page. Before JSF 1.2, it was not recommended to have HTML tags inside the JSF `<f:view>` tag, as they would sometimes not render properly. A common workaround to this limitation was to put standard HTML tags inside `<f:verbatim>` tags. As of JSF 1.2, this tag became somewhat redundant because it is now possible to safely place standard HTML tags inside the `<f:view>` tag.

The following markup segment illustrates typical usage of this tag:

```
<f:view>
  <f:verbatim><p></f:verbatim>
    This text will be rendered inside an HTML &lt;p&gt; tag.
  <f:verbatim></p></f:verbatim>
</f:view>
```

<f:view>

This tag is the parent tag for all JSF tags, both standard and custom.

The following markup segment illustrates typical usage of this tag:

```
<f:view>
  <h:outputText
      escape="true"
      value="All JSF components must be inside <f:view>"/>
</f:view>
```

JSF HTML Components

In previous examples, we only covered a subset of the standard JSF HTML components. In this section, we will list all standard JSF HTML components.

<h:column>

This tag is typically nested inside the `<h:dataTable>` tag. Any components inside this tag will be rendered as a single column inside the table rendered by `<h:dataTable>`.

The following markup segment illustrates typical usage of this tag.

```
<h:dataTable value="{Order.items}" var="item">
  <h:column>
    <f:facet name="header">
      <h:outputText value="Item Number" />
    </f:facet>
    <h:outputText value="#{item.itemNumber}" />
  </h:column>
  <h:column>
    <f:facet name="header">
      <h:outputText value="Item Description" />
    </f:facet>
    <h:outputText value="#{item.itemShortDesc}" />
  </h:column>
</h:dataTable>
```

<h:commandButton>

This tag renders an HTML submit button on the rendered page.

The following markup segment illustrates typical usage of this tag:

```
<h:form>
  <h:inputText label="First Name"
      value="#{Customer.firstName}"/>
  <h:commandButton action="save"
       value="Save"></h:commandButton>
</h:form>
```

<h:commandLink>

This tag renders a link that will submit the form defined by this tag's parent
`<h:form>` tag.

The following markup segment illustrates typical usage of this tag:

```
<h:form>
 <h:inputText label="First Name"
     value="#{Customer.firstName}"/>
 <h:commandLink action="save"
      value="Save"></h:commandLink>
</h:form>
```

<h:dataTable>

This tag builds a table dynamically based on the values of a Collection. The collection
holding the values must be defined by the tag's `value` attribute.

The following markup segment illustrates typical usage of this tag:

```
<h:dataTable value="{Order.items}" var="item">
 <h:column>
   <f:facet name="header">
     <h:outputText value="Item Number" />
   </f:facet>
   <h:outputText value="#{item.itemNumber}" />
 </h:column>
 <h:column>
   <f:facet name="header">
     <h:outputText value="Item Description" />
   </f:facet>
   <h:outputText value="#{item.itemShortDesc}" />
 </h:column>
</h:dataTable>
```

<h:form>

This tag renders an HTML form on the generated page.

The following markup segment illustrates typical usage of this tag:

```
<h:form>
 <h:inputText label="First Name"
     value="#{Customer.firstName}"/>
  <h:commandLink action="save"
      value="Save"></h:commandLink>
</h:form>
```

<h:graphicImage>

This tag renders an HTML `img` tag.

The following markup segment illustrates typical usage of this tag:

```
<h:graphicImage
    url="/images/logo.png">
</h:graphicImage>
```

<h:inputHidden>

This tag renders an HTML hidden field.

The following markup segment illustrates typical usage of this tag:

```
<h:inputHidden
    value="#{Customer.id}" />
```

<h:inputSecret>

This tag renders an HTML `input` field of type `password`.

The following markup segment illustrates typical usage of this tag:

```
<h:inputSecret redisplay="false"
   value="#{User.password}" />
```

<h:inputText>

This tag renders an HTML `input` field of type `text`.

The following markup segment illustrates typical usage of this tag:

```
<h:inputText label="First Name"
    value="#{Customer.firstName}"/>
```

<h:inputTextarea>

This tag renders an HTML `textarea` field.

The following markup segment illustrates typical usage of this tag:

```
<h:inputTextarea label="Comments"
    value="#{Order.comments}"/>
```

\<h:message\>

This tag renders messages for a single component. The component for which to render messages must use its `id` attribute to set an identifier for itself. This identifier then needs to be used as this element's `for` attribute.

The following markup segment illustrates typical usage of this tag:

```
<table>
  <tr>
    <td align="right">
      <h:outputLabel
            value="Login Name:"
              for="loginField"/></td>
    <td><h:inputText id="loginField" value="#{User.login}"
            required="true"/></td>
    <td><h:message for="loginField"/></td>
  </tr>
</table>
```

\<h:messages\>

This tag outputs messages for all components or global messages. If the tag's `globalOnly` attribute is set to `true`, then only global messages (messages not specific to any component) will be displayed.

The following markup segment illustrates typical usage of this tag:

```
<f:view>
  <h:messages/>
  <h:form>
    <h:inputText label="First Name"
        value="#{Customer.firstName}"/>
    <h:commandButton action="save"
          value="Save"/>
  </h:form>
<f:view>
```

\<h:outputFormat\>

This tag renders parameterized text. Parameters in this tag's value attribute are defined in a manner similar to the way they are defined in a resource bundle, that is, by placing integers between curly braces in the parameter locations. Parameters are substituted with values defined in any child \<f:param\> elements.

The following markup segment illustrates typical usage of this tag:

```
<h:outputFormat value="Hello, {0}">
  <f:param value="#{Customer.firstName}"/>
</h:outputFormat>
```

<h:outputLabel>

This tag renders an HTML `label` field.

The following markup segment illustrates typical usage of this tag:

```
<table>
  <tr>
    <td align="right">
      <h:outputLabel
          value="Login Name:"
          for="loginField"/></td>
    <td><h:inputText id="loginField" value="#{User.login}"
          required="true"/></td>
  </tr>
</table>
```

<h:outputLink>

This tag renders an HTML link as an `anchor` (a) element with an `href` attribute.

The following markup segment illustrates typical usage of this tag:

```
<h:outputLink
 value="http://ensode.net">
  <h:outputText value="Ensode"/>
</h:outputLink>
```

<h:outputText>

If the `dir`, `lang`, `style`, or `styleClass` attributes are defined, this tag renders an HTML `span` element containing the tag's `value` attribute. Otherwise, the value defined by the tag's value attribute is rendered, escaping any XML/HTML characters so that they are rendered properly. If the tag's escape attribute is set to `false`, then XML/HTML characters are not escaped.

The following markup segment illustrates typical usage of this tag:

```
<h:outputText value="#{Customer.firstName}"/>
```

<h:panelGrid>

This tag renders a static HTML table. The number of columns in the table is specified in the tag's `columns` attribute. Child components are then added to a subsequent row once the number of elements defined in the `columns` attribute have been added for the current row.

The following markup segment illustrates typical usage of this tag:

```
<h:panelGrid columns="2"
    columnClasses="rightAlign,leftAlign">
    <h:outputText value="First Name:">
    </h:outputText>
    <h:inputText label="First Name"
      value="#{Customer.firstName}"
      required="true">
      <f:validateLength minimum="2"
        maximum="30"></f:validateLength>
    </h:inputText>
    <h:outputText value="Last Name:"></h:outputText>
    <h:inputText label="Last Name"
      value="#{Customer.lastName}"
      required="true">
      <f:validateLength minimum="2"
        maximum="30"></f:validateLength>
    </h:inputText>
    <h:outputText value="Email:">
    </h:outputText>
    <h:inputText label="Email" value="#{Customer.email}">
       <f:validateLength minimum="3"
         maximum="30"></f:validateLength>
    </h:inputText>
    <h:panelGroup></h:panelGroup>
    <h:commandButton action="save"
      value="Save"></h:commandButton>
  </h:panelGrid>
```

<h:panelGroup>

This tag is used to group its child components together in a single cell of a parent `<h:panelGrid>` or `<h:dataTable>` tag. Can also be used to create an "empty" cell in a parent `<h:panelGrid>` tag.

The following markup segment illustrates typical usage of this tag:

```
<h:panelGrid columns="2"
      columnClasses="rightAlign,leftAlign">
      <h:outputText value="First Name:">
      </h:outputText>
      <h:inputText label="First Name"
        value="#{Customer.firstName}"
        required="true">
        <f:validateLength minimum="2"
          maximum="30"></f:validateLength>
      </h:inputText>
      <h:outputText value="Last Name:"></h:outputText>
      <h:inputText label="Last Name"
        value="#{Customer.lastName}"
        required="true">
        <f:validateLength minimum="2"
          maximum="30"></f:validateLength>
      </h:inputText>
      <h:outputText value="Email:">
      </h:outputText>
      <h:inputText label="Email" value="#{Customer.email}">
        <f:validateLength minimum="3"
          maximum="30"></f:validateLength>
      </h:inputText>
      <h:panelGroup></h:panelGroup>
      <h:commandButton action="save"
        value="Save"></h:commandButton>
  </h:panelGrid>
```

<h:selectBooleanCheckbox>

This tag renders a single HTML `input` field of type `checkbox`. The `value` attribute for this tag is usually set to a value-binding expression mapping to a Boolean property in a managed bean.

The following markup segment illustrates typical usage of this tag:

```
<h:selectBooleanCheckbox
  value="#{Customer.newsletterOk}" />
<h:outputText
  value="Would you like to receive our newsletter?"/>
```

<h:selectManyCheckbox>

This tag renders a series of related checkboxes. Values for the user to select are defined in any child `<f:selectItem>` or `<f:selectItems>` tags.

The following markup segment illustrates typical usage of this tag:

```
<h:selectManyCheckBox value="#{Order.items}">
  <f:selectItems value="#{ValueContainer.allItems} "/>
</h:selectManyCheckBox>
```

<h:selectManyListbox>

This tag renders an HTML `select` field of variable size that allows multiple selections. Values for the user to select are defined in any child `<f:selectItem>` or `<f:selectItems>` tags. The number of elements displayed at the same time is set by the tag's `size` attribute.

The following markup segment illustrates typical usage of this tag:

```
<h:selectManyListBox value="#{Order.items}">
  <f:selectItems value="#{ValueContainer.allItems} "/>
</h:selectManyListBox>
```

<h:selectManyMenu>

This tag renders an HTML `select` field that allows multiple selections. Values for the user to select are defined in any child `<f:selectItem>` or `<f:selectItems>` tags. This tag is identical to `<h:selectManyListbox>`, except that it always displays one element at a time, therefore it has no `size` attribute.

The following markup segment illustrates typical usage of this tag:

```
<h:selectManyMenu value="#{Order.items}">
  <f:selectItems value="#{ValueContainer.allItems} "/>
</h:selectManyMenu>
```

<h:selectOneListbox>

This tag renders an HTML `select` field of variable size that does not allow multiple selections. Values for the user to select are defined in any child `<f:selectItem>` or `<f:selectItems>` tags. The number of elements displayed at the same time is set by the tag's `size` attribute, which is optional. If the size attribute is not set, then all elements are displayed at the same time.

The following markup segment illustrates typical usage of this tag:

```
<h:selectOneListBox value="#{Order.selectedItem}">
  <f:selectItems value="#{ValueContainer.allItems} "/>
</h:selectOneListBox>
```

<h:selectOneMenu>

This tag renders an HTML "dropdown", which is to say it renders an HTML select field that does not allow multiple selections. Only one element is displayed at a time. Values for the user to select are defined in any child `<f:selectItem>` or `<f:selectItems>` tags.

The following markup segment illustrates typical usage of this tag:

```
<h:selectOneMenu value="#{Order.selectedItem}">
  <f:selectItems value="#{ValueContainer.allItems} "/>
</h:selectOneMenu>
```

<h:selectOneRadio>

This tag renders a series of related radio buttons. Values for the user to select are defined in any child `<f:selectItem>` or `<f:selectItems>` tags.

The following markup segment illustrates typical usage of this tag:

```
<h:selectOneRadio value="#{Order.selectedItem}">
  <f:selectItems value="#{ValueContainer.allItems} "/>
</h:selectOneRadio>
```

Additional JSF Tag Libraries

In addition to the standard JSF tag libraries, there are a number of third-party JSF tag libraries available. The following table lists some of the most popular ones:

Tag Library	Distributor	License	URL
MyFaces Tomahawk	Apache	Apache 2.0	http://myfaces.apache.org/tomahawk/
ICEfaces	ICEsoft	MPL 1.1	http://www.icefaces.org
RichFaces	Red Hat/ JBoss	LGPL	http://labs.jboss.com/portal/ jbossrichfaces/
Woodstock	Sun	CDDL	https://woodstock.dev.java.net

Summary

In this chapter, we covered how to develop web-based applications using JavaServer Faces, the standard component framework for the Java EE 5 platform. We covered how to write a simple application by creating JSPs containing JSF tags and managed beans. We also covered how to validate user input by using JSF's standard validators and by creating our own custom validators or by writing validator methods. Additionally, we covered how to customize standard JSF error messages, both the message text and the message style (font, color, etc.). Finally, we covered how to write applications by integrating JSF and the Java Persistence API (JPA).

Java Messaging Service

The Java Messaging Service API (JMS) provides a mechanism for Java EE applications to send messages to each other. JMS applications do not communicate directly; instead message producers send messages to a destination, and message consumers receive the message from the destination.

The message destination is a message queue when the Point-To-Point (PTP) Messaging Domain is used, or a message topic when the Publish/Subscribe (pub/sub) messaging domain is used.

In this chapter, we will cover the following topics:

- Setting up GlassFish for JMS
- Working with message queues
- Working with message topics

Setting Up GlassFish for JMS

Before we can start writing code to take advantage of the JMS API, we need to configure some GlassFish resources. Specifically, we need to set up a **JMS Connection Factory**, a **message queue**, and a **message topic**.

Setting Up a JMS Connection Factory

The easiest way to set up a JMS connection factory is via GlassFish's web console. Recall from Chapter 1 that the web console can be accessed by starting our domain by entering the following command in the command line:

```
asadmin start-domain domain1
```

then pointing the browser to `http://localhost:4848` and logging in.

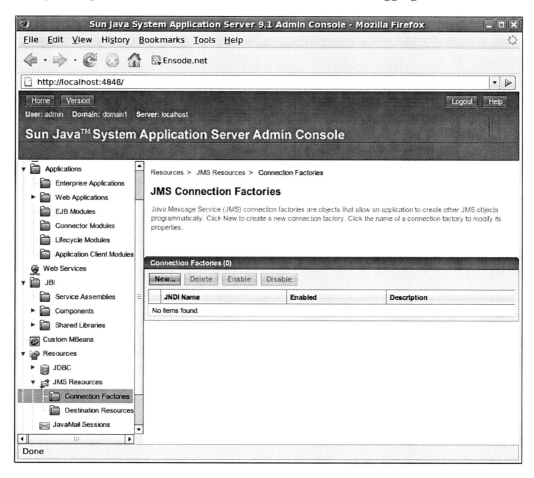

A connection factory can be added by expanding the **Resources** node in the tree at the left-hand side of the web console, expanding the **JMS Resources** node, clicking on the **Connection Factories** node, and then clicking on the **New...** button in the main area of the web console.

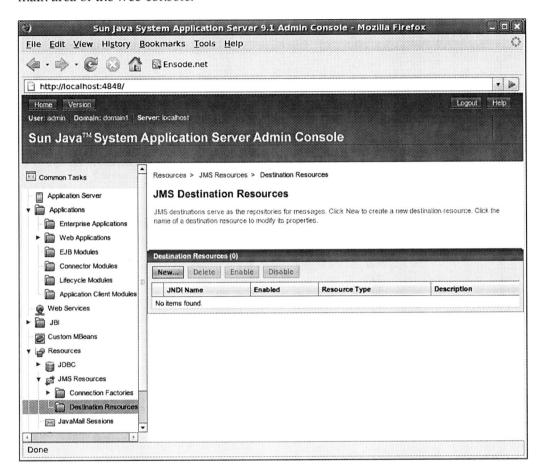

After clicking on the **New...** button and entering the appropriate information for our connection factory, we should then see our newly created message queue listed in the main area of the GlassFish web console.

New JMS Connection Factory   [OK] [Cancel]

The creation of a new Java Message Service (JMS) connection factory also creates a connector connection pool for the factory and a connector resource.

General Settings

JNDI Name: *   `jms/GlassFishBookConnectionFactory`

Resource Type: *   `javax.jms.ConnectionFactory` ▾

Description: `Used for book examples.`

Status: ☑ Enabled

Pool Settings

Initial and Minimum Pool Size: `8`   Connections
Minimum and initial number of connections maintained in the pool

Maximum Pool Size: `32`   Connections
Maximum number of connections that can be created to satisfy client requests

Pool Resize Quantity: `2`   Connections
Number of connections to be removed when pool idle timeout expires

Idle Timeout: `300`   Seconds
Maximum time that connection can remain idle in the pool

Max Wait Time: `60000`   Milliseconds
Amount of time caller waits before connection timeout is sent

On Any Failure: ☐ **Close All Connections**
Close all connections and reconnect on failure, otherwise reconnect only when used

Transaction Support: ▾
Level of transaction support. Overwrite the transaction support attribute in the Resource Adapter in a downward compatible way.

Connection Validation: ☐ **Required**
Validate connection before passing to container.

For our purposes, we can take most of the defaults; the only thing we need to do is enter a JNDI name and pick a resource type for our connection factory.

It is always a good idea to use a JNDI name starting with "jms/" when picking a JNDI name for JMS resources. This way, JMS resources can be easily identified when browsing a JNDI tree.

In the text field labeled **JNDI Name**, enter `jms/GlassFishBookConnectionFactory`. Our code examples later in this chapter will use this JNDI name to obtain a reference to this connection factory.

The **Resource Type** dropdown has three options:

- **javax.jms.TopicConnectionFactory**: used to create a connection factory that creates JMS topics for JMS clients using the pub/sub messaging domain

- **javax.jms.QueueConnectionFactory**: used to create a connection factory that creates JMS queues for JMS clients using the PTP messaging domain

- **javax.jms.ConnectionFactory**: used to create a connection factory that creates either JMS topics or JMS queues

For our example, we will select **javax.jms.ConnectionFactory**; this way we can use the same connection factory for all of our examples, those using the PTP messaging domain and those using the pub/sub messaging domain.

After entering the JNDI name for our connection factory, selecting a connection factory type, and optionally, entering a description for our connection factory, we must click on the **OK** button for the changes to take effect.

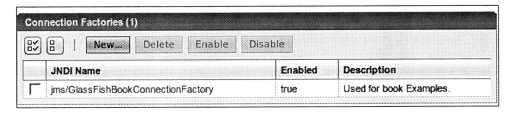

We should then see our newly created connection factory listed in the main area of the GlassFish web console.

Setting Up a JMS Message Queue

A JMS message queue can be added by expanding the **Resources** node in the tree at the left-hand side of the web console, expanding the **JMS Resources** node, and clicking on the **Destination Resources** node, then clicking on the **New...** button in the main area of the web console.

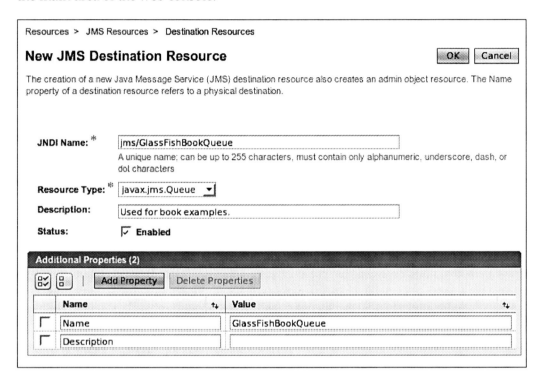

In our examples, the JNDI name of the message queue is jms/GlassFishBookQueue. The resource type for message queues must be javax.jms.Queue. Additionally, a value for the **Name** property must be entered. In the above example, we use GlassFishBookQueue as the value for this property.

After clicking on the **New...** button and entering the appropriate information for our message queue, we should now see the newly created queue.

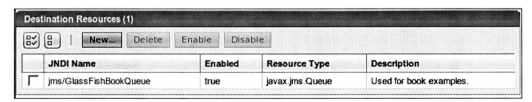

Setting Up a JMS Message Topic

Setting up a JMS message topic in GlassFish is very similar to setting up a message queue.

In the GlassFish web console, expand the **Resources** node in the tree at the left-hand side, then expand the **JMS Resouces** node, click on the **Destination** node, then click on the **New...** button in the main area of the web console.

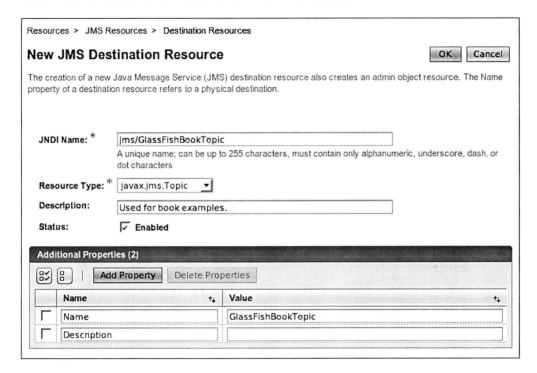

Our examples will use a **JNDI Name** of jms/GlassFishBookTopic. As this is a message topic, **Resource Type** must be javax.jms.Topic. The **Description** field is optional. The **Name** property is required; for our example, we will use GlassFishBookTopic as the value for the **Name** property.

After clicking the **OK** button, we can see our newly created message topic.

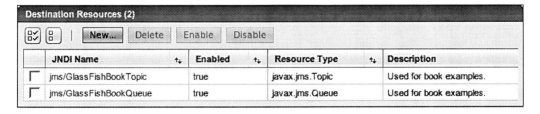

Now that we have set up a connection factory, a message queue, and a message topic, we are ready to start writing code using the JMS API.

Message Queues

As we mentioned earlier, message queues are used when our JMS code uses the Point-To-Point (PTP) messaging domain. For the PTP messaging domain, there is usually one message producer and one message consumer. The message producer and the message consumer don't need to be running concurrently in order to communicate. The messages placed in the message queue by the message producer will stay in the message queue until the message consumer executes and requests the messages from the queue.

Sending Messages to a Message Queue

The following example illustrates how to add messages to a message queue:

```
package net.ensode.glassfishbook;

import javax.annotation.Resource;
import javax.jms.Connection;
import javax.jms.ConnectionFactory;
import javax.jms.JMSException;
import javax.jms.MessageProducer;
import javax.jms.Queue;
import javax.jms.Session;
import javax.jms.TextMessage;

public class MessageSender
{

  @Resource(mappedName = "jms/GlassFishBookConnectionFactory")
  private static ConnectionFactory connectionFactory;

  @Resource(mappedName = "jms/GlassFishBookQueue")
  private static Queue queue;

  public void produceMessages()
  {
    MessageProducer messageProducer;
    TextMessage textMessage;
    try
    {
      Connection connection = connectionFactory.createConnection();
      Session session = connection.createSession(false,
          Session.AUTO_ACKNOWLEDGE);
      messageProducer = session.createProducer(queue);
```

```
            textMessage = session.createTextMessage();
            textMessage.setText(
                "Testing, 1, 2, 3. Can you hear me?");
            System.out.println("Sending the following message: "
                + textMessage.getText());
            messageProducer.send(textMessage);

            textMessage.setText("Do you copy?");
            System.out.println("Sending the following message: "
                + textMessage.getText());
            messageProducer.send(textMessage);

            textMessage.setText("Good bye!");
            System.out.println("Sending the following message: "
                + textMessage.getText());
            messageProducer.send(textMessage);

            messageProducer.close();
            session.close();
            connection.close();
        }
        catch (JMSException e)
        {
            e.printStackTrace();
        }
    }
    public static void main(String[] args)
    {
        new MessageSender().produceMessages();
    }
}
```

Before delving into the details of the above code, alert readers might have noticed that the above class is a standalone Java application, because it contains a `main` method. As this class is standalone, it executes outside the application server, yet we can see that some resources are injected into it, specifically the connection factory and queue. The reason we can inject resources into this code even though it runs outside the application server is because GlassFish includes a utility called `appclient`. This utility allows us to "wrap" an executable JAR file and allow it to have access to the application server resources. To execute the above code, assuming it is packaged in an executable JAR file called `jmsptpproducer.jar`, we would type the following in the command line:

`appclient -client jmsptpproducer.jar`

We would then see the following output on the console:

```
Sending the following message: Testing, 1, 2, 3. Can you hear me?
Sending the following message: Do you copy?
Sending the following message: Good bye!
```

The `appclient` executable can be found under `[GlassFish installation directory]/glassfish/bin`; the example assumes this directory is in your PATH variable; if it isn't the complete path to the `appclient` executable must be typed in the command line.

With that out of the way, we can now talk about the code.

The `produceMessages()` method performs all the necessary steps to send messages to a message queue.

The first thing this method does is obtain a JMS connection by invoking the `createConnection()` method on the injected instance of `javax.jms.ConnectionFactory`. Notice that the `mappedName` attribute of the `@Resource` annotation decorating the connection factory object matches the JNDI name of the connection factory that we set up in the GlassFish web console. Behind the scenes, a JNDI lookup is made using this name to obtain the connection factory object.

After obtaining a connection, the next step is to obtain a JMS session from the said connection. This can be accomplished by calling the `createSession()` method on the Connection object. As can be seen in the code, the `createSession()` method takes two parameters.

The first parameter of the `createSession()` method is a Boolean indicating if the session is transacted. If this value is `true`, several messages can be sent as part of a transaction by invoking the `commit()` method in the session object; similarly, they can be rolled back by invoking its `rollback()` method.

The second parameter of the `createSession()` method indicates how messages are acknowledged by the message receiver. Valid values for these parameters are defined as constants in the `javax.jms.Session` interface:

- `Session.AUTO_ACKNOWLEDGE`: indicates that the session will automatically acknowledge receipt of a message.
- `Session.CLIENT_ACKNOWLEDGE`: indicates that the message receiver must explicitly call the `acknowledge()` method on the message.
- `Session.DUPS_OK_ACKNOWLEDGE`: indicates that the session will lazily acknowledge the receipt of messages. Using this value might result in some messages being delivered more than once.

After obtaining a JMS session, an instance of `javax.jms.MessageProducer` is obtained by invoking the `createProducer()` method on the session object. The `MessageProducer` object is the one that will actually send messages to the message queue. The injected `Queue` instance is passed as a parameter to the `createProducer()` method; again, the value of the `mappedName` attribute for the `@Resource` annotation decorating this object must match the JNDI name that we gave our message queue when setting it up in the `GlassFish` web console.

After obtaining an instance of `MessageProducer`, the code creates a series of text messages by invoking the `createTextMessage()` method on the session object. This method returns an instance of a class implementing the `javax.jms.TextMessage` interface. This interface defines a method called `setText()`, which is used to set the actual text in the message. After creating each text message and setting its text, it is sent to the queue by invoking the `send()` method on the `MessageProducer` object.

After sending the messages, the code disconnects from the JMS queue by invoking the `close()` method on the `MessageProducer` object, on the `Session` object, and on the `Connection` object.

Although this example sends only text messages to the queue, we are not limited to this type of message. The JMS API provides several types of messages that can be sent and received by JMS applications. All message types are defined as interfaces in the `javax.jms` package. The following table lists all of the available message types:

Message Type	Description
BytesMessage	Allows sending an array of bytes as a message.
MapMessage	Allows sending an implementation of `java.util.Map` as a message.
ObjectMessage	Allows sending any Java object implementing `java.io.Serializable` as a message.
StreamMessage	Allows sending an array of bytes as a message. Differs from BytesMessage in that it stores the type of each primitive type added to the stream.
TextMessage	Allows sending a `java.lang.String` as a message.

For more information on all of the above message types, consult their JavaDoc documentation at `http://java.sun.com/javaee/5/docs/api/javax/jms/package-summary.html`.

Retrieving Messages from a Message Queue

Of course, there is no point in sending messages from a queue if nothing is going to receive them. The following example illustrates how to retrieve messages from a JMS message queue:

```java
package net.ensode.glassfishbook;

import javax.annotation.Resource;
import javax.jms.Connection;
import javax.jms.ConnectionFactory;
import javax.jms.JMSException;
import javax.jms.MessageConsumer;
import javax.jms.Queue;
import javax.jms.Session;
import javax.jms.TextMessage;

public class MessageReceiver
{
  @Resource(mappedName = "jms/GlassFishBookConnectionFactory")
  private static ConnectionFactory connectionFactory;
  @Resource(mappedName = "jms/GlassFishBookQueue")
  private static Queue queue;

  public void getMessages()
  {
    Connection connection;
    MessageConsumer messageConsumer;
    TextMessage textMessage;
    boolean goodByeReceived = false;

    try
    {
      connection = connectionFactory.createConnection();
      Session session = connection.createSession(false,
          Session.AUTO_ACKNOWLEDGE);
      messageConsumer = session.createConsumer(queue);
      connection.start();

      while (!goodByeReceived)
      {
        System.out.println("Waiting for messages...");
        textMessage = (TextMessage) messageConsumer.receive();

        if (textMessage != null)
        {
          System.out.print("Received the following message: ");
          System.out.println(textMessage.getText());
          System.out.println();
```

```
        }
        if (textMessage.getText() != null
            && textMessage.getText().equals("Good bye!"))
        {
          goodByeReceived = true;
        }
      }
      messageConsumer.close();
      session.close();
      connection.close();
    }
    catch (JMSException e)
    {
      e.printStackTrace();
    }
  }
  public static void main(String[] args)
  {
    new MessageReceiver().getMessages();
  }
}
```

Just as in the previous example, an instance of `javax.jms.ConnectionFactory` and an instance of `javax.jms.Queue` are injected by using the `@Resource` annotation. Getting a connection and a JMS session is exactly the same here as in the previous example.

In this example, we obtain an instance of `javax.jms.MessageConsumer` by calling the `createConsumer()` method on the JMS session object. When we are ready to start receiving messages from the message queue, we need to invoke the `start()` method on the JMS connection object.

Code not receiving messages?

A common mistake when writing JMS message consumers is to fail to call the `start()` method on the JMS connection object. If our code is not receiving messages it should be receiving, we need to make sure we didn't forget to call this method.

Messages are received by invoking the `receive()` method on the instance of `MessageConsumer` obtained from the JMS session. This method returns an instance of a class implementing the `javax.jms.Message` interface. It must be cast to the appropriate type in order to obtain the actual message.

In this particular example, we placed this method call in a `while` loop as we are expecting a message that will let us know that no more messages are coming. Specifically, we are looking for a message containing the text "Good bye!". Once we receive this message, we break out of the loop and continue processing. In this particular case, there is no more processing to do, therefore all we do is call the `close()` method on the message consumer object, on the session object, and on the connection object.

Just as in the previous example, using the `appclient` utility allows us to inject resources into the code, and prevents us from having to add any libraries to the CLASSPATH. After executing the code through the `appclient` utility, we should see the following output in the command line:

```
appclient -client target/jmsptpconsumer.jar
Waiting for messages...
Received the following message: Testing, 1, 2, 3. Can you hear me?

Waiting for messages...
Received the following message: Do you copy?

Waiting for messages...
Received the following message: Good bye!
```

This of course, assumes that the previous example was already executed and it placed messages in the message queue.

Asynchronously Receiving Messages from a Message Queue

The `MessageConsumer.receive()` method has a disadvantage; it blocks execution until a message is received from the queue. We can avoid this disadvantage by receiving messages asynchronously via an implementation of the `javax.jms.MessageListener` interface.

The `javax.jms.MessageListener` interface contains a single method called `onMessage`; it takes an instance of a class implementing the `javax.jms.Message` interface as its sole parameter. The following example illustrates a typical implementation of this interface:

```
package net.ensode.glassfishbook;
import javax.jms.JMSException;
import javax.jms.Message;
import javax.jms.MessageListener;
import javax.jms.TextMessage;
```

```
public class ExampleMessageListener implements MessageListener
{
  public void onMessage(Message message)
  {
    TextMessage textMessage = (TextMessage)message;
    try
    {
      System.out.print("Received the following message: ");
      System.out.println(textMessage.getText());
      System.out.println();
    }
    catch (JMSException e)
    {
      e.printStackTrace();
    }
  }
}
```

In this case, the onMessage() method simply outputs the message text to the console.

Our main code can now delegate message retrieval to our custom MessageListener implementation.

```
package net.ensode.glassfishbook;
import javax.annotation.Resource;
import javax.jms.Connection;
import javax.jms.ConnectionFactory;
import javax.jms.JMSException;
import javax.jms.MessageConsumer;
import javax.jms.Queue;
import javax.jms.Session;
public class AsynchMessReceiver
{
  @Resource(mappedName = "jms/GlassFishBookConnectionFactory")
  private static ConnectionFactory connectionFactory;
  @Resource(mappedName = "jms/GlassFishBookQueue")
  private static Queue queue;
  public void getMessages()
  {
    Connection connection;
    MessageConsumer messageConsumer;
    try
    {
      connection = connectionFactory.createConnection();
      Session session = connection.createSession(false,
          Session.AUTO_ACKNOWLEDGE);
```

```
        messageConsumer = session.createConsumer(queue);
        messageConsumer.setMessageListener(
            new ExampleMessageListener());
        connection.start();

        System.out.println("The above line will allow "
            + "the MessageListener implementation to "
                + "receive and process messages from "
                + "the queue.");
        Thread.sleep(1000);
        System.out.println("Our code does not have to block "
            + "while messages are received.");
        Thread.sleep(1000);
        System.out.println("It can do other stuff "
            + "(hopefully something more useful than sending "
            + "silly output to the console. :)");
        Thread.sleep(1000);

        messageConsumer.close();
        session.close();
        connection.close();
    }
    catch (JMSException e)
    {
      e.printStackTrace();
    }
    catch (InterruptedException e)
    {
      e.printStackTrace();
    }
  }
  public static void main(String[] args)
  {
    new AsynchMessReceiver().getMessages();
  }
}
```

The only relevant difference between this example and the one in the previous section is that in this case, we are calling the `setMessageListener()` method on the instance of `javax.jms.MessageConsumer` obtained from the JMS session. We pass an instance of our custom implementation of `javax.jms.MessageListener` to this method; its `onMessage()` method is automatically called whenever there is a message waiting in the queue. By using this approach, the main code does not block while waiting to receive messages.

Executing this example (using, of course, GlassFish's `appclient` utility), results in the following output:

```
appclient -client target/jmsptpasynchconsumer.jar
```

The above line will allow the MessageListener implementation to receive and process messages from the queue.

Received the following message: Testing, 1, 2, 3. Can you hear me?

Received the following message: Do you copy?

Received the following message: Good bye!

Our code does not have to block while messages are received.

It can do other stuff (hopefully something more useful than sending silly output to the console. :)

Notice how the messages were received and processed while the main thread was executing. We can tell this is the case because the output of our `MessageListener`'s `onMessage()` method can be seen between calls to `System.out.println()` in the primary class.

Browsing Message Queues

JMS provides a way to browse message queues without actually removing the messages from the queue. The following example illustrates how to do this:

```
package net.ensode.glassfishbook;

import java.util.Enumeration;

import javax.annotation.Resource;
import javax.jms.Connection;
import javax.jms.ConnectionFactory;
import javax.jms.JMSException;
import javax.jms.Queue;
import javax.jms.QueueBrowser;
import javax.jms.Session;
import javax.jms.TextMessage;

public class MessageQueueBrowser
{
  @Resource(mappedName = "jms/GlassFishBookConnectionFactory")
  private static ConnectionFactory connectionFactory;
  @Resource(mappedName = "jms/GlassFishBookQueue")
  private static Queue queue;
  public void browseMessages()
```

```
   {
     try
     {
       Enumeration messageEnumeration;
       TextMessage textMessage;
       Connection connection =
           connectionFactory.createConnection();
       Session session = connection.createSession(false,
           Session.AUTO_ACKNOWLEDGE);
       QueueBrowser browser = session.createBrowser(queue);
       messageEnumeration = browser.getEnumeration();
       if (messageEnumeration != null)
       {
         if (!messageEnumeration.hasMoreElements())
         {
           System.out.println(
               "There are no messages in the queue.");
         }
         else
         {
           System.out.println(
               "The following messages are in the queue:");
           while (messageEnumeration.hasMoreElements())
           {
             textMessage = (TextMessage)
                 messageEnumeration.nextElement();
             System.out.println(textMessage.getText());
           }
         }
       }
       session.close();
       connection.close();
     }
     catch (JMSException e)
     {
       e.printStackTrace();
     }
   }
   public static void main(String[] args)
   {
     new MessageQueueBrowser().browseMessages();
   }
 }
```

As we can see, the procedure to browse messages in a message queue is straightforward. We obtain a JMS connection and a JMS session in the usual way, then invoke the `createBrowser()` method on the JMS session object. This method returns an implementation of the `javax.jms.QueueBrowser` interface; this interface contains the `getEnumeration()` method, which we can invoke to obtain an Enumeration containing all messages in the queue. To examine the messages in the queue, we simply traverse this enumeration and obtain the messages one by one. In this example, we simply invoke the `getText()` method of each message in the queue.

Message Topics

Message topics are used when our JMS code uses the Publish/Subscribe (pub/sub) messaging domain. When using this messaging domain, the same message can be sent to all subscribers to the topic.

Sending Messages to a Message Topic

The following example illustrates how to send messages to a message topic:

```
package net.ensode.glassfishbook;
import javax.annotation.Resource;
import javax.jms.Connection;
import javax.jms.ConnectionFactory;
import javax.jms.JMSException;
import javax.jms.MessageProducer;
import javax.jms.Session;
import javax.jms.TextMessage;
import javax.jms.Topic;

public class MessageSender
{
  @Resource(mappedName = "jms/GlassFishBookConnectionFactory")
  private static ConnectionFactory connectionFactory;
  @Resource(mappedName = "jms/GlassFishBookTopic")
  private static Topic topic;

  public void produceMessages()
  {
    MessageProducer messageProducer;
    TextMessage textMessage;
    try
    {
      Connection connection =
          connectionFactory.createConnection();
```

```
        Session session = connection.createSession(false,
            Session.AUTO_ACKNOWLEDGE);
        messageProducer = session.createProducer(topic);

        textMessage = session.createTextMessage();

        textMessage.setText(
            "Testing, 1, 2, 3. Can you hear me?");
        System.out.println("Sending the following message: "
            + textMessage.getText());
        messageProducer.send(textMessage);

        textMessage.setText("Do you copy?");
        System.out.println("Sending the following message: "
            + textMessage.getText());
        messageProducer.send(textMessage);

        textMessage.setText("Good bye!");
        System.out.println("Sending the following message: "
            + textMessage.getText());
        messageProducer.send(textMessage);

        messageProducer.close();
        session.close();
        connection.close();
      }
      catch (JMSException e)
      {
        e.printStackTrace();
      }
    }
    public static void main(String[] args)
    {
      new MessageSender().produceMessages();
    }
  }
```

As we can see, this code is nearly identical to the MessageSender class we saw when we discussed Point-To-Point messaging. As a matter of fact, the only lines of code that are different are the ones that are highlighted. The JMS API was designed this way so that application developers do not have to learn two different APIs for the PTP and pub/sub domains.

As the code is nearly identical to the corresponding example in the Message Queues section, we will only explain the differences between the two examples. In this example, instead of declaring an instance of a class implementing javax.jms.Queue, we declare an instance of a class implementing javax.jms.Topic. Just as in previous examples, we use dependency injection to initialize the Topic object.

After obtaining a JMS connection and a JMS session, we pass the Topic object to the `createProducer()` method in the Session object. This method returns an instance of `javax.jms.MessageProducer` that we can use to send messages to the JMS topic.

Receiving Messages from a Message Topic

Just as sending messages to a Message Topic is nearly identical to sending messages to a Message Queue, receiving messages from a Message Topic is nearly identical to receiving messages from a Message Queue.

```
package net.ensode.glassfishbook;

import javax.annotation.Resource;
import javax.jms.Connection;
import javax.jms.ConnectionFactory;
import javax.jms.JMSException;
import javax.jms.MessageConsumer;
import javax.jms.Session;
import javax.jms.TextMessage;
import javax.jms.Topic;

public class MessageReceiver
{
  @Resource(mappedName = "jms/GlassFishBookConnectionFactory")
  private static ConnectionFactory connectionFactory;
  @Resource(mappedName = "jms/GlassFishBookTopic")
  private static Topic topic;

  public void getMessages()
  {
    Connection connection;
    MessageConsumer messageConsumer;
    TextMessage textMessage;
    boolean goodByeReceived = false;

    try
    {
      connection = connectionFactory.createConnection();
      Session session = connection.createSession(false,
          Session.AUTO_ACKNOWLEDGE);
      messageConsumer = session.createConsumer(topic);
      connection.start();

      while (!goodByeReceived)
      {
        System.out.println("Waiting for messages...");
        textMessage = (TextMessage) messageConsumer.receive();
```

```
      if (textMessage != null)
      {
        System.out.print("Received the following message: ");
        System.out.println(textMessage.getText());
        System.out.println();
      }
      if (textMessage.getText() != null
          && textMessage.getText().equals("Good bye!"))
      {
        goodByeReceived = true;
      }
    }
    messageConsumer.close();
    session.close();
    connection.close();
  }
  catch (JMSException e)
  {
    e.printStackTrace();
  }
}
public static void main(String[] args)
{
  new MessageReceiver().getMessages();
}
}
```

Once again the differences between this code and the corresponding code for PTP
are trivial. Instead of declaring an instance of a class implementing javax.jms.
Queue, we declare a class implementing javax.jms.Topic; we use the @Resource
annotation to inject an instance of this class into our code, using the JNDI name we
used when creating it in the GlassFish web console. After obtaining a JMS connection
and session, we pass the Topic object to the createConsumer() method in the
Session object. This method returns an instance of javax.jms.MessageConsumer
that we can use to receive messages from the JMS topic.

Using the pub/sub messaging domain, as illustrated in this section, has the
advantage that messages can be sent to several message consumers. We can easily
test this by concurrently executing two instances of the MessageReceiver class we
developed in this section, then executing the MessageSender class we developed in
the previous section. We should see console output for each instance, indicating that
both instances received all messages.

Just as with message queues, messages can be retrieved asynchronously from a message Topic. The procedure to do so is so similar to the message queue version that we will not show an example. To convert the asynchronous example shown earlier in this chapter to use a message topic, simply replace the `javax.jms.Queue` variable with an instance of `javax.jms.Topic` and inject the appropriate instance by using `"jms/GlassFishBookTopic"` as the value of the `mappedName` attribute of the `@Resource` annotation decorating the instance of `javax.jms.Topic`.

Creating Durable Subscribers

The disadvantage of using the pub/sub messaging domain is that message consumers must be executing when the messages are sent to the topic. If the message consumer is not executing at the time, it will not receive the messages, whereas in PTP, messages are kept in the queue until the message consumer executes. Fortunately, the JMS API provides a way to use the pub/sub messaging domain and keep messages in the topic until all subscribed message consumers execute and receive the messages. This can be accomplished by creating durable subscribers to a JMS Topic.

In order to be able to service durable subscribers, we need to set the `ClientId` property of our JMS connection factory. Each durable subscriber must have a unique client ID, therefore a unique connection factory must be declared for each potential durable subscriber.

InvalidClientIdException?

Only one JMS client can connect to a Topic for a specific client ID, if more than one JMS client attempts to obtain a JMS connection using the same connection factory, a JMSException stating that the Client ID is already in use will be thrown. The solution is to create a connection factory for each potential client that will be receiving messages from the durable Topic.

As we mentioned before, the easiest way to add a connection factory is through the GlassFish web console. Recall that to add a JMS connection factory through the GlassFish web console, we need to expand the **Resources** node on the left-hand side, then expand the **JMS Resources** node, click on the **Connection Factories** node, and then click on the **New...** button in the main area of the page.

Our next example will use the settings displayed in the following screenshot.

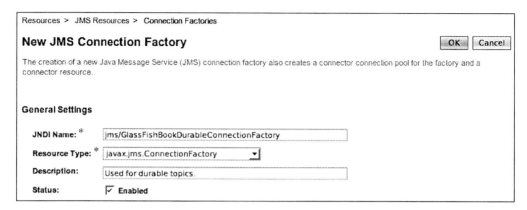

Before clicking on the **OK** button, we need to scroll to the bottom of the page, click on the **Add Property** button, and enter a new property named `ClientId`. Our example will use `ExampleId` as the value for this property.

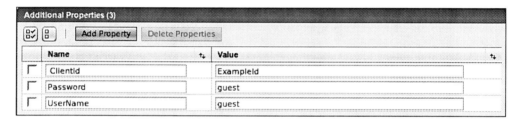

 Notice that GlassFish has two predefined properties called `Password` and `UserName`. We can modify the default values for those properties to require a user name and password in order to obtain a connection from the connection factory. Whenever a user name and password are required, we need to invoke an overloaded version of the `ConnectionFactory.getConnection()` method; this overloaded version takes two String parameters, the first one for the user name and the second one for the password.

Now that we have set up GlassFish to be able to provide durable subscriptions, we are ready to write some code to take advantage of them.

```
package net.ensode.glassfishbook;
import javax.annotation.Resource;
import javax.jms.Connection;
import javax.jms.ConnectionFactory;
import javax.jms.JMSException;
import javax.jms.MessageConsumer;
```

```
import javax.jms.Session;
import javax.jms.TextMessage;
import javax.jms.Topic;
public class MessageReceiver
{
  @Resource(mappedName =
      "jms/GlassFishBookDurableConnectionFactory")
  private static ConnectionFactory connectionFactory;
  @Resource(mappedName = "jms/GlassFishBookTopic")
  private static Topic topic;
  public void getMessages()
  {
    Connection connection;
    MessageConsumer messageConsumer;
    TextMessage textMessage;
    boolean goodByeReceived = false;
    try
    {
      connection = connectionFactory.createConnection();
      Session session = connection.createSession(false,
          Session.AUTO_ACKNOWLEDGE);
      messageConsumer = session.createDurableSubscriber(topic,
          "Subscriber1");
      connection.start();
      while (!goodByeReceived)
      {
        System.out.println("Waiting for messages...");
        textMessage = (TextMessage) messageConsumer.receive();
        if (textMessage != null)
        {
          System.out.print("Received the following message: ");
          System.out.println(textMessage.getText());
          System.out.println();
        }
        if (textMessage.getText() != null
            && textMessage.getText().equals("Good bye!"))
        {
          goodByeReceived = true;
        }
      }
      messageConsumer.close();
      session.close();
```

```
        connection.close();
      }
      catch (JMSException e)
      {
        e.printStackTrace();
      }
    }
    public static void main(String[] args)
    {
      new MessageReceiver().getMessages();
    }
  }
```

As you can see, this code is not much different from previous examples whose purpose was to retrieve messages. There are only two differences from previous examples: The instance of `ConnectionFactory` we are injecting is the one we set up earlier in this section to handle durable subscriptions, and instead of calling the `createSubscriber()` method on the JMS session object, we are calling `createDurableSubscriber()`. The `createDurableSubscriber()` method takes two arguments, a JMS `Topic` object to retrieve messages from and a String designating a name for this subscription. This second parameter must be unique among all subscribers to the durable topic.

Summary

In this chapter, we covered how to set up JMS connection factories, JMS message queues, and JMS message topics in GlassFish by using the GlassFish web console.

We also covered how to send messages to a message queue via the `javax.jms.MessageProducer` interface.

Additionally, we covered how to receive messages from a message queue via the `javax.jms.MessageConsumer` interface. We also covered how to asynchronously receive messages from a message queue by implementing the `javax.jms.MessageListener` interface.

We also saw how to use the above interfaces to send and receive messages to and from a JMS message topic.

We also covered how to browse messages in a message queue without removing the messages from the queue via the `javax.jms.QueueBrowser` interface.

Finally, we saw how to set up and interact with durable subscriptions to JMS topics.

8
Security

In this chapter, we will cover how to secure Java EE applications by taking advantage of GlassFish's built-in security features. Java EE security relies on the Java Authentication and Authorization Service (JAAS) API. As we shall see, securing Java EE applications requires very little coding; for the most part, securing an application is achieved by setting up users and security groups in a security realm in the application server, then configuring our applications to rely on a specific security realm for authentication and authorization.

Some of the topics we will cover include:

- The Admin realm
- The File realm
- The Certificate realm
  - ° Creating self-signed security certificates
- The JDBC realm
- Custom Realms

Security Realms

Security realms are, in essence, collections of users and related security groups. Users are application users. A user can belong to one or more security group; the groups that the user belongs to define what actions the system will allow the user to perform. For example, an application can have regular users who can only use the basic application functionality, and it can have administrators who, in addition to being able to use basic application functionality, can add additional users to the system.

Security realms store user information (user name, password, and security groups); applications don't need to implement this functionality, they can simply be configured to obtain this information from a security realm. A security realm can be used by more than one application.

Predefined Security Realms

GlassFish comes preconfigured with three predefined security realms: **admin-realm**, the **file realm**, and the **certificate realm**. **admin-realm** is used to manage user's access to the GlassFish web console and shouldn't be used for other applications. The file realm stores user information in a file. The certificate realm looks for a client-side certificate to authenticate the user.

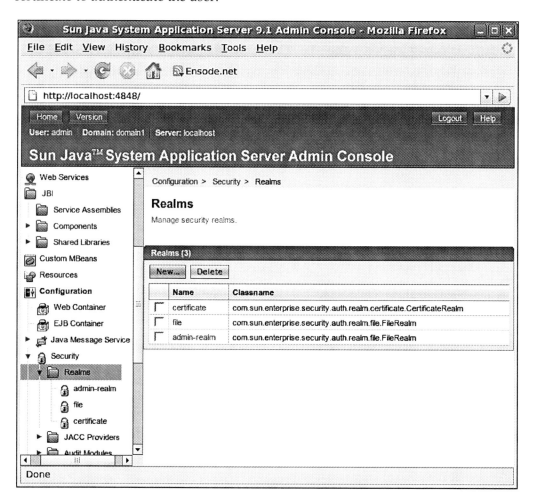

In addition to the predefined security realms, we can add additional realms with very little effort. We will cover how to do this later in this chapter, but first let's discuss GlassFish's predefined security realms.

admin-realm

To illustrate how to add users to a realm, let's add a new user to admin-realm. This will allow this additional user to log in to the GlassFish web console. In order to add a user to admin-realm, log in to the GlassFish web console, expand the **Configuation** node at the left-hand side, then expand the **Security** node, then the **Realms** node, and click on **admin-realm**. The main area of the page should look like the following screenshot:

To add a user to the realm, click on the button labeled **Manage Users** at the top left. The main area of the page should now look like this:

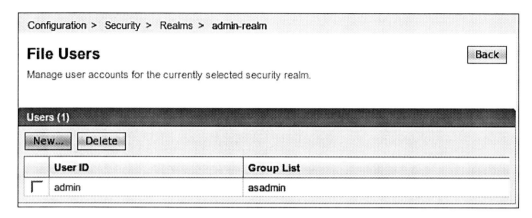

To add a new user to the realm, simply click on the **New...** button at the top left of the screen. Then enter the new user information.

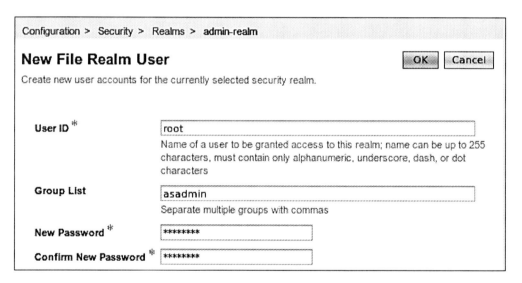

In the above screenshot, we added a new user named "root", added this user to the "asadmin" group, and entered this user's password.

 The GlassFish web console will only allow users in the "asadmin" group to log in. Failing to add our user to this security group would prevent him/her from logging in to the console.

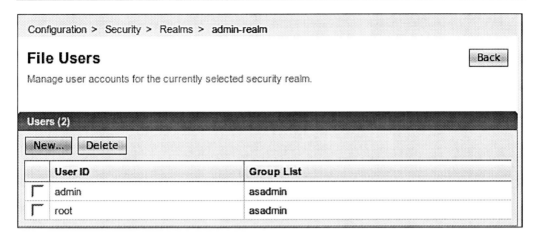

We have successfully added a new user for the GlassFish web console. We can test this new account by logging into the console with this new user's credentials.

The file Realm

The second predefined realm in GlassFish is the file realm. This realm stores user information encrypted in a text file. Adding users to this realm is very similar to adding users to admin-realm. We can add a user by expanding the **Configuration** node, then expanding the **Security** node, then the **Realms** node, then clicking on **file**, then clicking on the **Manage Users** button and clicking on the **New...** button.

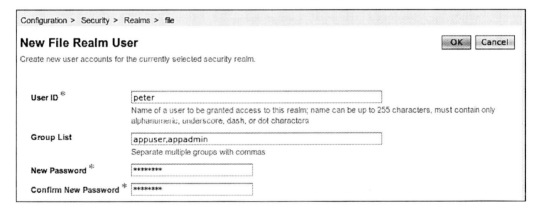

As this realm is meant for us to use for our applications, we can come up with our own groups. In this example, we added a user with a User ID of "peter" to the groups "appuser" and "appadmin".

Clicking the OK button should save the new user and take us to the user list for this realm.

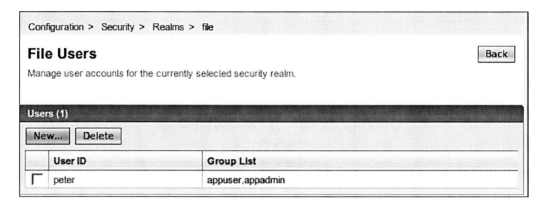

Clicking the **New...** button allows us to add additional users to the realm. Let's add an additional user called "joe" and belonging only to the "appuser" group.

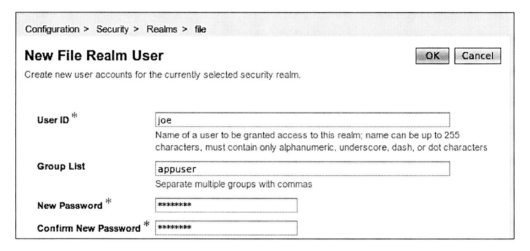

As we have seen in this section, adding users to the file realm is very simple. We will now illustrate how to authenticate and authorize users via the file realm.

File Realm Basic Authentication

In the previous section, we covered how to add users to the file realm and how to assign roles to these users. In this section, we will illustrate how to secure a web application so that only properly authenticated and authorized users can access it. This web application will use the file realm for user access control.

The application will consist of a few very simple JSPs. All authentication logic is taken care of by the application server, therefore the only place we need to make modifications in order to secure the application is in its deployment descriptors, web.xml and sun-web.xml. We will first discuss web.xml, which is shown next.

```xml
<web-app xmlns="http://java.sun.com/xml/ns/javaee" version="2.5"
    xmlns:xsi="http://www.w3.org/2001/XMLSchema-instance"
    xsi:schemaLocation="http://java.sun.com/xml/ns/javaee http://java.
sun.com/xml/ns/javaee/web-app_2_5.xsd">
    <security-constraint>
      <web-resource-collection>
        <web-resource-name>Admin Pages</web-resource-name>
        <url-pattern>/admin/*</url-pattern>
      </web-resource-collection>
      <auth-constraint>
        <role-name>admin</role-name>
      </auth-constraint>
    </security-constraint>
    <security-constraint>
      <web-resource-collection>
        <web-resource-name>All Pages</web-resource-name>
        <url-pattern>/*</url-pattern>
      </web-resource-collection>
      <auth-constraint>
        <role-name>user</role-name>
      </auth-constraint>
    </security-constraint>
    <login-config>
      <auth-method>BASIC</auth-method>
      <realm-name>file</realm-name>
</web-app>
```

The `<security-constraint>` element defines who can access pages matching a certain URL pattern. The URL pattern of the pages is defined inside the `<url-pattern>` element, which, as shown in the example, must be nested inside a `<web-resource-collection>` element. Roles allowed to access the pages are defined in the `<role-name>` element, which must be nested inside an `<auth-constraint>` element.

In the above example, we define two sets of pages to be protected. The first set of pages is any page whose URL starts with /admin. These pages can only be accessed by users with the role of admin. The second set of pages is all pages, defined by the URL pattern of /*. Only users with the role of user can access these pages. It is worth noting that the first set of pages is a subset of the second set, that is, any page whose URL matches `/admin/*` also matches `/*`; in cases like this the most specific case "wins". In this particular case, users with a role of user (and without the role of admin) will not be able to access any page whose URL starts with `/admin`.

The next element we need to add to `web.xml` in order to protect our pages is the `<login-config>` element. This element must contain an `<auth-method>` element that defines the authorization method for the application. Valid values for this element include `BASIC`, `DIGEST`, `FORM`, and `CLIENT-CERT`.

`BASIC` indicates that basic authentication will be used. This type of authentication will result in a browser-generated popup, prompting the user for a user name and password, being displayed the first time a user tries to access a protected page. Unless using the HTTPS protocol, when using basic authentication, the user's credentials are Base64 encoded, not encrypted. It would be fairly easy for an attacker to decode these credentials; therefore using basic authentication is not recommended.

`DIGEST` is similar to basic authentication except it uses an MD5 DIGEST to encrypt the user credentials instead of sending them Base64 encoded.

`FORM` uses a custom HTML or JSP page containing an HTML form with user name and password fields. The values in the form are then checked against the security realm for user authentication and authorization. Unless using HTTPS, user credentials are sent in clear text when using form-based authentication, therefore using HTTPS is recommended because it encrypts the data. We will cover setting up GlassFish to use HTTPS, later in this chapter.

`CLIENT-CERT` uses client-side certificates to authenticate and authorize the user.

The `<realm-name>` element of `<login-config>` indicate which security realm to use to authenticate and authorize the user. In this particular example, we are using the file realm.

All of the `web.xml` elements we have discussed in this section can be used with any security realm; they are not tied to the file realm. The only thing that ties our application to the file realm is the value of the `<realm-name>` element. Something else to keep in mind is that not all authentication methods are supported by all realms. The file realm supports only basic and form-based authentication.

Before we can successfully authenticate our users, we need to link the user roles defined in `web.xml` with the groups defined in the realm. We accomplish this in the `sun-web.xml` deployment descriptor.

```
<?xml version="1.0" encoding="UTF-8" standalone="no"?>
<!DOCTYPE sun-web-app PUBLIC "-//Sun Microsystems, Inc.//DTD
Application Server 9.0 Servlet 2.5//EN" "http://www.sun.com/software/
```

```
appserver/dtds/sun-web-app_2_5-0.dtd">
<sun-web-app>
   <security-role-mapping>
     <role-name>admin</role-name>
     <group-name>appadmin</group-name>
   </security-role-mapping>
   <security-role-mapping>
     <role-name>user</role-name>
     <group-name>appuser</group-name>
   </security-role-mapping>
</sun-web-app>
```

As can be seen in the example, the sun-web.xml deployment descriptor can have one or more <security-role-mapping> elements; one of these elements for each role defined in web.xml is needed. The <role-name> subelement indicates the role to map. Its value must match the value of the corresponding <role-name> element in web.xml. The <group-name> subelement must match the value of a security group in the realm used to authenticate users in the application.

In this example, the first <security-role-mapping> element maps the "admin" role defined in the application's web.xml deployment descriptor to the "appadmin" group we created when adding users to the file realm earlier in the chapter. The second <security-role-mapping> maps the "user" role in web.xml to the "appuser" group in the file realm.

As we mentioned earlier, there is nothing we need to do in our code in order to authenticate and authorize users. All we need to do is modify the application's deployment descriptors as described in this section. As our application is nothing but a few simple JSPs, we will not show the source code for them. The structure of our application is shown in the following screenshot:

Based on the way we set up our application in the deployment descriptors, users with a role of "user" will be able to access the two JSPs at the root of the application (`index.jsp` and `random.jsp`). Only users with the role of "admin" will be able to access any pages under the "admin" folder, which in this particular case is a single JSP named `index.jsp`.

After packaging and deploying our application and pointing the browser to the URL of any of its pages, we should see a popup asking for a user name and a password.

After entering the correct user name and password, we are directed to the page we were attempting to see.

At this point, the user can navigate to any page he or she is allowed to access in the application, either by following links or by typing the URL in the browser, without having to re-enter his/her user name and password.

Notice that we logged in as user joe; this user belongs only to the user role, therefore he does not have access to any page with a URL that starts with /admin. If joe tries to access one of these pages, he will see the following error message in the browser.

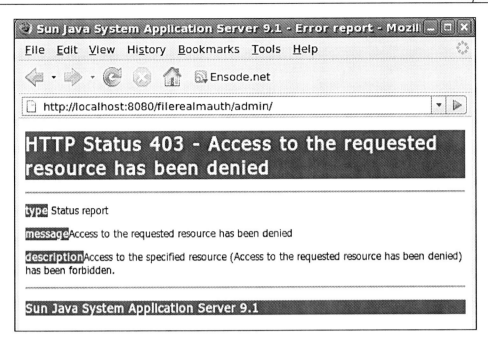

Only users belonging to the admin role can see pages that match the above URL. When we were adding users to the file realm, we added a user named peter that had this role. If we log in as peter, we will be able to see the requested page. For basic authentication, the only way possible to log out of the application is to close the browser, therefore to log in as peter we need to close and reopen the browser.

As we mentioned before, one disadvantage of the basic authentication method we used in this example is that login information is not encrypted. One way to get around this is to use the HTTPS (HTTP over SSL) protocol; when using this protocol all information between the browser and the server is encrypted.

The easiest way to use HTTPS is by modifying the application `web.xml` deployment descriptor.

```
<web-app xmlns="http://java.sun.com/xml/ns/javaee" version="2.5"
  xmlns:xsi="http://www.w3.org/2001/XMLSchema-instance"
  xsi:schemaLocation="http://java.sun.com/xml/ns/javaee http://java.
sun.com/xml/ns/javaee/web-app_2_5.xsd">
  <security-constraint>
    <web-resource-collection>
      <web-resource-name>Admin Pages</web-resource-name>
      <url-pattern>/admin/*</url-pattern>
    </web-resource-collection>
    <auth-constraint>
      <role-name>admin</role-name>
    </auth-constraint>
    <user-data-constraint>
      <transport-guarantee>CONFIDENTIAL</transport-guarantee>
    </user-data-constraint>
  </security-constraint>
  <security-constraint>
    <web-resource-collection>
      <web-resource-name>AllPages</web-resource-name>
      <url-pattern>/*</url-pattern>
    </web-resource-collection>
    <auth-constraint>
      <role-name>user</role-name>
    </auth-constraint>
    <user-data-constraint>
      <transport-guarantee>CONFIDENTIAL</transport-guarantee>
    </user-data-constraint>
  </security-constraint>
  <login-config>
    <auth-method>BASIC</auth-method>
    <realm-name>file</realm-name>
  </login-config>
</web-app>
```

As we can see, all we need to do to have the application be accessed only through HTTPS is to add a `<user-data-constraint>` element containing a nested `<transport-guarantee>` element to each set of pages we want to encrypt traffic. Sets of pages to be protected are declared in the `<security-constraint>` elements in the `web.xml` deployment descriptor.

Now, when we access the application through the (unsecure) HTTP port (by default this is 8080), the request is automatically forwarded to the (secure) HTTPS port (default of 8181).

In this example, we set the value of the `<transport-guarantee>` to CONFIDENTIAL. This has the effect of encrypting all the data between the browser and the server, also, if the request is made through the unsecured HTTP port, it is automatically forwarded to the secured HTTPS port.

Another valid value for the `<transport-guarantee>` element is INTEGRAL. When using this value, the integrity of the data between the browser and the server is guaranteed; in other words, the data cannot be changed in transit. When using this value, requests made over HTTP are not automatically forwarded to HTTPS; if a user attempts to access a secure page via HTTP when this value is used, the browser will deny the request and return a 403 (Access Denied) error.

The third and last valid value for the `<transport-guarantee>` is NONE. When using this value, no guarantees are made about the integrity or confidentiality of the data. NONE is the default value used when the `<transport-guarantee>` element is not present in the application's `web.xml` deployment descriptor.

After making the above modifications to the `web.xml` deployment descriptor, redeploying the application and pointing the browser to any of the pages in the application, we should see the following.

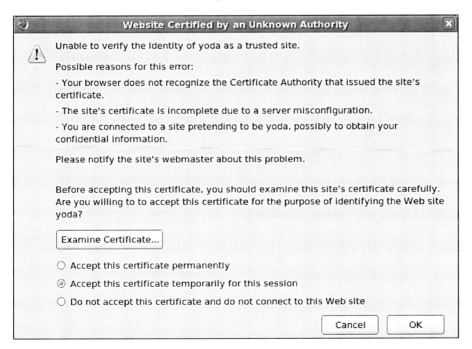

The reason we see this warning window is that, in order for a server to use the HTTPS protocol, it must have an SSL certificate. Typically, SSL certificates are issued by certificate authorities such as Verisign or Thawte. These certificate authorities digitally sign the certificate; by doing this they certify that the server belongs to the entity to which it claims to belong.

A digital certificate from one of these certificate authorities typically costs around $400 USD, and expires after a year. As the cost of these certificates may be prohibitive for development or testing purposes, GlassFish comes preconfigured with a self-signed SSL certificate. As this certificate has not being signed by a certificate authority, the browser pops up the above warning window when we try to access a secured page via HTTPS. We can simply click OK to accept the certificate.

Once we accept the certificate, we are prompted for a user name and password; after entering the appropriate credentials, we are allowed access to the requested page.

Notice the URL in the above screenshot; the protocol is set to HTTPS, and the port is 8181. The URL we pointed the browser to was `http://localhost:8080/filerealmauthhttps/random.jsp`; because of the modifications we made to the application's `web.xml` deployment descriptor, the request was automatically forwarded to this URL. Of course, users may directly type the secure URL and it will work without a problem.

Any data transferred over HTTPS is encrypted, including the user name and password entered at the pop-up window generated by the browser. Using HTTPS allows us to safely use basic authentication. However, basic authentication has another disadvantage, which is that the only way that a user can log out from the application is to close the browser. If we need to allow users to log out of the application without closing the browser, we need to use form-based authentication.

When using form-based authentication, we need to make some modifications to the application's `web.xml` deployment descriptor.

```xml
<web-app xmlns="http://java.sun.com/xml/ns/javaee" version="2.5"
  xmlns:xsi="http://www.w3.org/2001/XMLSchema-instance"
  xsi:schemaLocation="http://java.sun.com/xml/ns/javaee http://java.
sun.com/xml/ns/javaee/web-app_2_5.xsd">
  <security-constraint>
    <web-resource-collection>
      <web-resource-name>Admin Pages</web-resource-name>
      <url-pattern>/admin/*</url-pattern>
    </web-resource-collection>
    <auth-constraint>
      <role-name>admin</role-name>
    </auth-constraint>
  </security-constraint>
  <security-constraint>
    <web-resource-collection>
      <web-resource-name>AllPages</web-resource-name>
      <url-pattern>/*</url-pattern>
    </web-resource-collection>
    <auth-constraint>
      <role-name>user</role-name>
    </auth-constraint>
  </security-constraint>
  <login-config>
    <auth-method>FORM</auth-method>
    <realm-name>file</realm-name>
    <form-login-config>
      <form-login-page>/login.jsp</form-login-page>
      <form-error-page>/loginerror.jsp</form-error-page>
    </form-login-config>
  </login-config>
  <servlet>
    <servlet-name>LogoutServlet</servlet-name>
    <servlet-class>
      net.ensode.glassfishbook.LogoutServlet
    </servlet-class>
  </servlet>
  <servlet-mapping>
    <servlet-name>LogoutServlet</servlet-name>
    <url-pattern>/logout</url-pattern>
  </servlet-mapping>
</web-app>
```

When using form-based authentication, we simply use FORM as the value of the
<auth-method> element in web.xml. When using this authentication method, we
need to provide a login page and a login error page. We indicate the URLs for the
login and login error pages as the values of the <form-login-page> and <form-
error-page> elements, respectively. As can be seen in the example, these elements
must be nested inside the <form-login-config> element.

The markup for the login page for our application is shown next.

```
<%@ page language="java" contentType="text/html; charset=UTF-8"
  pageEncoding="UTF-8"%>
<!DOCTYPE html PUBLIC "-//W3C//DTD HTML 4.01 Transitional//EN"
"http://www.w3.org/TR/html4/loose.dtd">
<html>
<head>
<meta http-equiv="Content-Type" content="text/html; charset=UTF-8">
<title>Login</title>
</head>
<body>
<p>Please enter your username and password to access the application</
p>
<form method="POST" action="j_security_check">
<table cellpadding="0" cellspacing="0" border="0">
  <tr>
    <td align="right">Username: </td>
    <td>
      <input type="text" name="j_username">
    </td>
  </tr>
  <tr>
    <td align="right">Password: </td>
    <td>
      <input type="password" name="j_password">
    </td>
  </tr>
  <tr>
    <td></td>
    <td><input type="submit" value="Login"></td>
  </tr>
</table>
</form>
</body>
</html>
```

The login page for an application using form-based authentication must contain a form whose method is "POST" and whose action is "j_security_check". We don't need to implement a servlet or anything else to process this form. The code to process it is supplied by the application server.

The form in the login page must contain a text field named j_username; this text field is meant to hold the user's user name. Additionally, the form must contain a password field named j_password, meant for the user's password. Of course, the form must contain a submit button to submit the data to the server.

The only requirement for a login page is for it to have a form whose attributes match those in the preceding example, and the j_username and j_password input fields as described in the above paragraph.

There are no special requirements for the error page. Of course, it should show an error message telling the user that login was unsuccessful; however, it can contain anything we wish. The error page for our application simply tells the user that there was an error logging in, and links back to the login page to give the user a chance to try again.

In addition to a login page and a login error page, we added a servlet to our application. This servlet allows us to implement logout functionality, something that wasn't possible when we were using basic authentication.

```
package net.ensode.glassfishbook;
import java.io.IOException;
import javax.servlet.ServletException;
import javax.servlet.http.HttpServlet;
import javax.servlet.http.HttpServletRequest;
import javax.servlet.http.HttpServletResponse;
public class LogoutServlet extends HttpServlet
{
  @Override
  protected void doGet(HttpServletRequest request,
    HttpServletResponse response) throws ServletException, IOException
  {
    request.getSession().invalidate();
    response.sendRedirect("index.jsp");
  }
}
```

As you can see, all we need to do to log out the user is invalidate the session. In our servlet, we redirect the response to the index.jsp page; as the session is invalid at this point, the security mechanism will "kick in" and automatically direct the user to the login page.

We are now ready to test form-based authentication; after building our application, deploying it, and pointing the browser to any of its pages, we should see our login page rendered in the browser.

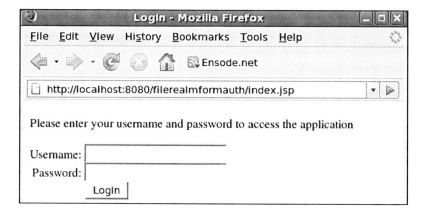

If we submit invalid credentials, we are automatically forwarded to the login error page.

We can click on the **Try again** link to try again. After entering valid credentials, we are allowed into the application.

As you can see, we added a logout link to the page; this page directs the user to the logout servlet, which as we mentioned before simply invalidates the session. From the user's point of view, this link will simply log them out and direct them to the login screen.

The certificate Realm

The certificate realm uses client-side certificates for authentication. Just like server-side certificates, client side certificates are typically obtained from a certificate authority like Verisign or Thawte. These certificate authorities verify that the certificate really belongs to the entity to which it claims to belong.

Obtaining a certificate from a certificate authority costs money and takes some time. It might not be practical to obtain a certificate from one of the certificate authorities when we are developing and or testing our application. Fortunately, we can create self-signed certificates for testing purposes.

Creating Self-Signed Certificates

We can create self-signed certificates with little effort using the keytool utility included with the Java Development Kit.

 We will only briefly cover some of the keytool utility functionality; specifically, we will cover what is necessary to create and import self-signed certificates into GlassFish and into the browser. To learn more about the keytool utility, refer to `http://java.sun.com/ j2se/1.5.0/docs/tooldocs/solaris/keytool.html`.

Generating a self-signed certificate can be accomplished by typing the following command in the command line:

```
keytool -genkey -v -alias selfsignedkey -keyalg RSA -storetype PKCS12 -
keystore client_keystore.p12 -storepass wonttellyou -keypass wonttellyou
```

The above command assumes that the `keytool` utility is in the system PATH. This tool can be found under the `bin` directory, under the directory where the Java Development Kit is installed.

Substitute the values for the `-storepass` and `-keypass` parameters with your own password; both of these passwords must be the same in order to successfully use the certificate to authenticate the client. You may choose any value for the `-alias` parameter. You may also choose any value for the `-keystore` parameter; however, the value must end in `.p12`, as this command generates a file that needs to be imported into the web browser, and this file won't be recognized unless it has the `p12` extension.

After entering this command from the command line, keytool will prompt for some information.

```
What is your first and last name?
  [Unknown]:  David Heffelfinger
What is the name of your organizational unit?
  [Unknown]:  Book Writing Division
What is the name of your organization?
  [Unknown]:  Ensode.net
What is the name of your City or Locality?
  [Unknown]:  Fairfax
What is the name of your State or Province?
  [Unknown]:  Virginia
What is the two-letter country code for this unit?
  [Unknown]:  US
Is CN=David Heffelfinger, OU=Ensode.net, O=Book Writing Division,
L=Fairfax, ST=Virginia, C=US correct?
  [no]:  y

Generating 1,024 bit RSA key pair and self-signed certificate
(SHA1withRSA) with a validity of 90 days
        for: CN=David Heffelfinger, OU=Ensode.net, O=Book Writing
Division, L=Fairfax, ST=Virginia, C=US
[Storing client_keystore.p12]
```

After you enter the data for each prompt, keytool will generate the certificate; it will be stored in the current directory. The name of the file will be the value we used for the `-keystore` parameter (`client_keystore.p12` in the example).

To be able to use this certificate to authenticate ourselves, we need to import it into the browser. The procedure, although similar, varies from browser to browser. In Firefox, this can be accomplished by going to **Edit|Preferences**, then clicking on the **Advanced** icon at the top of the resulting pop-up window, then clicking on the **Encryption** tab.

We then need to click on the **View Certificates** button, click on the Import button on the resulting window, then navigate and select our certificate from the directory in which it was created. At this point, Firefox will ask us for the password used to encrypt the certificate; in our example, we used *wonttellyou* as the password. After entering the password, we should see a pop-up window confirming that our certificate was successfully imported. We should then see it in the list of certificates.

We have now added our certificate to Firefox so that it can be used to authenticate ourselves. If you are using another web browsers, the procedure will be similar. Consult your browser's documentation for details.

The certificate we created in the previous step needs to be exported into a format that GlassFish can understand:

```
keytool -export -alias selfsignedkey -keystore client_keystore.p12 -
storetype PKCS12 -storepass wonttellyou -rfc -file selfsigned.cer
```

The values for the `-alias`, `-keystore`, and `-storepass` parameters must match the values used in the previous command. You may choose any value for the `-file` parameter, but it is recommended for the value to end in the `.cer` extension.

As our certificate was not issued by a certificate authority, GlassFish by default will not recognize it as a valid certificate. GlassFish knows what certificates to trust based on the certificate authority that created them. The way this is implemented is that certificates for these various authorities are stored in a keystore named `cacerts.jks`. This keystore can be found in the following location:

```
[glassfish installation directory]/glassfish/domains/domain1/config/
cacerts.jks.
```

In order for GlassFish to accept our certificate, we need to import it into the cacerts keystore. This can be accomplished by issuing the following command from the command line:

```
keytool -import -file selfsigned.cer -keystore [glassfish installation
directory]/glassfish/domains/domain1/config/cacerts.jks -keypass changeit
-storepass changeit
```

At this point, keytool will display the certificate information in the command line and ask us if we want to trust it.

```
Owner: CN=David Heffelfinger, OU=Book Writing Division, O=Ensode.net,
L=Fairfax, ST=Virginia, C=US

Issuer: CN=David Heffelfinger, OU=Book Writing Division, O=Ensode.net,
L=Fairfax, ST=Virginia, C=US

Serial number: 464f452f

Valid from: Sat May 19 14:42:55 EDT 2007 until: Fri Aug 17 14:42:55 EDT
2007

Certificate fingerprints:
        MD5:  A9:22:8E:2D:A3:06:BB:09:47:A7:02:E3:17:86:A2:6B

        SHA1: 16:E2:85:BC:BF:19:77:D8:02:49:31:22:FE:A8:3A:D8:
              A7:3F:62:03

        Signature algorithm name: SHA1withRSA

        Version: 3

Trust this certificate? [no]:  y

Certificate was added to keystore
```

Once we add the certificate to the `cacerts.jks` keystore, we need to restart the domain for the change to take effect.

What we are effectively doing here is adding ourselves as a certificate authority that GlassFish will trust. This of course should not be done in a production system.

The value for the `-file` parameter must match the value we used for this same parameter when we exported the certificate.

"changeit" is the default password for the `-keypass` and `-storepass` parameters for the `cacerts.jks` keystore. This value can be changed by issuing the following command:

`[glassfish installation directory]/glassfish/bin/asadmin change-master-password --savemasterpassword=true`

This command will prompt for the existing master password and for the new master password. The `–savemasterpassword=true` parameter is optional; it saves the master password into a file called `master-password` in the root directory for the domain. If we don't use this parameter when changing the master password, then we will need to enter the master password every time we want to start the domain.

Now that we have created a self-signed certificate, imported it into our browser, and established ourselves as a certificate authority that GlassFish will trust, we are ready to develop an application that will use client-side certificates for authentication.

Configuring Applications to Use the Certificate Realm

As we are taking advantage of Java EE 5 security features, we don't need to modify any code at all in order to use the certificate realm. All we need to do is modify the application's configuration in its deployment descriptors, `web.xml` and `sun-web.xml`.

```
<web-app xmlns="http://java.sun.com/xml/ns/javaee" version="2.5"
  xmlns:xsi="http://www.w3.org/2001/XMLSchema-instance"
  xsi:schemaLocation="http://java.sun.com/xml/ns/javaee http://
                      java.sun.com/xml/ns/javaee/web-app_2_5.xsd">
  <security-constraint>
    <web-resource-collection>
      <web-resource-name>AllPages</web-resource-name>
      <url-pattern>/*</url-pattern>
    </web-resource-collection>
    <auth-constraint>
      <role-name>users</role-name>
    </auth-constraint>
```

```
        <user-data-constraint>
          <transport-guarantee>CONFIDENTIAL</transport-guarantee>
        </user-data-constraint>
      </security-constraint>
      <login-config>
        <auth-method>CLIENT-CERT</auth-method>
        <realm-name>certificate</realm-name>
      </login-config>
    </web-app>
```

The main difference between this web.xml deployment descriptor and the one we saw in the previous section is the contents of the <login-config> element. In this case, we declared CLIENT-CERT as the authorization method and certificate as the realm to use to authenticate. This will have the effect of GlassFish asking the browser for a client certificate before allowing a user into the application.

When using client-certificate authentication, the request must always be done via HTTPS, therefore; it is a good idea to add the <transport-guarantee> element with a value of CONFIDENTIAL to the web.xml deployment descriptor. Recall from the previous section that this has the effect of forwarding any requests through the HTTP port to the HTTPS port. If we don't add this value to the web.xml deployment descriptor, any requests through the HTTP port will fail because client-certificate authentication cannot be done through the HTTP protocol.

Notice that we declared that only users in the role of users can access any page in the system; we did this by adding the role of users to the <role-name> element nested inside the <auth-constraint> element of the <security-constraint> element in the web.xml deployment descriptor. In order to allow access to authorized users, we need to add them to this role. This is done in the sun-web.xml deployment descriptor.

```
    <?xml version="1.0" encoding="UTF-8" standalone="no"?>
    <!DOCTYPE sun-web-app PUBLIC "-//Sun Microsystems, Inc.//DTD
    Application Server 9.0 Servlet 2.5//EN" "http://www.sun.com/software/
    appserver/dtds/sun-web-app_2_5-0.dtd">
    <sun-web-app>
      <security-role-mapping>
        <role-name>users</role-name>
        <principal-name>CN=David Heffelfinger, OU=Book Writing Division,
    O=Ensode.net, L=Fairfax, ST=Virginia, C=US</principal-name>
      </security-role-mapping>
    </sun-web-app>
```

This assignment is done by mapping the principal (user) to a role in a `<security-role-mapping>` element in the `sun-web.xml` deployment descriptor; its `<role-name>` subelement must contain the role name, and the `<principal-name>` subelement contains the user name. This user name is taken from the certificate.

If you are not sure of the name to use, this name can be obtained from the certificate with the keytool utility.

```
keytool -printcert -file selfsigned.cer
Owner: CN=David Heffelfinger, OU=Book Writing Division, O=Ensode.net,
L=Fairfax, ST=Virginia, C=US
Issuer: CN=David Heffelfinger, OU=Book Writing Division, O=Ensode.net,
L=Fairfax, ST=Virginia, C=US
Serial number: 464f452f
Valid from: Sat May 19 14:42:55 EDT 2007 until: Fri Aug 17 14:42:55 EDT
2007
Certificate fingerprints:
        MD5:  A9:22:8E:2D:A3:06:BB:09:47:A7:02:E3:17:86:A2:6B
        SHA1: 16:E2:85:BC:BF:19:77:D8:02:49:31:22:FE:A8:3A:D8:
A7:3F:62:03
        Signature algorithm name: SHA1withRSA
        Version: 3
```

The value to use as `<principal-name>` is the line after **Owner:**. Please note that the value of `<principal-name>` must be in the same line as its opening and closing tags (`<principal-name>` and `</principal-name>`); if there are newline or carriage return characters before or after the value, they are interpreted as being part of the value and validation will fail.

As our application has a single user and a single role, we are ready to deploy it. If we had more users we would have to add additional `<security-role-mapping>` elements to our `sun-web.xml` deployment descriptor, at least one per user. If we had users that belong to more than one role, then we would add a `<security-role-mapping>` element for each role to which the user belongs, using the `<principal-name>` value corresponding to the user's certificate for each one of them.

We are now ready to test our application; after we deploy it and point the browser to any page in the application, we should see a screen like the following (assuming the browser hasn't been configured to provide a default certificate any time a server requests one):

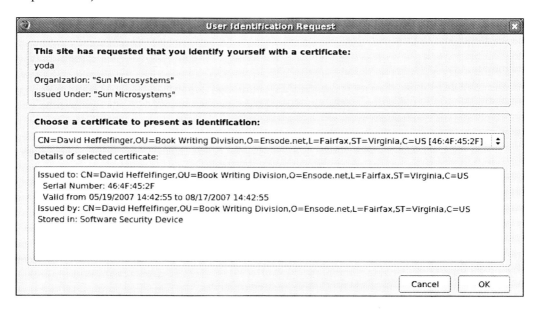

After clicking the **OK** button, we are allowed to access the application.

Before allowing access to the application, GlassFish checks the certificate authority that issued the certificate (as we self-signed the certificate, the owner of the certificate and the certificate authority are the same), and checks against the list of trusted certificate authorities. Because we added ourselves as a trusted authority by importing our self-signed certificate into the cacerts.jks keystore, GlassFish recognizes the certificate authority as a valid one. It then gets the principal name from the certificate and compares it against entries in the application's sun-web. xml; because we added ourselves to this deployment descriptor and gave ourselves a valid role, we are allowed into the application.

Defining Additional Realms

In addition to the three pre-configured security realms we discussed in the previous section, we can create additional realms for application authentication. We can create realms that behave exactly like the file or admin-realm realms; we can also create realms that behave like the certificate realm. Additionally, we can create realms that use other methods of authentication. We can authenticate users against an LDAP database; we can also authenticate users against a relational database, and when GlassFish is installed on a Solaris server, we can use Solaris authentication within GlassFish. Also, if none of the above authentication mechanisms fits our needs, we can implement our own.

Defining Additional File Realms

Expand the **Configuration** node, expand the **Security** node, click on the **Realms** node, then click on the **New...** button on the resulting page in the main area of the web console. We should now see a screen like the following:

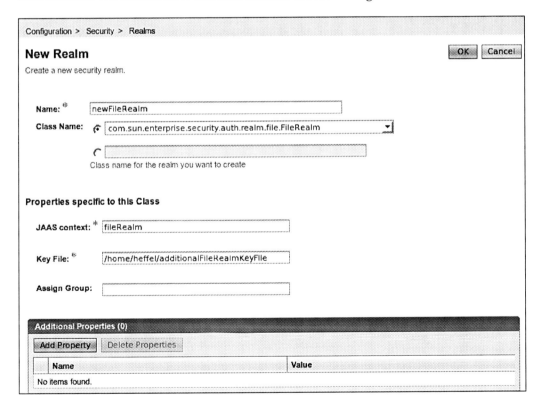

All we need to do to create an additional realm is enter a unique name for it in the **Name** field, pick `com.sun.enterprise.security.auth.realm.file.FileRealm` for the **Class Name** field (should be the default), and enter a value for the **Key File** field; the value for this field must be the absolute path to a file where user information will be stored. The JAAS context field will default to `fileRealm`; this default should not be changed.

After entering all of the above information, we can click on the **OK** button and our new realm will be created. We can then use it just like the predefined file realm. Applications wishing to authenticate against this new realm must use its name as the value of the `<realm-name>` element in the application's `web.xml` deployment descriptor.

Defining Additional Certificate Realms

To define an additional certificate realm, we simply need to enter its name in the **Name** field and pick `com.sun.enterprise.security.auth.realm.certificate.CertificateRealm` as the value of the **Class Name** field, then click **OK** to create our new realm.

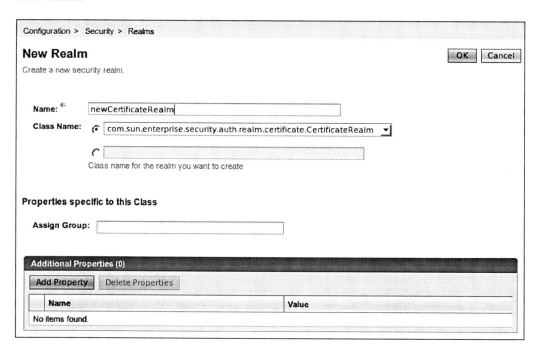

Applications wishing to use this new realm for authentication must use its name as the value of the `<realm-name>` element in the `web.xml` deployment descriptor, and specify `CLIENT-CERT` as the value of its `<auth-method>` element. Of course, client certificates must be present and configured as explained in the *Configuring Applications to Use the Certificate Realm* section.

Defining an LDAP Realm

We can easily set up a realm to authenticate against an LDAP (Lightweight Directory Access Protocol) database. In order to do this we need, in addition to the obvious step of entering a name for the realm, to select `com.sun.enterprise.security.auth.realm.ldap.LDAPRealm` as the Class Name value for a new realm.

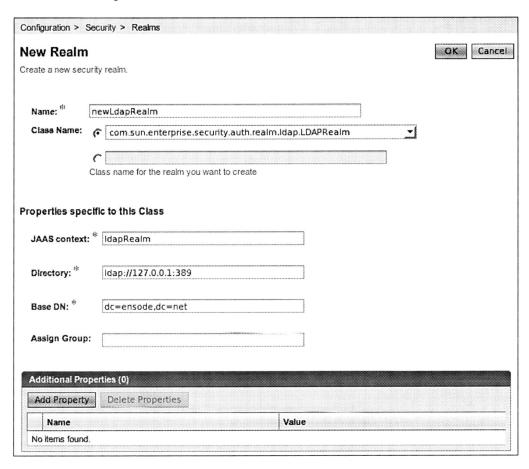

We then need to enter a URL for the directory server in the **Directory** field, and the Base Distinguished Name (DN) to be used to search user data as the value of the **Base DN** field.

After creation of an LDAP realm, applications can use it to authenticate against the LDAP database. The name of the realm needs to be used as the value of the `<realm-name>` element in the application's `web.xml` deployment descriptor; the value of the `<auth-method>` element must be either `BASIC` or `FORM`. Users and roles in the LDAP database can be mapped to groups in the application's `sun-web.xml` deployment descriptor, using the `<principal-name>`, `<role-name>`, and `<group-name>` elements as discussed earlier in this chapter.

Defining a Solaris Realm

When GlassFish is installed in a Solaris server, it can "piggyback" on the operating system authentication mechanism via a Solaris Realm. There are no special properties for this type of realm, all we need to do to create one is pick a name for it and select `com.sun.enterprise.security.auth.realm.solaris.SolarisRealm` as the value of the **Class Name** field.

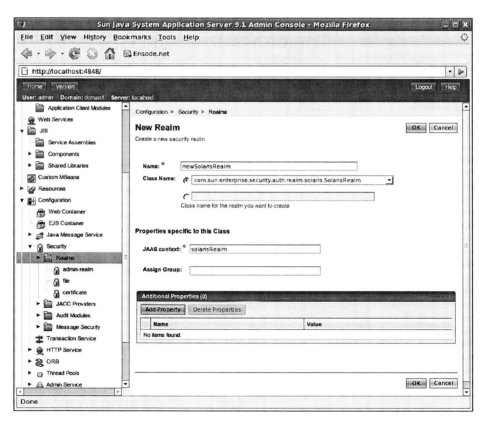

The **JAAS context** field will default to `solarisRealm`; this default should not be changed. After addition of the realm, applications can authenticate against it using basic or form-based authentication. Operating-system groups and users can be mapped to application roles defined in the application's `web.xml` deployment descriptor via the `<principal-name>`, `<role-name>`, and `<group-name>` elements in its `sun-web.xml` deployment descriptor.

Defining a JDBC Realm

Another type of realm we can create is a JDBC realm. This type of realm uses user information stored in database tables for user authentication.

In order to illustrate how to authenticate against a JDBC realm, we need to create a database to hold user information.

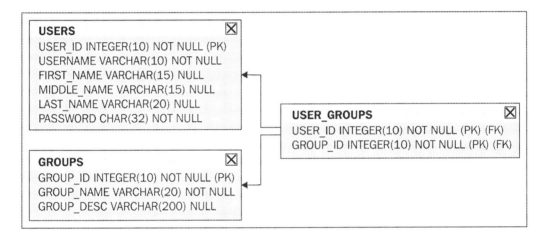

Our database consists of three tables. A `USERS` table holding user information, a `GROUPS` table holding group information, and as there is a many-to-many relationship between `USERS` and `GROUPS`, we need to add a join table to preserve data normalization. The name of this table is `USER_GROUPS`.

Notice that the `PASSWORD` column of the `USERS` table is of type `CHAR(32)`. The reason we chose this type instead of `VARCHAR` is that by default, the JDBC realm expects passwords to be encrypted as an MD5 hash, and these hashes are always 32 characters.

Passwords can be easily encrypted in the format expected by default, by using the `java.security.MessageDigest` class included with the JDK. The following example code will take a clear text password and create an encrypted MD5 hash out of it.

```
package net.ensode.glassfishbook;

import java.security.MessageDigest;
import java.security.NoSuchAlgorithmException;

public class EncryptPassword
{
  public static String encryptPassword(String password)
      throws NoSuchAlgorithmException
  {
    MessageDigest messageDigest =
        MessageDigest.getInstance("MD5");
    byte[] bs;
    messageDigest.reset();
    bs = messageDigest.digest(password.getBytes());

    StringBuilder stringBuilder = new StringBuilder();
    //hex encode the digest
    for (int i = 0; i < bs.length; i++)
    {
      String hexVal = Integer.toHexString(0xFF & bs[i]);
      if (hexVal.length() == 1)
      {
        stringBuilder.append("0");
      }
      stringBuilder.append(hexVal);
    }

    return stringBuilder.toString();
  }

  public static void main(String[] args)
  {
    String encryptedPassword = null;

    try
    {
      if (args.length == 0)
      {
        System.err.println("Usage: java " +
            "net.ensode.glassfishbook.EncryptPassword " +
            "cleartext");
      }
      else
      {
        encryptedPassword = encryptPassword(args[0]);
        System.out.println(encryptedPassword);
```

```
        }
      }
    catch (NoSuchAlgorithmException e)
    {
      e.printStackTrace();
    }
  }
}
```

The "meat" of this class is its `encryptPassword()` method. It basically takes a clear text string and digests it using the MD5 algorithm by using the `digest()` method of an instance of `java.security.MessageDigest`. It then encodes the digest as a series of hexadecimal numbers. The reason this encoding is necessary is because GlassFish, by default, expects MD5 digested passwords to be hex encoded.

When using JDBC realms, the Glassfish users and groups are not added to the realm via the GlassFish console; instead, they are added by inserting data into the appropriate tables.

Once we have the database that will hold user credentials in place, we are ready to create a new JDBC realm.

We can create a JDBC realm by entering its name in the **Name** field of the New Realm form in the GlassFish web console, then selecting `com.sun.enterprise.security.auth.realm.jdbc.JDBCRealm` as the value of the **Class Name** field.

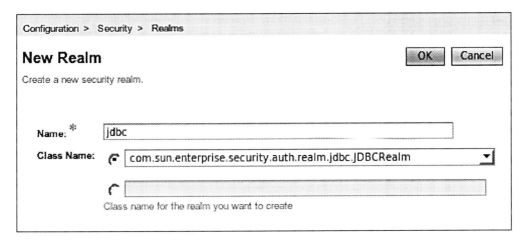

There are a number of other properties we need to set for our new JDBC realm.

Properties specific to this Class

JAAS context: *	jdbcRealm
JNDI: *	jdbc/_UserAuthPool
User Table: *	V_USER_ROLE
User Name: *	USERNAME
Password: *	PASSWORD
Group Table: *	V_USER_ROLE
Group Name: *	GROUP_NAME
Assign Group:	
Database User:	
Database Password:	
Digest:	
Encoding:	
Charset:	

The **JAAS context** field will default to **jdbcRealm** for JDBC realms; this default should not be changed. The value of the **JNDI** property must be the JNDI name of the data source corresponding to the database that contains the realm's user and group data. The value of the **User Table** property must be the name of the table that contains user-name and password information.

Notice, in the screenshot that, that we used V_USER_GROUPS as the value for this property. V_USER_GROUPS is a database view that contains both user and group information. The reason we didn't use the USERS table directly is because GlassFish assumes that both the user table and the group table contain a column containing the user name. Doing this results in having duplicate data. To avoid this situation, we created a view that we could use as the value of both the User Table Property and the Group Table Property (to be discussed shortly).

The User Name property must contain the column in the User Table that contains the user names. The Password property value must be the name of the column in the User Table that contains the user's password. The value of the Group Table property must be the name of the table containing user groups. The Group Name property must contain the name of the column in the **Group Table** containing user group names.

All other properties are optional and, in most cases, left blank. Of special interest is the Digest property. This property allows us to specify the message digest algorithm to use to encrypt the user's password. Valid values for this property include all algorithms supported by the JDK; these algorithms are MD2, MD5, SHA-1, SHA-256, SHA-384, and SHA-512. Additionally, if we wish to store user passwords in clear text, we can do so by using the value "none" for this property.

Once we have defined our JDBC realm, we need to configure our application via its `web.xml` and `sun-web.xml` deployment descriptors. Configuring an application to rely on a JDBC realm for authorization and authentication is done just as when using any other type of realm.

```
<web-app xmlns="http://java.sun.com/xml/ns/javaee" version="2.5"
  xmlns:xsi="http://www.w3.org/2001/XMLSchema-instance"
  xsi:schemaLocation="http://java.sun.com/xml/ns/javaee http://
                      java.sun.com/xml/ns/javaee/web-app_2_5.xsd">
  <security-constraint>
    <web-resource-collection>
      <web-resource-name>Admin Pages</web-resource-name>
      <url-pattern>/admin/*</url-pattern>
    </web-resource-collection>
    <auth-constraint>
      <role-name>admin</role-name>
    </auth-constraint>
  </security-constraint>
  <security-constraint>
    <web-resource-collection>
      <web-resource-name>AllPages</web-resource-name>
      <url-pattern>/*</url-pattern>
```

```
      </web-resource-collection>
      <auth-constraint>
        <role-name>user</role-name>
      </auth-constraint>
    </security-constraint>
    <login-config>
      <auth-method>FORM</auth-method>
      <realm-name>jdbc</realm-name>
      <form-login-config>
        <form-login-page>/login.jsp</form-login-page>
        <form-error-page>/loginerror.jsp</form-error-page>
      </form-login-config>
    </login-config>
    <servlet>
      <servlet-name>LogoutServlet</servlet-name>
      <servlet-class>
        net.ensode.glassfishbook.LogoutServlet
      </servlet-class>
    </servlet>
    <servlet-mapping>
      <servlet-name>LogoutServlet</servlet-name>
      <url-pattern>/logout</url-pattern>
    </servlet-mapping>
  </web-app>
```

In the above example, we set the value of the `<realm-name>` element in the `web.xml` deployment descriptor to `jdbc`; this is the name we chose to give our realm when we configured it through the GlassFish console.

In this example, we chose to use form-based authentication, but we could have used basic authentication instead.

In addition to declaring that we will rely on the JDBC realm for authentication and authorization, just as with other types of realms, we need to map the roles defined in the `web.xml` deployment descriptor to security group names. This is accomplished in the `sun-web.xml` deployment descriptor.

```
<?xml version="1.0" encoding="UTF-8" standalone="no"?>
<!DOCTYPE sun-web-app PUBLIC "-//Sun Microsystems, Inc.//DTD
Application Server 9.0 Servlet 2.5//EN" "http://www.sun.com/software/
appserver/dtds/sun-web-app_2_5-0.dtd">
<sun-web-app>
  <security-role-mapping>
    <role-name>admin</role-name>
    <group-name>Admin</group-name>
```

```
    </security-role-mapping>
    <security-role-mapping>
      <role-name>user</role-name>
      <group-name>Users</group-name>
    </security-role-mapping>
  </sun-web-app>
```

The value of the `<role-name>` elements must match the corresponding `<role-name>` elements in `web.xml`. The value of `<group-name>` must be a value in the column specified by the `Group Name Column` property of the JDBC realm, as specified when it was configured in the GlassFish web console.

Defining Custom Realms

The predefined realm types should cover the vast majority of cases. However, we can create custom realm types if the predefined ones don't meet our needs. Doing so involves coding custom Realm and LoginModule classes. Let's first discuss the custom realm class.

```java
package net.ensode.glassfishbook;

import java.util.Enumeration;
import java.util.Vector;

import com.sun.enterprise.security.auth.realm.IASRealm;
import com.sun.enterprise.security.auth.realm.
InvalidOperationException;
import com.sun.enterprise.security.auth.realm.NoSuchUserException;

public class SimpleRealm extends IASRealm
{
  @Override
  public Enumeration getGroupNames(String userName)
      throws InvalidOperationException, NoSuchUserException
  {
    Vector vector = new Vector();

    vector.add("Users");
    vector.add("Admin");

    return vector.elements();
  }

  @Override
  public String getAuthType()
  {
    return "simple";
  }
```

```
@Override
public String getJAASContext()
{
  return "simpleRealm";
}

public boolean loginUser(String userName, String password)
{
  boolean loginSuccessful = false;
  if ("glassfish".equals(userName) &&
      "secret".equals(password))
  {
    loginSuccessful = true;
  }
  return loginSuccessful;
}
}
```

Our custom realm class must extend com.sun.enterprise.security.auth.realm. IASRealm; this class can be found inside the appserv-rt.jar file; therefore this JAR file must be added to the CLASSPATH before our Realm can be successfully compiled.

 appserv-rt.jar can be found under [glassfish installation directory]/glassfish/lib.

Our class must override a method called getGroupNames(). This method takes a single String as a parameter and returns an Enumeration. The String parameter is for the user name for the user that is attempting to log into the realm. The Enumeration must contain a collection of Strings indicating what groups the user belongs to. In our simple example, we basically hard-coded the groups. In a real application, these groups would be obtained from some kind of persistent storage (database, file, etc.).

The next method our realm class must override is the getAuthType() method. This method must return a String containing a description of the type of authentication used by this realm.

The above two methods are declared as abstract in the IASRealm (parent) class. Though the getJAASContext() method is not abstract, we should nevertheless override it, because the value it returns is used to determine the type of authentication to use from the application server's login.conf file. The return value of this method is used to map the realm to the corresponding login module.

Finally, our realm class must contain a method to authenticate the user; we are free to call it anything we want; additionally, we can use as many parameters of any type as we wish. Our simple example simply has the values for a single user name and password hard-coded; again a real application would obtain valid credentials from some kind of persistent storage. This method is meant to be called from the corresponding login module class.

```
package net.ensode.glassfishbook;

import java.util.Enumeration;

import javax.security.auth.login.LoginException;

import com.sun.appserv.security.AppservPasswordLoginModule;
import com.sun.enterprise.security.auth.realm.
InvalidOperationException;
import com.sun.enterprise.security.auth.realm.NoSuchUserException;

public class SimpleLoginModule extends
    AppservPasswordLoginModule
{
  @Override
  protected void authenticateUser() throws LoginException
  {
    Enumeration userGroupsEnum = null;
    String[] userGroupsArray = null;
    SimpleRealm simpleRealm;

    if (!(_currentRealm instanceof SimpleRealm))
    {
      throw new LoginException();
    }
    else
    {
      simpleRealm = (SimpleRealm) _currentRealm;
    }

    if (simpleRealm.loginUser(_username, _password))
    {
      try
      {
        userGroupsEnum = simpleRealm.getGroupNames(_username);
      }
      catch (InvalidOperationException e)
      {
        throw new LoginException(e.getMessage());
      }
      catch (NoSuchUserException e)
      {
```

```
        throw new LoginException(e.getMessage());
      }
      userGroupsArray = new String[2];
      int i = 0;
      while (userGroupsEnum.hasMoreElements())
      {
        userGroupsArray[i++] =
            ((String) userGroupsEnum.nextElement());
      }
    }
    else
    {
      throw new LoginException();
    }
    commitUserAuthentication(userGroupsArray);
  }
}
```

Our login module class must extend the `com.sun.appserv.security.`
`AppservPasswordLoginModule` class which is also inside the `appserv-rt.jar` file; it
only needs to override a single method, `authenticateUser()`. This method takes no
parameters and must throw a `LoginException` if user authentication is unsuccessful.
The `_currentRealm` variable is defined in the parent class; it is of type `com.sun.`
`enterprise.security.auth.realm.Realm`, the parent class of all realm classes.
This variable is initialized before the `authenticateUser()` method is executed. The
login module class must verify that this class is of the expected type (`SimpleRealm` in
our example); if it is not, a `LoginException` must be thrown.

Another two variables that are defined in the parent class and initialized before the
`authenticateUser()` method is executed are `_username` and `_password`; these
variables contain the credentials that the user entered in the login form (for form-based
authentication) or pop-up window (for basic authentication). Our example simply
passes these values to the realm class so that it can verify the user credentials.

The `authenticateUser()` method must call the `commitUserAuthentication()`
method of the parent class upon a successful authentication. This method takes
an array of String objects containing the group the user belongs to. Our example
simply invokes the `getGroupNames()` method defined in the realm class and adds
the elements of the Enumeration it returns to an array, then passes that array to
`commitUserAuthentication()`.

Obviously, GlassFish is unaware of the existence of our custom realm and login
module classes. We need to add these classes to GlassFish's CLASSPATH; the easiest
way to do this is through the web console.

We can add directories and JAR files to GlassFish's CLASSPATH by clicking on the
Application Server node, clicking on the **JVM Settings** tab, then clicking on the
Path Settings sub-tab, then entering the path of the folder or JAR file in the text area
labeled **Classpath Suffix**. The domain needs to be restarted for this change to
take effect.

The last step we need to follow before we can authenticate applications against our
custom realm is to add our new custom realm to the domain's login.conf file.

```
/*  Copyright 2004 Sun Microsystems, Inc.  All rights reserved.   */
/*  SUN PROPRIETARY/CONFIDENTIAL. Use is subject to license terms. */
fileRealm {
com.sun.enterprise.security.auth.login.FileLoginModule required;
```

```
            };
ldapRealm {
com.sun.enterprise.security.auth.login.LDAPLoginModule required;
            };
solarisRealm {
com.sun.enterprise.security.auth.login.SolarisLoginModule required;
                };
jdbcRealm {
com.sun.enterprise.security.auth.login.JDBCLoginModule required;
            };
simpleRealm {

        net.ensode.glassfishbook.SimpleLoginModule required;

            };
```

The value before the opening brace must match the return value of the
`getJAASContext()` method defined in the realm class. It is in this file that the realm
and login module classes are linked to each other. The GlassFish domain needs to be
restarted for this change to take effect.

We are now ready to use our custom realm to authenticate users in our applications.
We need to add a new realm of the type we created via GlassFish's admin console.

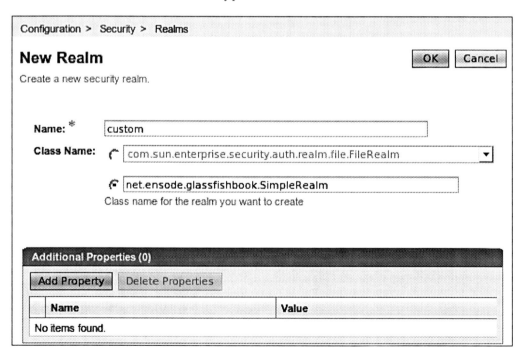

To create our realm, as usual we need to give it a name. Instead of selecting a class name from the dropdown, we need to type it into the text field. Our custom realm didn't have any properties, therefore we don't have to add any in this example. If it did, they would be added by clicking on the **Add Property** button and entering the property name and corresponding value. Our realm would then get the properties by overriding the `init()` method from its parent class. This method has the following signature:

```
protected void init(Properties arg0) throws
    BadRealmException, NoSuchRealmException
```

The instance of `java.util.Properties` that it takes as a parameter would be pre-populated with the properties entered in the page shown in the previous screenshot (our custom realm doesn't have any properties, but for those that do, properties are entered in this page).

Once we have added the pertinent information for our new custom realm, we can use it just as we use any of the predefined realms. Applications need to specify its name as the value of the `<realm-name>` element of the application's `web.xml` deployment descriptor. Nothing out of the ordinary needs to be done at the application level.

Summary

In this chapter, we covered how to use GlassFish's default realms to authenticate our web applications. We covered the file realm, which stores user information in a flat file, and the certificate realm, which requires client-side certificates for user authentication.

Additionally, we covered how to create additional realms that behave just like the default realms by using the realm classes included with GlassFish.

We also covered how to use additional realm classes included in GlassFish to create realms that authenticate against an LDAP Database, or against a relational database, and how to create realms that "piggyback" into a Solaris server's authentication mechanism.

Finally, we covered how to create custom realm classes for cases where the included ones do not meet our needs.

Enterprise JavaBeans

Enterprise JavaBeans are server-side components that encapsulate application business logic. Enterprise JavaBeans simplify application development by automatically taking care of transaction management and security. There are two types of Enterprise JavaBeans: Session Beans, which perform business logic; and Message-Driven Beans, which act as a message listener.

Readers familiar with previous versions of J2EE will notice that Entity Beans were not mentioned in the above paragraph. In Java EE 5, Entity Beans have been deprecated in favor of the Java Persistence API (JPA). Entity Beans are still supported for backwards compatibility; however, the preferred way of doing Object Relational Mapping with Java EE 5 is through JPA. Refer to Chapter 4 for a detailed discussion on JPA.

The following topics will be covered in this chapter:

- Session Beans
    - A simple session bean
    - A more realistic example
    - Using a session bean to implement the DAO design pattern
- Message-driven beans
- Transactions in Enterprise Java beans
    - Container-managed transactions
    - Bean-managed transactions
- Enterprise JavaBeans life cycles
    - Stateful session bean life cycle
    - Stateless session bean life cycle
    - Message-driven bean life cycle
- EJB timer service
- EJB security

Session Beans

As we previously mentioned, session beans typically encapsulate business logic. In Java EE 5, only two artifacts need to be created in order to create a session bean: the bean itself, and a business interface. These artifacts need to be decorated with the proper annotations to let the EJB container know they are session beans.

Previous versions of J2EE required application developers to create several artifacts in order to create a session bean. These artifacts included the bean itself, a local or remote interface (or both), a local home or a remote home interface (or both) and a deployment descriptor. As we shall see in this chapter, EJB development has been greatly simplified in Java EE 5.

Simple Session Bean

The following example illustrates a very simple session bean:

```
package net.ensode.glassfishbook;
import javax.ejb.Stateless;
@Stateless
public class SimpleSessionBean implements SimpleSession
{
  private String message =
      "If you don't see this, it didn't work!";
  public String getMessage()
  {
    return message;
  }
}
```

The `@Stateless` annotation lets the EJB container know that this class is a **stateless session bean**. There are two types of session beans, stateless and stateful. Before we explain the difference between these two types of session beans, we need to clarify how an instance of an EJB is provided to an EJB client application.

When EJBs (both session beans and message-driven beans) are deployed, the EJB container creates a series of instances of each EJB. This is what is typically referred to as the **EJB pool**. When an EJB client application obtains an instance of an EJB, one of the instances in the pool is provided to this client application.

The difference between stateful and stateless session beans is that stateful session beans maintain **conversational state** with the client, where stateless session beans do not. In simple terms, what this means is that when an EJB client application obtains an instance of a stateful session bean, the same instance of the EJB is provided for each method invocation, therefore, it is safe to modify any instance variables on a stateful session bean, as they will retain their value for the next method call.

The EJB container may provide any instance of an EJB in the pool when an EJB client application requests an instance of a stateless session bean. As we are not guaranteed the same instance for every method call, values set to any instance variables in a stateless session bean may be "lost" (they are not really lost; the modification is in another instance of the EJB in the pool).

Other than being decorated with the `@Stateless` annotation, there is nothing special about this class. Notice that it implements an interface called `SimpleSession`. This interface is the bean's business interface. The `SimpleSession` interface is shown next:

```
package net.ensode.glassfishbook;

import javax.ejb.Remote;

@Remote
public interface SimpleSession
{
    public String getMessage();
}
```

The only peculiar thing about this interface is that it is decorated with the `@Remote` annotation. This annotation indicates that this is a **remote business interface**. What this means is that the interface may be in a different JVM than the client application invoking it. Remote business interfaces may even be invoked across the network.

Business interfaces may also be decorated with the `@Local` interface. This annotation indicates that the business interface is a **local business interface**. Local business interface implementations must be in the same JVM as the client application invoking their methods.

As remote business interfaces can be invoked either from the same JVM or from a different JVM than the client application, at first glance, we might be tempted to make all of our business interfaces remote. Before doing so, we must be aware of the fact that the flexibility provided by remote business interfaces comes with a performance penalty, because method invocations are made under the assumption that they will be made across the network. As a matter of fact, most typical Java EE application consist of web applications acting as client applications for EJBs; in this case, the client application and the EJB are running on the same JVM, therefore, local interfaces are used a lot more frequently than remote business interfaces.

Once we have compiled the session bean and its corresponding business interface, we need to place them in a JAR file and deploy them. Just as with WAR files, the easiest way to deploy an EJB JAR file is to copy it to `[glassfish installation directory]/glassfish/domains/domain1/autodeploy`.

Now that we have seen the session bean and its corresponding business interface, let's take a look at a client sample application:

```
package net.ensode.glassfishbook;

import javax.ejb.EJB;

public class SessionBeanClient
{
  @EJB
  private static SimpleSession simpleSession;

  private void invokeSessionBeanMethods()
  {
    System.out.println(simpleSession.getMessage());

    System.out.println("\nSimpleSession is of type: "
        + simpleSession.getClass().getName());
  }

  public static void main(String[] args)
  {
    new SessionBeanClient().invokeSessionBeanMethods();
  }
}
```

The above code simply declares an instance variable of type net.ensode. SimpleSession, which is the business interface for our session bean. The instance variable is decorated with the @EJB annotation; this annotation lets the EJB container know that this variable is a business interface for a session bean. The EJB container then injects an implementation of the business interface for the client code to use.

As our client is a stand-alone application (as opposed to a Java EE artifact such as a WAR file) in order for it to be able to access code deployed in the server, it must be placed in a JAR file and executed through the **appclient** utility. This utility can be found at [glassfish installation directory]/glassfish/bin/. Assuming this path is in the PATH environment variable, and assuming we placed our client code in a JAR file called simplesessionbeanclient.jar, we would execute the above client code by typing the following command in the command line:

appclient -client simplesessionbeanclient.jar

Executing the above command results in the following console output:

If you don't see this, it didn't work!

SimpleSession is of type: net.ensode.glassfishbook._SimpleSession_Wrapper

which is the output of the SessionBeanClient class.

The first line of output is simply the return value of the `getMessage()` method we implemented in the session bean. The second line of output displays the fully qualified class name of the class implementing the business interface. Notice that the class name is not the fully qualified name of the session bean we wrote; instead, what is actually provided is an implementation of the business interface created behind the scenes by the EJB container.

A More Realistic Example

In the previous section, we saw a very simple, "Hello world" type of example. In this section, we will show a more realistic example. Session beans are frequently used as Data Access Objects (DAOs). Sometimes, they are used as a wrapper for JDBC calls, other times they are used to wrap calls to obtain or modify JPA entities. In this section, we will take the latter approach.

The following example illustrates how to implement the DAO design pattern in a session bean. Before looking at the bean implementation, let's look at the business interface corresponding to it:

```
package net.ensode.glassfishbook;

import javax.ejb.Remote;

@Remote
public interface CustomerDao
{
  public void saveCustomer(Customer customer);

  public Customer getCustomer(Long customerId);

  public void deleteCustomer(Customer customer);
}
```

As we can see, the above is a remote interface implementing three methods; the `saveCustomer()` method saves customer data to the database, the `getCustomer()` method obtains data for a customer from the database, and the `deleteCustomer()` method deletes customer data from the database. All of these methods take or return an instance of the `Customer` entity we developed in Chapter 4 as a parameter.

Let's now take a look at the session bean implementing the above business interface. As we are about to see, there are some differences between the way JPA code is implemented in a session bean versus in a plain old Java object.

```
package net.ensode.glassfishbook;

import java.sql.Connection;
import java.sql.PreparedStatement;
import java.sql.ResultSet;
import java.sql.SQLException;
```

```java
import javax.annotation.Resource;
import javax.ejb.Stateless;
import javax.persistence.EntityManager;
import javax.persistence.PersistenceContext;
import javax.sql.DataSource;

@Stateless
public class CustomerDaoBean implements CustomerDao
{
  @PersistenceContext
  private EntityManager entityManager;
  @Resource(name = "jdbc/__CustomerDBPool")
  private DataSource dataSource;
  public void saveCustomer(Customer customer)
  {
    if (customer.getCustomerId() == null)
    {
      saveNewCustomer(customer);
    }
    else
    {
      updateCustomer(customer);
    }
  }
  private void saveNewCustomer(Customer customer)
  {
    customer.setCustomerId(getNewCustomerId());
    entityManager.persist(customer);
  }
  private void updateCustomer(Customer customer)
  {
    entityManager.merge(customer);
  }
  public Customer getCustomer(Long customerId)
  {
    Customer customer;
    customer = entityManager.find(Customer.class, customerId);
    return customer;
  }
  public void deleteCustomer(Customer customer)
  {
    entityManager.remove(customer);
  }
```

```java
private Long getNewCustomerId()
{
  Connection connection;
  Long newCustomerId = null;
  try
  {
    connection = dataSource.getConnection();
    PreparedStatement preparedStatement = connection
        .prepareStatement(
          "select max(customer_id)+1 as new_customer_id "
        + "from customers");
    ResultSet resultSet = preparedStatement.executeQuery();
    if (resultSet != null && resultSet.next())
    {
      newCustomerId = resultSet.getLong("new_customer_id");
    }
    connection.close();
  }
  catch (SQLException e)
  {
    e.printStackTrace();
  }
  return newCustomerId;
  }
}
```

The first difference we should notice is that an instance of `javax.persistence.EntityManager` is directly injected into the session bean. In previous JPA examples, we had to inject an instance of `javax.persistence.EntityManagerFactory`, then use the injected `EntityManagerFactory` instance to obtain an instance of `EntityManager`.

The reason we had to do this was that our previous examples were not thread safe. What this means is that potentially the same code could be executed concurrently by more than one user. As `EntityManager` is not designed to be used concurrently by more than one thread, we used an `EntityManagerFactory` instance to provide each thread with its own instance of `EntityManager`. Since the EJB container assigns a session bean to a single client at time, session beans are inherently thread safe, therefore, we can inject an instance of `EntityManager` directly into a session bean.

The next difference between this session bean and previous JPA examples is that in previous examples, JPA calls were wrapped between calls to `UserTransaction.`
`begin()` and `UserTransaction.commit()`. The reason we had to do this is because JPA calls are required to be in wrapped in a transaction, if they are not in a transaction, most JPA calls will throw a `TransactionRequiredException`. The reason we don't have to explicitly wrap JPA calls in a transaction as in previous examples is because session bean methods are implicitly transactional; there is nothing we need to do to make them that way. This default behavior is what is known as **Container-Managed Transactions**. Container-Managed Transactions are discussed in detail later in this chapter.

 As mentioned in Chapter 4, when a JPA entity is retrieved in one transaction and updated in a different transaction, the `EntityManager.` `merge()` method needs to be invoked to update the data in the database. Invoking `EntityManager.persist()` in this case will result in a "Cannot persist detached object" exception.

Invoking Session Beans from Web Applications

Frequently, Java EE applications consist of web applications acting as clients for EJBs. The most common way of deploying a Java EE application that consists of both a web application and one or more session beans is to package both the WAR file for the web application and the EJB JAR files into an EAR (Enterprise ARchive) file.

In this section, we will modify the example we saw in the section titled *Integrating JSF and JPA* from Chapter 6 so that the web application acts as a client to the DAO session bean we saw in the previous section. In order to make this application act as an EJB client, we will modify the `CustomerController` managed bean so that it delegates the logic to save a new customer to the database to the `CustomerDaoBean` session bean we developed in the previous section.

```
package net.ensode.glassfishbook.jsfjpa;

import javax.ejb.EJB;

import net.ensode.glassfishbook.Customer;
import net.ensode.glassfishbook.CustomerDao;

public class CustomerController
{
  @EJB
  CustomerDao customerDao;
  private Customer customer;
```

```
public String saveCustomer()
{
  String returnValue = "success";
  try
  {
    customerDao.saveCustomer(customer);
  }
  catch (Exception e)
  {
    e.printStackTrace();
    returnValue = "failure";
  }
  return returnValue;
}
public Customer getCustomer()
{
  return customer;
}
public void setCustomer(Customer customer)
{
  this.customer = customer;
}
}
```

As you can see, all we had to do was to declare an instance of the CustomerDao business interface, and decorate it with the @EJB annotation so that an instance of the corresponding EJB is injected, and replace the code to save data to the database with an invocation to the saveCustomer() method, which is defined in the CustomerDao business interface.

Now that we have modified our web application to be a client for our session bean, we need to package it in a WAR file. Then we need to package the WAR file, along with the EJB JAR file containing the session bean, in an EAR file.

An EAR file is a compressed ZIP file containing WAR files, EJB JAR files, and any additional libraries that either the web application or the EJB might depend on. An EAR file also contains an application.xml deployment descriptor. This deployment descriptor must be placed in a META-INF directory inside the EAR file.

The structure of our EAR file is shown in the following screenshot.

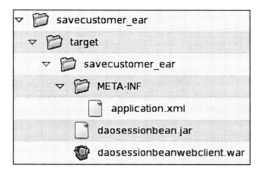

The `application.xml` deployment descriptor declares all the Java EE modules that are included in the EAR file.

```xml
<?xml version="1.0" encoding="UTF-8"?>
<!DOCTYPE application PUBLIC
    "-//Sun Microsystems, Inc.//DTD J2EE Application 1.3//EN"
    "http://java.sun.com/dtd/application_1_3.dtd">
<application>
  <display-name>savecustomer_ear</display-name>
  <module>
    <web>
      <web-uri>daosessionbeanwebclient.war</web-uri>
      <context-root>/daosessionbeanwebclient</context-root>
    </web>
  </module>
  <module>
    <ejb>daosessionbean.jar</ejb>
  </module>
</application>
```

Each module must be nested inside a `<module>` element, followed by either an `<ejb>` element for EJB modules, a `<web>` element for web modules, or a `<java>` element for EJB clients that are not web applications.

`<ejb>` and `<java>` elements specify the name of the JAR file to be deployed. `<web>` elements contain a required `<web-uri>` element indicating the name of the WAR file to be deployed, and an optional `<context-root>` element used to specify the context root of the web application. If no `<context-root>` element is present, then the base name of the WAR file is used as its context root.

An EAR file can be created by using a ZIP tool (WinZip, 7-Zip, etc.) to create a ZIP file with its contents, or, more likely, an IDE or build tool such as Eclipse, NetBeans, ANT or Maven can be used to automate its creation. An EAR file must end with a `.ear` extension. Once the EAR file is created, the easiest way to deploy it is to copy it into the `autodeploy` directory under `[glassfish installation directory]/glassfish/domains/domain1`.

Message-Driven Beans

The purpose of a message-driven bean is to consume messages from a JMS Queue or a JMS topic, depending on the messaging domain used (refer to Chapter 7). A message-driven bean must be decorated with the `@MessageDriven` annotation. The `mappedName` attribute of this annotation must contain the JNDI name of the JMS message queue or JMS message topic from which the bean will be consuming messages. The following example illustrates a simple message-driven bean:

```
package net.ensode.glassfishbook;

import javax.ejb.MessageDriven;
import javax.jms.JMSException;
import javax.jms.Message;
import javax.jms.MessageListener;
import javax.jms.TextMessage;

@MessageDriven(mappedName = "jms/GlassFishBookQueue")
public class ExampleMessageDrivenBean implements MessageListener
{
  public void onMessage(Message message)
  {
    TextMessage textMessage = (TextMessage) message;
    try
    {
      System.out.print("Received the following message: ");
      System.out.println(textMessage.getText());
      System.out.println();
    }
    catch (JMSException e)
    {
      e.printStackTrace();
    }
  }
}
```

As we can see, this class is nearly identical to the `ExampleMessageListener` class we saw in the previous chapter; the only differences are the class name and the fact that this example is decorated with the **@MessageDriven** interface. It is recommended, but not required for message-driven beans to implement the `javax.jms.MessageListener` interface, however; message-driven beans must have a method called `onMessage()` whose signature is identical to this example.

Client applications never invoke a message-driven bean's methods directly, instead they put messages in the message queue or topic, then the bean consumes those messages and acts as appropriate. The preceding example simply prints the message to standard output; as message-driven beans execute inside an EJB container, standard output gets redirected to a log. To see the messages in GlassFish's server log, open the `[GlassFish installation directory]/glassfish/domains/domain1/logs/server.log` file.

Transactions in Enterprise Java Beans

As we mentioned earlier in this chapter, by default, any EJB methods are automatically wrapped in a transaction. This default behavior is known as **Container-Managed Transactions**, because transactions are managed by the EJB container. Application developers may also choose to manage transactions themselves; this can be accomplished by using Bean-Managed Transactions. Both of these approaches are discussed in the following sections.

Container-Managed Transactions

Because EJB methods are transactional by default, we run into an interesting dilemma when a session bean is invoked from client code that is already a transaction. How should the EJB container behave? Should it suspend the client transaction, execute its method in a new transaction, then resume the client transaction? Should it not create a new transaction and execute its method as part of the client transaction? Should it throw an exception?

By default, if an EJB method is invoked by client code that is already in a transaction, the EJB container will simply execute the session bean method as part of the client transaction. If this is not the behavior we need, we can change it by decorating the method with the `@TransactionAttribute` annotation. This annotation has a `value` attribute that determines how the EJB container will behave when the session bean method is invoked within an existing transaction and when it is invoked outside any transactions. The value of the `value` attribute is typically a constant defined in the `javax.ejb.TransactionAttributeType` enum. The following table lists the possible values for the `@TransactionAttribute` annotation:

@TransactionAttribute value	Description
TransactionAttributeType.MANDATORY	Forces the method to be invoked as part of a client transaction. If the method is called outside any transactions, it will throw a `TransactionRequiredException`.
TransactionAttributeType.NEVER	The method is never executed in a transaction. If the method is invoked as part of a client transaction, it will throw a `RemoteException`. No transaction is created if the method is not invoked inside a client transaction.
TransactionAttributeType.NOT_SUPPORTED	If the method is invoked as part of a client transaction, the client transaction is suspended; the method is executed outside any transaction. After the method completes, the client transaction is resumed. No transaction is created if the method is not invoked inside a client transaction.
TransactionAttributeType.REQUIRED	If the method is invoked as part of a client transaction, the method is executed as part of that transaction. If the method is invoked outside any transaction, a new transaction is created for the method. This is the default behavior.
TransactionAttributeType.REQUIRES_NEW	If the method is invoked as part of a client transaction, that transaction is suspended, and a new transaction is created for the method. Once the method completes, the client transaction is resumed. If the method is called outside any transactions, a new transaction is created for the method.
TransactionAttributeType.SUPPORTS	If the method is invoked as part of a client transaction, it is executed as part of that transaction. If the method is invoked outside a transaction, no new transaction is created for the method.

Although the default transaction attribute is reasonable in most cases, it is good to be able to override this default, if necessary. For example, transactions have a performance impact, therefore being able to turn off transactions for a method that does not need them is beneficial. For a case like this, we would decorate our method as illustrated in the following code snippet:

```
@TransactionAttribute(value=TransactionAttributeType.NEVER)
public void doitAsFastAsPossible()
{
    //performance critical code goes here.
}
```

Other transaction attribute types can be declared by annotating the methods with the corresponding constant in the `TransactionAttributeType` enum.

If we wish to override the default transaction attribute consistently across all methods in a session bean, we can decorate the session bean class with the `@TransactionAttribute` annotation. The value of its `value` attribute will be applied to every method in the session bean.

Container-managed transactions are automatically rolled back whenever an exception is thrown inside an EJB method. Additionally, we can programmatically roll back a container-managed transaction by invoking the `setRollbackOnly()` method on an instance of `javax.ejb.EJBContext` corresponding to the session bean in question. The following example is a new version of the session bean we saw earlier in this chapter, modified to roll back transactions if necessary.

```
package net.ensode.glassfishbook;

import java.sql.Connection;
import java.sql.PreparedStatement;
import java.sql.ResultSet;
import java.sql.SQLException;

import javax.annotation.Resource;
import javax.ejb.EJBContext;
import javax.ejb.Stateless;
import javax.persistence.EntityManager;
import javax.persistence.PersistenceContext;
import javax.sql.DataSource;

@Stateless
public class CustomerDaoRollbackBean implements CustomerDaoRollback
{
    @Resource
    private EJBContext ejbContext;

    @PersistenceContext
```

```
private EntityManager entityManager;
@Resource(name = "jdbc/__CustomerDBPool")
private DataSource dataSource;
public void saveNewCustomer(Customer customer)
{
  if (customer == null || customer.getCustomerId() != null)
  {
    ejbContext.setRollbackOnly();
  }
  else
  {
    customer.setCustomerId(getNewCustomerId());
    entityManager.persist(customer);
  }
}
public void updateCustomer(Customer customer)
{
  if (customer == null || customer.getCustomerId() == null)
  {
    ejbContext.setRollbackOnly();
  }
  else
  {
    entityManager.merge(customer);
  }
}
//Additional method omitted for brevity.

}
```

In this version of the DAO session bean, we deleted the saveCustomer() method and made the saveNewCustomer() and updateCustomer() methods public. Each of these methods now checks to see if the customerId field is set correctly for the operation we are trying to perform (null for inserts and not null for updates). It also checks to make sure the object to be persisted is not null. If any of the checks results in invalid data, the method simply rolls back the transaction by invoking the setRollBackOnly() method on the injected instance of EJBContext and does not update the database.

Bean-Managed Transactions

As we have seen, container-managed transactions make it ridiculously easy to write code that is wrapped in a transaction; after all, there is nothing special that we need to do to make them that way. As a matter of fact, some developers are sometimes not even aware that they are writing code that will be transactional in nature when they develop session beans. Container-managed transactions cover most of the typical cases that we will encounter; however, they do have a limitation: each method can be wrapped in a single transaction or with no transaction. With container-managed transactions, it is not possible to implement a method that generates more than one transaction, but this can be accomplished by using **Bean-Managed Transactions**.

```
package net.ensode.glassfishbook;
import java.sql.Connection;
import java.sql.PreparedStatement;
import java.sql.ResultSet;
import java.sql.SQLException;
import java.util.List;
import javax.annotation.Resource;
import javax.ejb.Stateless;
import javax.ejb.TransactionManagement;
import javax.ejb.TransactionManagementType;
import javax.persistence.EntityManager;
import javax.persistence.PersistenceContext;
import javax.sql.DataSource;
import javax.transaction.UserTransaction;
@Stateless
@TransactionManagement(value = TransactionManagementType.BEAN)
public class CustomerDaoBmtBean implements CustomerDaoBmt
{
  @Resource
  private UserTransaction userTransaction;
  @PersistenceContext
  private EntityManager entityManager;
  @Resource(name = "jdbc/__CustomerDBPool")
  private DataSource dataSource;
  public void saveMultipleNewCustomers(
      List<Customer> customerList)
  {
    for (Customer customer : customerList)
    {
      try
      {
        userTransaction.begin();
        customer.setCustomerId(getNewCustomerId());
```

```
        entityManager.persist(customer);
        userTransaction.commit();
      }
      catch (Exception e)
      {
        e.printStackTrace();
      }
    }
  }
  private Long getNewCustomerId()
  {
    Connection connection;
    Long newCustomerId = null;
    try
    {
      connection = dataSource.getConnection();
      PreparedStatement preparedStatement =
          connection.prepareStatement("select " +
          "max(customer_id)+1 as new_customer_id " +
          "from customers");
      ResultSet resultSet = preparedStatement.executeQuery();
      if (resultSet != null && resultSet.next())
      {
        newCustomerId = resultSet.getLong("new_customer_id");
      }
      connection.close();
    }
    catch (SQLException e)
    {
      e.printStackTrace();
    }
    return newCustomerId;
  }
}
```

In this example, we implemented a method named `saveMultipleNewCustomers()`. This method takes an `ArrayList` of customers as its sole parameter. The intention of this method is to save as many elements in the `ArrayList` as possible. An exception saving one of the entities should not stop the method from attempting to save the remaining elements. This behavior is not possible using container-managed transactions, because an exception thrown when saving one of the entities would roll back the whole transaction. The only way to achieve this behavior is through bean-managed transactions.

As can be seen in the example, we declare that the session bean uses bean-managed transactions by decorating the class with the `@TransactionManagement` annotation, and using `TransactionManagementType.BEAN` as the value for its `value` attribute (The only other valid value for this attribute is `TransactionManagementType.CONTAINER`, but because this is the default value, it is not necessary to specify it.)

To be able to programmatically control transactions, we inject an instance of `javax.transaction.UserTransaction`, which is then used in the `for` loop inside the `getNewCustomerId()` method to begin and commit a transaction in each iteration of the loop.

If we need to roll back a bean-managed transaction, we can do it by simply calling the `rollback()` method on the appropriate instance of `javax.transaction.UserTransaction`.

Before moving on, it is worth noting that even though all the examples in this section were session beans, the concepts explained apply to message-driven beans as well.

Enterprise JavaBean Life Cycles

Enterprise JavaBeans go through different states in their life cycle. Each type of EJB has different states. States specific to each type of EJB are discussed in the next sections.

Stateful Session Bean Life Cycle

Readers experienced with previous versions of J2EE may remember that in previous versions of the specification, session beans were required to implement the `javax.ejb.SessionBean` interface. This interface provides methods to be executed at certain points in the session bean's life cycle. Methods provided by the `SessionBean` interface include:

- `ejbActivate()`
- `ejbPassivate()`
- `ejbRemove()`
- `setSessionContext(SessionContext ctx)`

The first three methods are meant to be executed at certain points in the bean's life cycle. In most cases, there is nothing to do in the implementation of these methods. This fact resulted in the vast majority of session beans implementing empty versions of these methods. Thankfully, in Java EE 5, it is no longer necessary to implement the `SessionBean` interface; however, if necessary, we can still write methods that

will get executed at certain points in the bean's life cycle. We can achieve this by decorating methods with specific annotations.

Before explaining the annotations available to implement life-cycle methods, a brief explanation of the session bean life cycle is in order. The life cycle of a stateful session bean is different from the life cycle of a stateless session bean.

A stateful session bean life cycle contains three states: **Does Not Exist**, **Ready**, and **Passive**, as shown in the following screenshot.

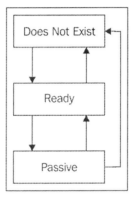

Before a stateful session bean is deployed, it is in the Does Not Exist state. Upon a successful deployment, the EJB container does any required dependency injection on the bean and it goes into the Ready state. At this point, the bean is ready to have its methods called by a client application.

When a stateful session bean is in the Ready state, the EJB container may decide to passivate it, that is, to move it from main memory to secondary storage; when this happens the bean goes into Passive state.

If an instance of a stateful session bean hasn't been accessed for a period of time, the EJB container will set the bean to the Does Not Exist state. By default, a stateful session bean will be sent to the Does Not Exist state after 90 minutes of inactivity. This default can be changed by going to the GlassFish administration console, expanding the **Configuration** node in the tree at the left-hand side, clicking on the **EJB Container** node, then scrolling down towards the bottom of the page and modifying the value of the **Removal Timeout** text field, then clicking on the **Save** button at the bottom-right of the main page.

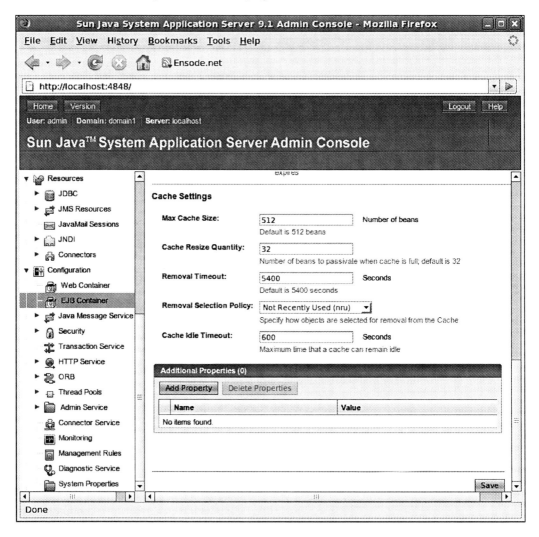

However, this technique sets the timeout value for all stateful session beans. If we need to modify the timeout value for a specific session bean, we need to include a `sun-ejb-jar.xml` deployment descriptor in the JAR file containing the session bean. In this deployment descriptor, we can set the timeout value as the value of the `<removal-timeout-in-seconds>` element.

```
<?xml version="1.0" encoding="UTF-8" standalone="no"?>
<!DOCTYPE sun-ejb-jar PUBLIC "-//Sun Microsystems, Inc.//DTD
Application Server 9.0 EJB 3.0//EN" "http://www.sun.com/software/
appserver/dtds/sun-ejb-jar_3_0-0.dtd">
<sun-ejb-jar>
  <enterprise-beans>
    <ejb>
      <ejb-name>MyStatefulSessionBean</ejb-name>
      <bean-cache>
        <removal-timeout-in-seconds>
           600
        </removal-timeout-in-seconds>
      </bean-cache>
    </ejb>
  </enterprise-beans>
</sun-ejb-jar>
```

Even though we are not required to create an `ejb-jar.xml` file for our session beans anymore (this used to be the case in previous versions of the J2EE specification), we can still write one if we wish to do so. The `<ejb-name>` element in the `sun-ejb-jar.xml` deployment descriptor must match the value of the element of the same name in `ejb-jar.xml`. If we choose not to create an `ejb-jar.xml` file, then this value must match the name of the EJB class. The timeout value for the stateful session bean must be the value of the `<removal-timeout-in-seconds>` element; as the name of the element suggests, the unit of time to use is seconds. In the above example, we set the timeout value to 600 seconds, or 10 minutes.

Any of the methods in a stateful session bean decorated with the `@PostActivate` annotation will be invoked just after the stateful session bean has been activated. This is equivalent to implementing the `ejbActivate()` method in previous versions of J2EE. Similarly, any method decorated with the `@PrePassivate` annotation will be invoked just before the stateful session bean is passivated. This is equivalent to implementing the `ejbPassivate()` method in previous versions of J2EE.

When a stateful session bean that is in the Ready state times out and is sent to the Does not Exist state, any method decorated with the `@PreDestroy` annotation is executed. If the session bean is in the Passive state and it times out, methods decorated with the `@PreDestroy` annotation are not executed. Additionally, if a client of the stateful session bean executes any method decorated with the `@Remove` annotation, any methods decorated with the `@PreDestroy` annotation are executed and the bean is marked for garbage collection. Decorating a method with the `@Remove` annotation is equivalent to implementing the `ejbRemove()` method in previous versions of the J2EE specification.

The `@PostActivate`, `@PrePassivate`, and `@Remove` annotations are valid only for stateful session beans. The `@PreDestroy` and `@PostConstruct` annotations are valid for stateful session beans, stateless session beans, and message-driven beans.

Stateless Session Bean Life Cycle

A stateless session bean life cycle, as shown in the following screenshot, contains only the **Does Not Exist** and **Ready** states.

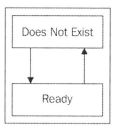

Stateless session beans are never passivated. A stateless session bean's methods can be decorated with the `@PostConstruct` and the `@PreDestroy` annotations. Just as in stateful session beans, any methods decorated with the `@PostConstruct` annotation will be executed when the stateless session bean goes from the Does Not Exist to the Ready state, and any methods decorated with the `@PreDestroy` annotation will be executed when a stateless session bean goes from the Ready state to the Does Not Exist state. Since stateless session beans are never passivated, therefore any `@PrePassivate` and `@PostActivate` annotations in a stateless session bean are simply ignored by the EJB container.

Message-Driven Bean Life Cycle

Just like stateless session beans, message-driven beans, as shown in the following screenshot, contain only the Does Not Exist and Ready states.

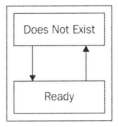

The above image is exactly the same as the previous one. Message-driven beans have the same life cycle as stateless session beans.

A message-driven bean can have methods decorated with the `@PostConstruct` and `@PreDestroy` methods. Methods decorated with the `@PostConstruct` are executed just before the bean goes to the Ready state. Methods decorated with the `@PreDestroy` annotation are executed just before the bean goes to the Does Not Exist state.

EJB Timer Service

Stateless session beans and message-driven beans can have a method that is executed periodically at regular intervals of time. This can be accomplished by using the **EJB Timer Service**. The following example illustrates how to take advantage of this service.

```
package net.ensode.glassfishbook;

import java.io.Serializable;
import java.util.Collection;
import java.util.Date;
import java.util.logging.Logger;

import javax.annotation.Resource;
import javax.ejb.EJBContext;
import javax.ejb.Stateless;
import javax.ejb.Timeout;
import javax.ejb.Timer;
import javax.ejb.TimerService;
```

```
@Stateless
public class EjbTimerExampleBean implements EjbTimerExample
{
  private static Logger logger = Logger.getLogger(EjbTimerExampleBean.
   class.getName());
  @Resource
  TimerService timerService;
  public void startTimer(Serializable info)
  {
    Timer timer = timerService.createTimer
       (new Date(), 5000, info);
  }
  public void stopTimer(Serializable info)
  {
    Timer timer;
    Collection timers = timerService.getTimers();
    for (Object object : timers)
    {
      timer = ((Timer) object);
      if (timer.getInfo().equals(info))
      {
        timer.cancel();
        break;
      }
    }
  }
  @Timeout
  public void logMessage(Timer timer)
  {
    logger.info("This message was triggered by :" +
        timer.getInfo() + " at "
        + System.currentTimeMillis());
  }
}
```

In the above example, we inject an implementation of the `javax.ejb.TimerService` interface by decorating an instance variable of this type with the `@Resource` annotation. We can then create a timer by invoking the `createTimer()` method of this `TimerService` instance.

There are several overloaded versions of the `createTimer()` method; the one we chose to use takes an instance of `java.util.Date` as its first parameter. This parameter is used to indicate the first time the timer should expire ("go off"). In the example, we chose to use a brand-new instance of the `Date` class, which in effect makes the timer expire immediately. The second parameter of the `createTimer()` method is the amount of time to wait, in milliseconds, before the timer expires again. In this example, the timer will expire every five seconds. The third parameter of the `createTimer()` method can be an instance of any class implementing the `java.io.Serializable` interface. As a single EJB can have several timers executing concurrently, this third parameter is used to uniquely identify each of the timers. If we don't need to identify the timers, null can be passed as a value for this parameter.

> The EJB method invoking `TimerService.createTimer()` must be called from an EJB client. Placing this call in an EJB method decorated with the `@PostConstruct` annotation to start the timer automatically when the bean is placed in Ready state will result in an `IllegalStateException` being thrown.

We can stop a timer by invoking its `cancel()` method. There is no way to directly obtain a single timer associated with an EJB; what we need to do is invoke the `getTimers()` method on the instance of `TimerService` that is linked to the EJB. This method will return a Collection containing all the timers associated with the EJB. We can then iterate through the collection and cancel the correct one by invoking its `getInfo()` method. This method will return the `Serializable` object we passed as a parameter to the `createTimer()` method.

Finally, any EJB method decorated with the `@Timeout` annotation will be executed when a timer expires. Methods decorated with this annotation must return void and take a single parameter of type `javax.ejb.Timer`. In our example, the method simply writes a message to the server log.

The following class is a stand-alone client for this EJB.

```
package net.ensode.glassfishbook;
import javax.ejb.EJB;
public class Client
{
  @EJB
  private static EjbTimerExample ejbTimerExample;
  public static void main(String[] args)
  {
    try
    {
      System.out.println("Starting timer 1...");
      ejbTimerExample.startTimer("Timer 1");
      System.out.println("Sleeping for 2 seconds...");
      Thread.sleep(2000);
```

```
        System.out.println("Starting timer 2...");
        ejbTimerExample.startTimer("Timer 2");
        System.out.println("Sleeping for 30 seconds...");
        Thread.sleep(30000);
        System.out.println("Stopping timer 1...");
        ejbTimerExample.stopTimer("Timer 1");
        System.out.println("Stopping timer 2...");
        ejbTimerExample.stopTimer("Timer 2");
        System.out.println("Done.");
    }
    catch (InterruptedException e)
    {
        e.printStackTrace();
    }
  }
}
```

The example simply starts a timer, waits for a couple of seconds, then starts a second timer. It then sleeps for 30 seconds and then stops both timers. After deploying the EJB and executing the client, we should see some entries like this in the server log:

```
[#|2007-05-05T20:41:39.518-0400|INFO|sun-appserver9.1|net.ensode.
glassfishbook.EjbTimerExampleBean|_ThreadID=22;_ThreadName=p:
thread-pool-1; w: 16;|This message was triggered by :Timer 1 at
1178412099518|#]

[#|2007-05-05T20:41:41.536-0400|INFO|sun-appserver9.1|net.ensode.
glassfishbook.EjbTimerExampleBean|_ThreadID=22;_ThreadName=p:
thread-pool-1; w: 16;|This message was triggered by :Timer 2 at
1178412101536|#]

[#|2007-05-05T20:41:46.537-0400|INFO|sun-appserver9.1|net.ensode.
glassfishbook.EjbTimerExampleBean|_ThreadID=22;_ThreadName=p:
thread-pool-1; w: 16;|This message was triggered by :Timer 1 at
1178412106537|#]

[#|2007-05-05T20:41:48.556-0400|INFO|sun-appserver9.1|net.ensode.
glassfishbook.EjbTimerExampleBean|_ThreadID=22;_ThreadName=p:
thread-pool-1; w: 16;|This message was triggered by :Timer 2 at
1178412108556|#]
```

These entries are created each time one of the timer expires.

EJB Security

Enterprise JavaBeans allow us to declaratively decide which users can access their methods. For example, some methods might only be available to users in certain roles. A typical scenario is that only users with a role of administrator can add, delete, or modify other users in the system.

The following example is a slightly modified version of the DAO session bean we saw earlier in this chapter. In this version, some methods that were previously private were made public. Additionally, the session bean was modified to allow only users in certain roles to access its methods.

```java
package net.ensode.glassfishbook;

import java.sql.Connection;
import java.sql.PreparedStatement;
import java.sql.ResultSet;
import java.sql.SQLException;

import javax.annotation.Resource;
import javax.annotation.security.RolesAllowed;
import javax.ejb.Stateless;
import javax.persistence.EntityManager;
import javax.persistence.PersistenceContext;
import javax.sql.DataSource;

@Stateless
@RolesAllowed("appadmin")
public class CustomerDaoBean implements CustomerDao
{
  @PersistenceContext
  private EntityManager entityManager;

  @Resource(name = "jdbc/__CustomerDBPool")
  private DataSource dataSource;

  public void saveCustomer(Customer customer)
  {
    if (customer.getCustomerId() == null)
    {
      saveNewCustomer(customer);
    }
    else
    {
      updateCustomer(customer);
    }
  }

  public Long saveNewCustomer(Customer customer)
  {
    customer.setCustomerId(getNewCustomerId());
    entityManager.persist(customer);

    return customer.getCustomerId();
  }

  public void updateCustomer(Customer customer)
  {
```

```
    entityManager.merge(customer);
  }
  @RolesAllowed(
  { "appuser", "appadmin" })
  public Customer getCustomer(Long customerId)
  {
    Customer customer;
    customer = entityManager.find(Customer.class, customerId);
    return customer;
  }
  public void deleteCustomer(Customer customer)
  {
    entityManager.remove(customer);
  }
  private Long getNewCustomerId()
  {
    Connection connection;
    Long newCustomerId = null;
    try
    {
      connection = dataSource.getConnection();
      PreparedStatement preparedStatement =
          connection
          .prepareStatement("select max(customer_id)+1 "
          "as new_customer_id from customers");
      ResultSet resultSet = preparedStatement.executeQuery();
      if (resultSet != null && resultSet.next())
      {
        newCustomerId = resultSet.getLong("new_customer_id");
      }
      connection.close();
    }
    catch (SQLException e)
    {
      e.printStackTrace();
    }
    return newCustomerId;
  }
}
```

As you can see, we declare what roles have access to the methods by using the `@RolesAllowed` annotation. This annotation can take either a single String or an array of Strings as a parameter. When a single String is used as a parameter for this annotation, only users with the role specified by the parameter can access the method. If an array of Strings is used as a parameter, users with any of the roles specified by the array's elements can access the method.

The `@RolesAllowed` annotation can be used to decorate an EJB class, in which case its values apply to all the methods in the EJB, or to decorate one or more methods. In this second case, its values apply only to the method(s) the annotation is decorating. If, as in our example, both the EJB class and one or more of its methods are decorated with the `@RolesAllowed` annotation, the method-level annotation takes precedence.

Application roles need to be mapped to a security realm's group name. This mapping, along with what realm to use, is set in the `sun-ejb-jar.xml` deployment descriptor.

```xml
<?xml version="1.0" encoding="UTF-8"?>
<!DOCTYPE sun-ejb-jar PUBLIC "-//Sun Microsystems, Inc.//DTD
Application Server 9.0 EJB 3.0//EN" "http://www.sun.com/software/
appserver/dtds/sun-ejb-jar_3_0-0.dtd">
<sun-ejb-jar>
  <security-role-mapping>
    <role-name>appuser</role-name>
    <group-name>appuser</group-name>
  </security-role-mapping>
  <security-role-mapping>
    <role-name>appadmin</role-name>
    <group-name>appadmin</group-name>
  </security-role-mapping>
  <enterprise-beans>
    <ejb>
      <ejb-name>CustomerDaoBean</ejb-name>
      <ior security-config>
        <as-context>
          <auth-method>username_password</auth-method>
          <realm>file</realm>
          <required>true</required>
        </as-context>
      </ior-security-config>
    </ejb>
  </enterprise-beans>
</sun-ejb-jar>
```

The `<security-role-mapping>` element of the `sun-ejb-jar.xml` file does the mapping between application roles and the security realm's group. The value of the `<role-name>` sub-element must contain the application role; this value must match the value used in the `@RolesAllowed` annotation. The value of the `<group-name>` sub-element must contain the name of the security group in the security realm used by the EJB. In this example, we map two application roles to the corresponding groups in the security realm. Although in this particular example the name of the application role and the security group match, this does not need to be the case.

Automatically Matching Roles to Security Groups

It is possible to automatically match any application roles to identically named security groups in the security realm. This can be accomplished by logging in to the GlassFish web console, clicking on the **Configuration** node, clicking on **Security**, then clicking on the checkbox labeled **Default Principal To Role Mapping**, and saving this configuration change.

As can be seen in the example, the security realm to use for authentication is defined in the `<realm>` sub-element of the `<as-context>` element. The value of this sub-element must match the name of a valid security realm in the application server. Other sub elements of the `<as-context>` element include `<auth-method>`, the only valid value for which is `username_password`, and `<required>`, whose only valid values are `true` and `false`.

Client Authentication

If the client code accessing a secured EJB is part of a web application whose user has already authenticated, then the user's credentials will be used to determine if the user should be allowed to access the method he/she is trying to execute.

Stand-alone clients must be executed through the `appclient` utility. The following code illustrates a typical client for our, secured session bean.

```
package net.ensode.glassfishbook;
import javax.ejb.EJB;
public class Client
{
  @EJB
  private static CustomerDao customerDao;
  public static void main(String[] args)
  {
    Long newCustomerId;
```

```
Customer customer = new Customer();
customer.setFirstName("Mark");
customer.setLastName("Butcher");
customer.setEmail("butcher@phony.org");

System.out.println("Saving New Customer...");
newCustomerId = customerDao.saveNewCustomer(customer);

System.out.println("Retrieving customer...");
customer = customerDao.getCustomer(newCustomerId);
System.out.println(customer);
    }
}
```

As you can see, there is nothing the code is doing in order to authenticate the user. The session bean is simply injected into the code via the @EJB annotation and it is used as usual. The reason this works is because the appclient utility takes care of authenticating the user. Passing the -user and -password arguments with the appropriate values will authenticate the user:

```
appclient -client ejbsecurityclient.jar -user peter -password secret
```

The above command will authenticate a user with a user name of "peter" and a password of "secret". Assuming the credentials are correct and that the user has the appropriate permissions, the EJB code will execute and we should see the expected output from the Client class above:

```
Saving New Customer...

Retrieving customer...

customerId = 29

firstName = Mark

lastName = Butcher

email = butcher@phony.org
```

If we don't enter the user name and password from the command line, appclient will prompt us for a user name and password through a graphical window. In our example, entering the following command:

```
appclient -client ejbsecurityclient.jar
```

will result in a pop-up window like the following to show up.

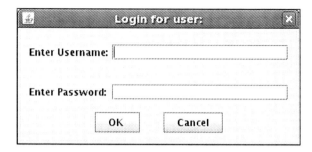

We can simply enter our user name and password in the appropriate fields, and after validating the credentials, the application will execute as expected.

Summary

In this chapter, we covered how to implement business logic via stateless and stateful session beans. We also explained how to take advantage of the transactional nature of EJBs to simplify implementing the Data Access Object (DAO) pattern.

Additionally, we explained the concept of Container-Managed Transactions, and how to control them by using the appropriate annotations. We also explained how to implement Bean-Managed Transaction, for cases in which Container-Managed Transactions are not enough to satisfy our requirements.

Life cycles for the different types of Enterprise Java beans were covered, including an explanation on how to have EJB methods automatically invoked by the EJB container at certain points in the life cycle.

We also covered how to have EJB methods invoked periodically by the EJB container by taking advantage of the EJB timer service.

Finally, we explained how to make sure EJB methods are only invoked by authorized users by annotating the EJB classes and/or methods and by adding the appropriate entries to the `sun-ejb-jar.xml` deployment descriptor.

10
Web Services

The Java EE 5 specification includes the JAX-WS API as one of its technologies. JAX-WS is used to easily develop web services. It stands for Java API for XML Web Services. JAX-WS is a high-level API. Invoking web services via JAX-WS is done via remote procedure calls. JAX-WS is a very natural API for Java developers.

Some of the topics we will cover are:

- Developing web services with the JAX-WS API
- Developing web service clients with JAX-WS
- Adding attachments to web service calls
- Exposing EJBs as web services
- Securing web services

Developing Web Services with JAX-WS

JAX-WS is a high level API that simplifies development of web services. Developing a web service via JAX-WS consists of writing a class with public methods to be exposed as web services. Both the class and the methods need to be decorated with annotations specifying that the methods are to be exposed as web services. The following example illustrates this process:

```
package net.ensode.glassfishbook;

import javax.jws.WebMethod;
import javax.jws.WebService;

@WebService
public class Calculator
{
  @WebMethod
```

```
    public int add(int first, int second)
    {
      return first + second;
    }

    @WebMethod
    public int subtract(int first, int second)
    {
      return first - second;
    }
  }
```

The above class exposes its two methods as web services. The add() method simply adds the two int primitives that it receives as parameters and returns the result. The substract() method subtracts its two parameters and returns the result.

We indicate that the class implements a web service by decorating it with the @WebService annotation. Any methods that we would like exposed as web services need to be decorated with the @WebMethod annotation. Only public methods can be exposed as web services.

To deploy our web service, we need to package it in a WAR file. Like any valid WAR file, our WAR file must contain a web.xml deployment descriptor in its META-INF directory. Nothing needs to be added to the WAR file's web.xml in order to successfully deploy our web service; as a matter of fact, if no additional servlets are deployed in the WAR file, then simply having an empty <web-app> element in the deployment descriptor will be enough to successfully deploy our WAR file. That is the approach we took for our example.

```
<?xml version="1.0" encoding="UTF-8"?>
<web-app xmlns="http://java.sun.com/xml/ns/javaee" version="2.5"
  xmlns:xsi="http://www.w3.org/2001/XMLSchema"
  xsi:schemaLocation="http://java.sun.com/xml/ns/javaee http://java.
sun.com/xml/ns/javaee/web-app_2_5.xsd">
</web-app>
```

After compiling and packaging the above code and deployment descriptor in a WAR file and deploying it, we can verify that it was successfully deployed by logging into the GlassFish admin web console and expanding the **Web Services** node at the left-hand side. We should see our newly deployed web service listed under this node.

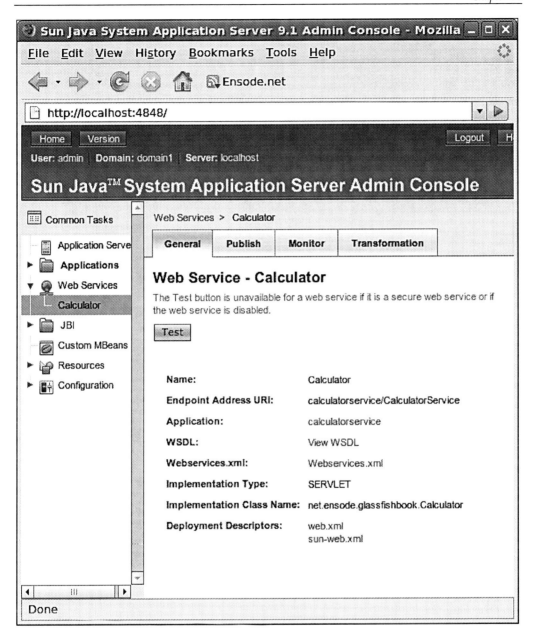

Now that we know that our web service has been successfully deployed, we can easily test it by clicking on the **Test** button.

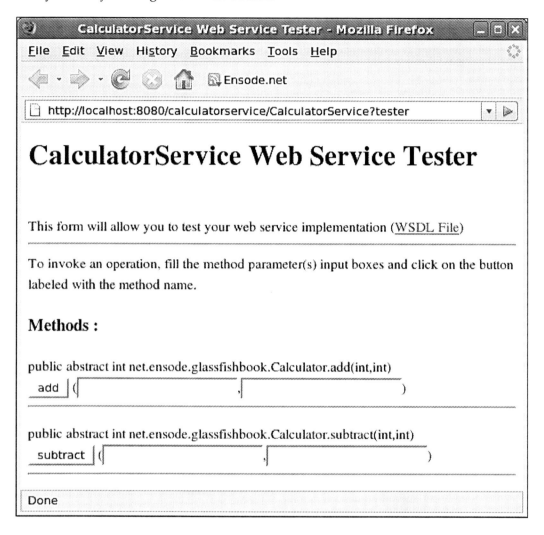

To test the methods, we can simply enter some parameters in the text fields and click on the appropriate button. For example, entering the values **2** and **3** in the text fields corresponding to the add method, and clicking on the **add** button would result in the following output:

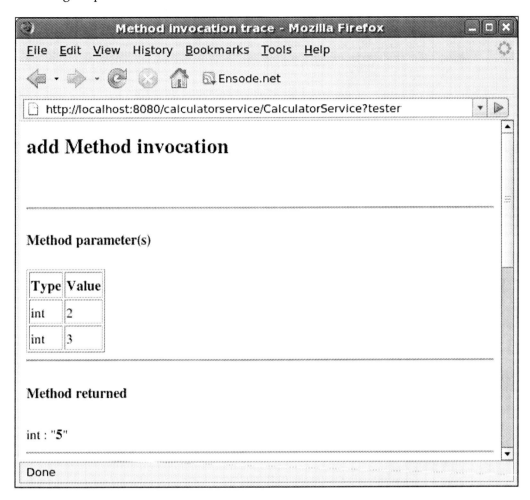

JAX-WS uses the SOAP protocol, behind the scenes, to exchange information between web service clients and servers. By scrolling down the page, we can see the SOAP request and response generated by our test.

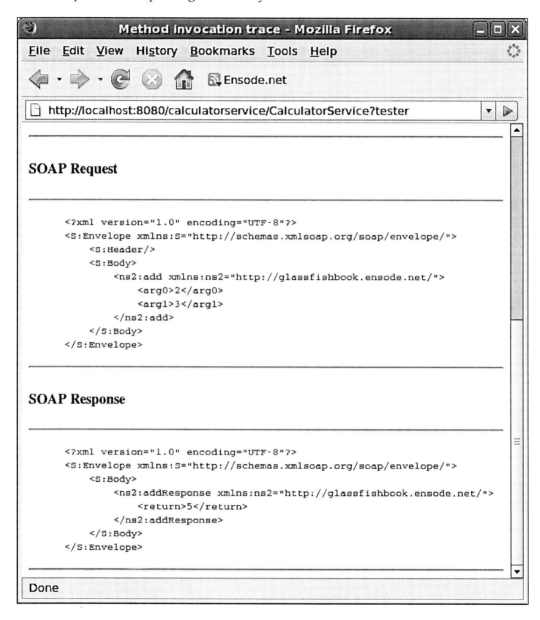

As application developers, we don't need to concern ourselves too much with these SOAP requests, because they are automatically taken care of by the JAX-WS API.

Web service clients need a WSDL (Web Services Definition Language) file in order to generate executable code that they can use to invoke the web service. WSDL files are typically placed in a web server and accessed by the client via its URL. When deploying web services developed using JAX-WS, a WSDL is automatically generated for us. We can see it, along with its URL, by clicking on the **View WSDL** link that is shown when we click on our web service in GlassFish's web console.

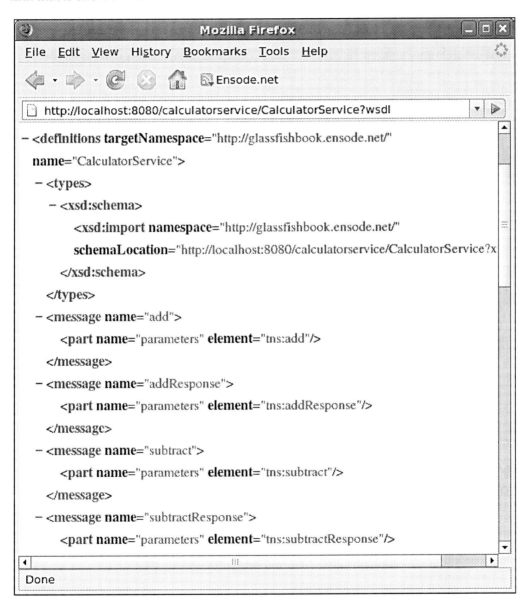

Notice the WSDL's URL in the browser's location text field; we will need this URL when developing a client for our web service.

Developing a Web Service Client

As we mentioned earlier, executable code needs to be generated from a web service's WSDL. A web service client will then invoke this executable code to access the web service.

GlassFish includes a utility to generate Java code from a WSDL. The name of the utility is `wsimport`. It can be found under `[glassfish installation directory]/glassfish/bin/`. The only required argument for `wsimport` is the URL of the WSDL corresponding to the web service.

```
wsimport http://localhost:8080/calculatorservice/CalculatorService?wsdl
```

The above command will generate a number of compiled Java classes that allow client applications to access our web service:

- `Add.class`
- `AddResponse.class`
- `Calculator.class`
- `CalculatorService.class`
- `ObjectFactory.class`
- `package-info.class`
- `Subtract.class`
- `SubtractResponse.class`

Keeping Generated Source Code

By default, the source code for the generated class files is automatically deleted. It can be kept by passing the `-keep` parameter to `wsimport`.

These classes need to be added to the client's CLASSPATH in order for them to be accessible to the client's code.

In addition to the command-line tool, Glassfish includes a custom ANT task to generate code from a WSDL. The following ANT build script illustrates its usage:

```
<project name="calculatorserviceclient" default="wsimport"
basedir=".">
  <target name="wsimport">
    <taskdef name="wsimport"
```

```
            classname="com.sun.tools.ws.ant.WsImport">
        <classpath
            path="/opt/glassfish/lib/webservices-tools.jar"/>
        <classpath path="/opt/glassfish/lib/webservices-rt.jar"/>
        <classpath path="/opt/glassfish/lib/javaee.jar"/>
    </taskdef>
        <wsimport wsdl="http://localhost:8080/calculatorservice/
    CalculatorService?wsdl" />
    </target>
</project>
```

The above example is a very minimal ANT build script that only illustrates how to set up the custom `<wsimport>` ANT target; in reality the ANT build script for the project would have several other targets for compilation, building a WAR file, etc.

As `<wsimport>` is a custom ANT target and it is not standard, we need to add a `<taskdef>` element to our ANT build script. We need to set the its `name` and `classname` attributes as illustrated in the example. Additionally, we need to add the following JAr files to the task's CLASSPATH via nested `<classpath>` elements:

- `webservices-tools.jar`
- `webservices-rt.jar`
- `javaee.jar`

All three of these JAR files can be found under the `[glassfish installation directory]/glassfish/lib` directory.

Once we set up the custom `<wsimport>` task via the `<taskdef>` element, we are ready to use it. We need to indicate the WSDL location via its `wsdl` attribute. Once this task executes, the Java code needed to access the web service defined by the WSDL is generated.

In addition to the custom ANT target for `wsimport`, there is a plugin for Maven 2 that implements this functionality as well. Its use is illustrated in the following `pom.xml` file:

```
<?xml version="1.0" encoding="UTF-8"?>
<project xmlns="http://maven.apache.org/POM/4.0.0"
    xmlns:xsi="http://www.w3.org/2001/XMLSchema-instance"
    xsi:schemaLocation="http://maven.apache.org/POM/4.0.0 http://
                        maven.apache.org/maven-v4_0_0.xsd">
    <modelVersion>4.0.0</modelVersion>
    <groupId>net.ensode.glassfishbook</groupId>
    <artifactId>calculatorserviceclient</artifactId>
    <packaging>jar</packaging>
    <name>Simple Web Service Client</name>
```

```
<version>1.0</version>
<url>http://maven.apache.org</url>
<repositories>
  <repository>
    <id>java.net</id>
    <url>https://maven-repository.dev.java.net/nonav/repository</url>
    <layout>legacy</layout>
  </repository>
</repositories>
<dependencies>
  <dependency>
    <groupId>com.sun.xml.ws</groupId>
    <artifactId>jaxws-rt</artifactId>
    <version>2.1</version>
  </dependency>
  <dependency>
    <groupId>javaee</groupId>
    <artifactId>javaee-api</artifactId>
    <version>5</version>
    <scope>provided</scope>
  </dependency>
</dependencies>
<build>
  <finalName>calculatorserviceclient</finalName>
  <plugins>
    <plugin>
      <groupId>org.codehaus.mojo</groupId>
      <artifactId>jaxws-maven-plugin</artifactId>
      <version>1.0-beta-1-SNAPSHOT</version>
      <executions>
        <execution>
          <goals>
            <goal>wsimport</goal>
          </goals>
          <configuration>
            <wsdlUrls>
              <wsdlUrl>
                http://localhost:8080/calculatorservice/
                  CalculatorService?wsdl
              </wsdlUrl>
            </wsdlUrls>
          </configuration>
```

```
            </execution>
          </executions>
        </plugin>
        <plugin>
          <groupId>org.apache.maven.plugins</groupId>
          <artifactId>maven-jar-plugin</artifactId>
          <configuration>
            <archive>
              <manifest>
                <mainClass>
                  net.ensode.glassfishbook.CalculatorServiceClient
                </mainClass>
                <addClasspath>true</addClasspath>
              </manifest>
            </archive>
          </configuration>
        </plugin>
        <plugin>
          <groupId>org.apache.maven.plugins</groupId>
          <artifactId>maven-compiler-plugin</artifactId>
          <configuration>
            <source>1.5</source>
            <target>1.5</target>
          </configuration>
        </plugin>
      </plugins>
    </build>
</project>
```

In order for the plugin to execute correctly, we need to add a dependency to the
`jaxws-rt` artifact under the `com.sun.xml.ws` group. Once we do that, we need
to set it up via the `<plugin>` sub-element of the `<build>` element in the `pom.xml`
file. The WSDL location needs to be specified in the `<wsdlUrl>` sub-element of the
`<configuration>` element. This plugin executes automatically when we build our
code from Maven 2. Just like the ANT task, it generates code we can use to access the
web service from a client.

We will now develop a simple client to access our web service.

```
package net.ensode.glassfishbook;

import javax.xml.ws.WebServiceRef;

public class CalculatorServiceClient
{
  @WebServiceRef(wsdlLocation =
```

```
        "http://localhost:8080/calculatorservice/" +
        "CalculatorService?wsdl")
    private static CalculatorService calculatorService;
    public void calculate()
    {
      Calculator calculator =
          calculatorService.getCalculatorPort();
      System.out.println("1 + 2 = "
          + calculator.add(1, 2));
      System.out.println("1 - 2 = "
          + calculator.subtract(1, 2));
    }
    public static void main(String[] args)
    {
      new CalculatorServiceClient().calculate();
    }
}
```

The @WebServiceRef annotation injects an instance of the web service into our client application. Its wsdlLocation attribute contains the URL of the WSDL corresponding to the web service we are invoking.

Notice that the web service class is an instance of a class called CalculatorService. This class was created when we invoked the wsimport utility; wsimport always generates a class whose name is the name of the class we implemented plus the "Service" suffix. We use this service class to obtain an instance of the web service class we developed. In our example, we do this by invoking the getCalculatorPort() method on the CalculatorService instance. In general, the method to invoke to get an instance of our web service class follows the pattern getNamePort(), where Name is the name of the class we wrote to implement the web service. Once we get an instance of our web service class, we can simply invoke its methods as with any regular Java object.

Strictly speaking, the getNamePort() method of the service class returns an instance of a class implementing an interface generated by wsimport. This interface is given the name of our web service class and declares all of the methods we declared to be web services. For all practical purposes, the object returned is equivalent to our web service class.

Recall from Chapter 9 that in order for resource injection to work in a stand-alone client (that does not get deployed to GlassFish), we need to execute it through the `appclient` utility. Assuming we packaged our client in a JAR file called `calculatorserviceclient.jar`, the command to execute would be:

```
appclient -client calculatorserviceclient.jar
```

After entering the above command in the command line, we should see the output of our client on the console.

```
1 + 2 = 3
1 - 2 = -1
```

In this example, we passed primitive types as parameters and return values; of course it is also possible to pass objects both as parameters and as return values. Unfortunately, not all standard Java classes or primitive types can be used as method parameters or return values when invoking web services. The reason for this is that, behind the scenes, method parameters and return types get mapped to XML definitions, and not all types can be properly mapped.

Valid types that can be used in JAX-WS web service calls are listed below:

- java.awt.Image
- java.lang.Object
- Java.lang.String
- java.math.BigDecimal
- java.math.BigInteger
- java.net.URI
- java.util.Calendar
- java.util.Date
- java.util.UUID
- javax.activation.DataHandler
- javax.xml.datatype.Duration
- javax.xml.datatype.XMLGregorianCalendar
- javax.xml.namespace.QName
- javax.xml.transform.Source

Additionally, the following primitive types can be used:

- boolean
- byte
- byte
- double
- float
- int
- long
- short

We can also use our own custom classes as method parameters and/or return values for web service method, but member variables of our classes must be one of the listed types.

Additionally, it is legal to use arrays as both method parameters and return values; however, when executing `wsimport`, these arrays get converted to Lists, generating a mismatch between the method signature in the web service and the method call invoked in the client. For this reason, it is preferred to use Lists as method parameters and/or return values, because this is also legal and does not create the mismatch between the client and the server.

 JAX-WS internally uses the Java Architecture for XML Binding to create SOAP messages from method calls. The types we are allowed to use for method calls and return values are the ones that JAXB supports. For more information on JAXB, see `https://jaxb.dev.java.net/`.

Sending Attachments to Web Services

In addition to sending and accepting the data types discussed in the previous sections, web service methods can send and accept file attachments. The following example illustrates how to do this:

```
package net.ensode.glassfishbook;

import java.io.FileOutputStream;
import java.io.IOException;
import javax.activation.DataHandler;
import javax.jws.WebMethod;
import javax.jws.WebService;

@WebService
```

```
public class FileAttachment
{
  @WebMethod
  public void attachFile(DataHandler dataHandler)
  {
    FileOutputStream fileOutputStream;
    try
    {
      //substitute "/tmp/attachment.gif" with
      // a valid path, if necessary.
      fileOutputStream = new FileOutputStream("/tmp/attachment.gif");

      dataHandler.writeTo(fileOutputStream);

      fileOutputStream.flush();
      fileOutputStream.close();
    }
    catch (IOException e)
    {
      e.printStackTrace();
    }
  }
}
```

In order to write a web service method that receives one or more attachments, all we need to do is to add a parameter of type `javax.activation.DataHandler` for each attachment the method will receive. In the above example, the `attachFile()` method takes a single parameter of this type and simply writes it to the file system.

Just as with any standard web service, the above code needs to be packaged in a WAR file and deployed. Once deployed, a WSDL will automatically be generated. We then need to execute the `wsimport` utility to generate code that our web service client can use to access the web service. As previously discussed, `wsimport` can be invoked directly from the command line, via a custom ANT target, or via a Maven 2 plugin. Once we have executed `wsimport` to generate code to access the web service, we can write and compile our client code package `net.ensode.glassfishbook`;

```
import java.io.File;
import java.io.FileInputStream;
import java.io.IOException;
import java.nio.ByteBuffer;
import java.nio.channels.FileChannel;

import javax.xml.ws.WebServiceRef;

public class FileAttachmentServiceClient
```

```
  {
    @WebServiceRef(wsdlLocation =
        "http://localhost:8080/fileattachmentservice/" +
        "FileAttachmentService?wsdl")
    private static FileAttachmentService fileAttachmentService;
    public static void main(String[] args)
    {
      FileAttachment fileAttachment = fileAttachmentService
          .getFileAttachmentPort();
      File fileToAttach = new File("src/main/resources/logo.gif");
      byte[] fileBytes = fileToByteArray(fileToAttach);

      fileAttachment.attachFile(fileBytes);
      System.out.println("Successfully sent attachment.");
    }
    static byte[] fileToByteArray(File file)
    {
      byte[] fileBytes = null;
      try
      {
        FileInputStream fileInputStream;
        fileInputStream = new FileInputStream(file);

        FileChannel fileChannel = fileInputStream.getChannel();
        fileBytes = new byte[(int) fileChannel.size()];
        ByteBuffer byteBuffer = ByteBuffer.wrap(fileBytes);
        fileChannel.read(byteBuffer);
      }
      catch (IOException e)
      {
        e.printStackTrace();
      }
      return fileBytes;
    }
  }
}
```

A web service client that needs to send one or more attachments to the web service first obtains an instance of the web service as usual. It then creates an instance of java.io.File passing the location of the file to attach as its constructor's parameter.

Once we have an instance of the java.io.File, containing the file we wish to attach, we then need to convert the file to a byte array, and pass this byte array to the web service method that expects an attachment.

Notice that, unlike when passing standard parameters, the parameter type used when the client invokes a method expecting a parameter is different from the parameter type of the method in the web server code. The method in the web server code expects an instance of `javax.activation.DataHandler` for each attachment. However, the code generated by `wsimport` expects an array of bytes for each attachment. These arrays of bytes are converted to the right type (`javax.activation.DataHandler`), behind the scenes, by the `wsimport`-generated code. We, as application developers, don't need to concern ourselves with the details of why this happens. We just need to keep in mind that when sending attachments to a web service method, the parameter types will be different in the web service code and in the client invocation of the corresponding method in the `wsimport`-generated code.

Exposing EJBs as Web Services

In addition to creating web services as described in the previous section, public methods of stateless session beans can easily be exposed as web services. The following example illustrates how to do this:

```
package net.ensode.glassfishbook;

import javax.ejb.Stateless;
import javax.jws.WebService;

@Stateless
@WebService
public class DecToHexBean
{
  public String convertDecToHex(int i)
  {
    return Integer.toHexString(i);
  }
}
```

As you can see, the only thing we need to do to expose a stateless session bean's public methods is decorate its class declaration with the `@WebService` annotation. Needless to say, as the class is a session bean, it also needs to be decorated with the `@Stateless` annotation.

Just like regular stateless session beans, session beans exposed as web services need to be deployed in a JAR file. Once deployed, we can see the new web service under the **Web Services** node in the GlassFish administration web console.

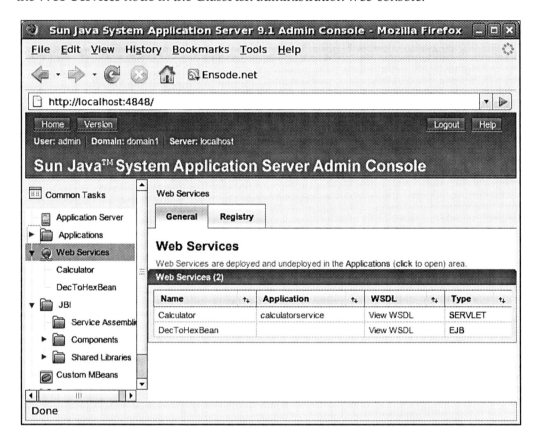

Notice that the value in the **Type** column at the far right of the screenshot for our new web service is **EJB**.

Just like standard web services, EJB web services automatically generate a WSDL for use by their clients upon deployment.

EJB Web Service Clients

The following class illustrates the procedure to be followed to access EJB web service methods from a client application.

```
package net.ensode.glassfishbook;

import javax.xml.ws.WebServiceRef;

public class DecToHexClient
```

```
{
  @WebServiceRef(wsdlLocation = "http://localhost:8080/
              DecToHexBeanService/DecToHexBean?wsdl")
  private static DecToHexBeanService decToHexBeanService;

  public void convert()
  {
    DecToHexBean decToHexBean =
        decToHexBeanService.getDecToHexBeanPort();

    System.out.println("decimal 4013 in hex is: "
        + decToHexBean.convertDecToHex(4013));
  }
  public static void main(String[] args)
  {
    new DecToHexClient().convert();
  }
}
```

As you can see, nothing special needs to be done when accessing an EJB web service from a client. The procedure is the same as with standard web services.

As the above example is a stand-alone application, it needs to be executed via the `appclient` application.

```
appclient -client ejbwsclient.jar
```

The above command results in the following output:

```
decimal 4013 in hex is: fad
```

Securing Web Services

Just as with regular web applications, web services can be secured so that only authorized users can access them. This can be accomplished by modifying the web service's `web.xml` deployment descriptor.

```
<?xml version="1.0" encoding="UTF-8"?>
<web-app xmlns="http://java.sun.com/xml/ns/javaee" version="2.5"
  xmlns:xsi="http://www.w3.org/2001/XMLSchema"
  xsi:schemaLocation="http://java.sun.com/xml/ns/javaee http://java.
sun.com/xml/ns/javaee/web-app_2_5.xsd">
  <security-constraint>
    <web-resource-collection>
      <web-resource-name>
        Calculator Web Service
      </web-resource-name>
```

```
      <url-pattern>/CalculatorService/*</url-pattern>
      <http-method>POST</http-method>
    </web-resource-collection>
    <auth-constraint>
      <role-name>user</role-name>
    </auth-constraint>
  </security-constraint>
  <login-config>
    <auth-method>BASIC</auth-method>
    <realm-name>file</realm-name>
  </login-config>
</web-app>
```

In this example, we modify our calculator service so that only authorized users can access it. Notice that the modifications needed to secure the web service are no different from the modifications needed to secure any regular web application. The URL pattern to use for the <url-pattern> element can be obtained by clicking on the **View WSDL** link corresponding to our service. In our example, the URL for the link is:

```
http://localhost:8080/calculatorservice/CalculatorService?wsdl
```

The value to use for <url-pattern> is the value right after the context root (/CalculatorService in our example) and before the question mark, followed by a slash and an asterisk.

Notice that the above web.xml deployment descriptor only secures HTTP POST requests; the reason for this is that wsimport uses a GET request to obtain the WSDL and generate the appropriate code. If GET requests are secured, wsimport will fail because it will be denied access to the WSDL. Future versions of wsimport will allow us to specify a user name and password for authentication. In the meantime, the workaround is to secure only POST requests.

The following code illustrates how a stand-alone client can access a secured web service:

```
package net.ensode.glassfishbook;
import javax.xml.ws.BindingProvider;
import javax.xml.ws.WebServiceRef;
public class CalculatorServiceClient
{
  @WebServiceRef(wsdlLocation = "http://localhost:8080/
securecalculatorservice/CalculatorService?wsdl")
  private static CalculatorService calculatorService;
```

```
public void calculate()
{
  Calculator calculator =
      calculatorService.getCalculatorPort();
  ((BindingProvider) calculator).getRequestContext().put(
      BindingProvider.USERNAME_PROPERTY, "joe");
  ((BindingProvider) calculator).getRequestContext().put(
      BindingProvider.PASSWORD_PROPERTY, "password");
  System.out.println("1 + 2 = " + calculator.add(1, 2));
  System.out.println("1 - 2 = " + calculator.subtract(1, 2));
}
public static void main(String[] args)
{
  new CalculatorServiceClient().calculate();
}
}
```

The above code is a modified version of the Calculator service stand-alone client we saw before. This version was modified to access the secure version of the service. As can be seen in the code, all we need to do to access the secured version of the server is to put a user name and a password in the request context. The user name and password must be valid for the realm used to authenticate the web service.

We can add the user name and password to the request context by casting our web service endpoint class to `javax.xml.ws.BindingProvider` and calling its `getRequestContext()` method. This method returns a `java.util.Map` instance. We can then simply add the user name and password by calling the Map's put method and using the constants `USERNAME_PROPERTY` and `PASSWORD_PROPERTY` defined in `BindingProvider` as keys, and the corresponding String objects as values.

Securing EJB Web Services

Just like standard web services, EJBs exposed as web services can be secured so that only authorized clients can access them. This can be accomplished by configuration of the EJB via the `sun-ejb-jar.xml` file.

```
<?xml version="1.0" encoding="UTF-8"?>
<!DOCTYPE sun-ejb-jar PUBLIC "-//Sun Microsystems, Inc.//DTD
Application Server 9.0 EJB 3.0//EN" "http://www.sun.com/software/
appserver/dtds/sun-ejb-jar_3_0-0.dtd">
<sun-ejb-jar>
  <enterprise-beans>
    <ejb>
      <ejb-name>SecureDecToHexBean</ejb-name>
```

```
        <webservice-endpoint>
          <port-component-name>
            SecureDecToHexBean
          </port-component-name>
          <login-config>
            <auth-method>BASIC</auth-method>
            <realm>file</realm>
          </login-config>
        </webservice-endpoint>
      </ejb>
    </enterprise-beans>
  </sun-ejb-jar>
```

As can be seen in the above deployment descriptor, security is set up differently for EJBs exposed as web services than with standard EJBs. For EJBs exposed as web services, the security configuration is done inside the `<webservice-endpoint>` element of the `sun-ejb-jar.xml` file.

The `<port-component-name>` element must be set to the name of the EJB we are exposing as a webservice. This name is defined in the `<ejb-name>` element for the EJB.

The `<login-config>` element is very similar to the corresponding element in a web application's `web.xml` deployment descriptor. The `<login-config>` element must contain an authorization method, defined by its `<auth-method>` sub-element, and a realm to use for authentication, which is defined by the `<realm>` sub-element.

> Do not use the `@RolesAllowed` annotation for EJBs intended to be exposed as web services. This annotation is intended for when the EJB methods are accessed through its remote or local interface. If an EJB or one or more of its methods is decorated with this annotation, then invoking the method will fail with a security exception.

Once we configure an EJB web service for authentication, package it in a JAR file, and deploy it as usual, the EJB web service is now ready to be accessed by clients.

The following code example illustrates how an EJB web service client can access a secure EJB web service:

```
package net.ensode.glassfishbook;
import javax.xml.ws.BindingProvider;
import javax.xml.ws.WebServiceRef;
public class DecToHexClient
{
  @WebServiceRef(wsdlLocation = "http://localhost:8080/
```

```
                     SecureDecToHexBeanService/SecureDecToHexBean?wsdl")
   private static SecureDecToHexBeanService secureDecToHexBeanService;

   public void convert()
   {
     SecureDecToHexBean secureDecToHexBean =
         secureDecToHexBeanService
         .getSecureDecToHexBeanPort();
     ((BindingProvider) secureDecToHexBean).getRequestContext().put(
         BindingProvider.USERNAME_PROPERTY, "joe");
     ((BindingProvider) secureDecToHexBean).getRequestContext().put(
         BindingProvider.PASSWORD_PROPERTY, "password");

     System.out.println("decimal 4013 in hex is: "
         + secureDecToHexBean.convertDecToHex(4013));
   }
   public static void main(String[] args)
   {
     new DecToHexClient().convert();
   }
}
```

As you can see in the above example, the procedure for accessing an EJB exposed as a web service is identical to accessing a standard web service. The implementation of the web service is irrelevant to the client.

Summary

In this chapter, we covered how to develop web services and web service clients via the JAX-WS API. We explained how to incorporate web service code generation for web service clients when using ANT or Maven 2 as a build tool. We also covered the valid types that can be used for remote method calls via JAX-WS. Additionally, we discussed how to send attachments to a web service. We also covered how to expose an EJB's methods as web services. Lastly, we covered how to secure web services so that they are not accessible to unauthorized clients.

11
Beyond Java EE

In previous chapters, we have covered all major Java EE technologies and APIs. In this chapter, we will cover additional frameworks that build upon Java EE.

Some of the topics that we will cover include:

- Facelets
- Ajax4jsf
- Seam

Facelets is an open-source alternative view technology that can be used when developing JSF applications.

Ajax4jsf is a JSF component library that greatly eases "ajaxifying" JSF applications.

Seam is a framework built on top of JSF and EJB3 that eases the development of applications that use these two technologies.

Facelets

Facelets is an alternative view technology for JavaServer Faces applications that offers a number of advantages over JSPs.

- Facelets allows the creation of pages using XHTML markup that can be created with WYSIWYG tools and can be previewed in a browser without having to deploy a WAR file.
- Facelets allows the modification of a web application's visual layout with very little effort.
- Facelets was designed specifically for JSF, where as JSP predates JSF. Therefore its life cycle is different from the JSF life cycle.

More information about Facelets can be found at `https://facelets.dev.java.net/`.

Downloading Facelets

Facelets can be downloaded by pointing the browser to `https://facelets.dev.java.net/servlets/ProjectDocumentList`, clicking on the **releases** link, then clicking on the latest stable version.

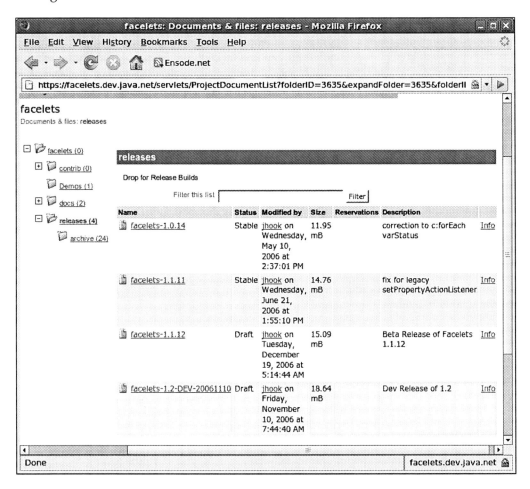

A single JAR file will be downloaded; this JAR file needs to be placed in the `WEB-INF/lib` directory in the application's WAR file.

If we are using Maven as our build tool, we just need to take advantage of Maven's dependency-management mechanism to download Facelets. The relevant section of the application's `pom.xml` file would look like this:

```
<dependencies>
    <dependency>
        <groupId>com.sun.facelets</groupId>
```

```
    <artifactId>jsf-facelets</artifactId>
    <version>[1.1.10,)</version>
  </dependency>
  <!-- Additional dependencies can be added -->
</dependencies>
```

Maven would then download the Facelets library from a central repository automatically when building the code for the first time, and it will place the Facelets JAR file to the appropriate location in the application's WAR file when packaging the application.

Configuring Our Facelets Application

Before we can use Facelets in our web application, we need to configure it by modifying its web.xml deployment descriptor.

```
<web-app xmlns="http://java.sun.com/xml/ns/javaee" version="2.5"
  xmlns:xsi="http://www.w3.org/2001/XMLSchema-instance"
  xsi:schemaLocation="http://java.sun.com/xml/ns/
      javaee http://java.sun.com/xml/ns/javaee/web-app_2_5.xsd">
  <context-param>
    <param-name>javax.faces.DEFAULT_SUFFIX</param-name>
    <param-value>.xhtml</param-value>
  </context-param>
  <context-param>
    <param-name>facelets.DEVELOPMENT</param-name>
    <param-value>true</param-value>
  </context-param>
  <context-param>
    <param-name>com.sun.faces.validateXml</param-name>
    <param-value>true</param-value>
  </context-param>
  <context-param>
    <param-name>com.sun.faces.verifyObjects</param-name>
    <param-value>true</param-value>
  </context-param>
  <servlet>
    <servlet-name>Faces Servlet</servlet-name>
    <servlet-class>javax.faces.webapp.FacesServlet</servlet-class>
    <load-on-startup>1</load-on-startup>
  </servlet>
  <servlet-mapping>
```

```
    <servlet-name>Faces Servlet</servlet-name>
    <url-pattern>*.jsf</url-pattern>
  </servlet-mapping>
</web-app>
```

The `<context-param>` elements in `web.xml` contain the application servlet context initialization parameters. The `javax.faces.DEFAULT_SUFFIX` parameter specifies the file extension for pages that contain JSF components. The default is `.jsp`; as Facelets does not use JSPs, we need to modify this value. Facelets typically uses XHTML for its view technology, therefore .xhtml is typically used as the value for this context parameter when developing web applications with Facelets.

Setting the `facelets.DEVELOPMENT` initialization parameter to `true` instructs Facelets to generate output useful for debugging.

The `com.sun.faces.validateXml` context parameter instructs the JSF reference implementation (included with GlassFish) to validate the `faces-config.xml` file.

The `com.sun.faces.verifyObjects` context parameter instructs the JSF reference implementation to verify that all components, converters, renderers, and validators in the application can be successfully created.

Additionally, some configuration needs to take place in the application's `faces-config.xml` file in order to successfully deploy a JSF web application using Facelets as its view technology.

```
<faces-config xmlns="http://java.sun.com/xml/ns/javaee"
  xmlns:xsi="http://www.w3.org/2001/XMLSchema-instance"
  xsi:schemaLocation="http://java.sun.com/xml/ns/javaee http://java.
sun.com/xml/ns/javaee/web-facesconfig_1_2.xsd"
  version="1.2">
  <application>
    <view-handler>
      com.sun.facelets.FaceletViewHandler
    </view-handler>
  </application>
</faces-config>
```

A **view handler** is a class that handles the JSF view creation and rendering. All JSF implementations must provide a default view handler class, and this default implementation is used unless we instruct JSF to use an alternative one. Facelets comes with a custom view handler that we need to use in order to develop JSF applications using Facelets as its view technology.

As can be seen in the example, we specify the view handler as the value of the
`<view-handler>` element in `faces-config.xml`. Facelet's view handler is `com.sun.
facelets.FaceletViewHandler`.

After configuring our application, we are ready to start writing our
Facelets application.

Writing a Facelets Application

Other than the additional necessary configuration, the only difference between a JSF
application using Facelets and one using JSPs is the view technology used. Facelets
applications typically use XHTML pages for the view.

In this section, we will develop a fictitious pizza ordering system. The markup for
the data entry page looks like this:

```
<?xml version="1.0" encoding="UTF-8" ?>
<!DOCTYPE html PUBLIC "-//W3C//DTD XHTML 1.0 Transitional//EN"
"http://www.w3.org/TR/xhtml1/DTD/xhtml1-transitional.dtd">
<html xmlns="http://www.w3.org/1999/xhtml"
  xmlns:h="http://java.sun.com/jsf/html"
  xmlns:f="http://java.sun.com/jsf/core">
<head>
<meta http-equiv="Content-Type" content="text/html; charset=UTF-8" />
<title>Pizza Builder</title>
</head>
<body>
<h2>Customize Your Pizza</h2>
<h:messages/>
<form jsfc="h:form" id="pizzaForm">
<table cellspacing="0" cellpadding="0" border="0">
  <tr>
    <td align="right"><b>Crust:</b> </td>
    <td>
      <h:selectOneRadio id="crustItems" value="#{pizza.crust}">
        <input type="radio" jsfc="f:selectItem"
          itemValue="Hand Tossed"
          id="htItem" itemLabel="Hand Tossed"/>
        <label jsfc="h:outputLabel" for="htItem"
          rendered="false">Hand Tossed</label> 
        <input type="radio" jsfc="f:selectItem"
          itemValue="Thin"
          itemLabel="Thin" id="thinItem" />
```

```
      <label jsfc="h:outputLabel"
        for="thinItem" rendered="false">
      Thin</label>
    </h:selectOneRadio>
  </td>
</tr>
<tr>
  <td align="right"><b>Toppings:</b> </td>
  <td>
    <h:selectManyCheckbox value="#{pizza.toppings}"
      id="toppingItems">
      <input type="checkbox" jsfc="f:selectItem"
        itemValue="Sausage"
        id="sausageItem" itemLabel="Sausage"/>
      <label jsfc="h:outputLabel" for="sausageItem"
        rendered="false">Sausage</label>
          
      <input type="checkbox" jsfc="f:selectItem"
        itemValue="Pepperoni"
        id="pepperoniItem" itemLabel="Pepperoni" />
      <label jsfc="h:outputLabel" for="pepperoniItem"
        rendered="false">Pepperoni</label>  
      <input type="checkbox" jsfc="f:selectItem"
        itemValue="Green Peppers" id="greenPeppersItem"
        itemLabel="Green Peppers" />
      <label jsfc="h:outputLabel" for="greenPeppersItem"
        rendered="false">Green Peppers</label>  
      <input type="checkbox" jsfc="f:selectItem"
        itemValue="Onions"
        id="onionsItem" itemLabel="Onions" />
      <label jsfc="h:outputLabel" for="onionsItem"
        rendered="false">Onions</label>
    </h:selectManyCheckbox>
  </td>
</tr>
<tr>
  <td align="right"><b>Comments:</b> </td>
  <td>
    <input type="text" size="40" jsfc="h:inputText"
      value="#{pizza.comments}" id="commentField"/>
  </td>
```

```
    </tr>
    <tr>
      <td> </td>
      <td>
        <input type="Submit" value="Submit"
          jsfc="h:commandButton"
          action="submit" id="submitButton"/>
      </td>
    </tr>
  </table>
  </form>
  </body>
  </html>
```

The first thing to notice about this markup is that we use XML Namespaces to include JSF components in our XHTML file. In the above example, standard JSF components are included via the following two lines:

```
xmlns:h="http://java.sun.com/jsf/html"
xmlns:f="http://java.sun.com/jsf/core"
```

Recall from Chapter 6 that when using JSPs, the taglib directive is used for this purpose.

We should also notice that a lot of the XHTML elements contain a non-standard jsfc attribute. What this attribute does is convert the XHTML element into the JSF component specified as the value for the jsfc attribute.

A couple of components used in the page have no XHTML equivalent, namely the <h:selectOneRadio> and the <h:selectManyCheckbox components>. We can simply add them to the page and they will be ignored by the browser.

<f:selectItem> components declare their label as the value of their itemlabel attribute; as this attribute is not a valid attribute of the XHTML input field , it is ignored by the browser, therefore it does not preview properly when opening the page in the browser. If we add a standard XHTML label to the markup, the label is rendered twice when rendering the page from JSF (once from the itemLabel attribute and once from the <label> element); to get around this issue, we added <label> elements with a jsfc attribute of h:outputLabel and set their rendered attribute to false. As the rendered attribute is not a valid XHTML attribute, it is ignored by the browser and the labels are visible when previewing the page. However, when rendering the page from JSF, the rendered attribute is interpreted and the labels are not displayed.

The following screenshot shows how this file is rendered when opening it directly in the browser.

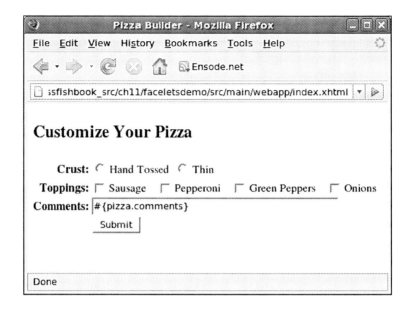

The **Comments** field shows a value-binding expression. This expression is replaced with its value when the page is rendered through JSF. This and all other value binding expressions refer to a managed bean called pizza. The code for this backing bean is shown next.

```
package net.ensode.glassfishbook;

public class Pizza
{
  private String crust;
  private String[] toppings;
  private String comments;

  public String getComments()
  {
    return comments;
  }

  public void setComments(String comments)
  {
    this.comments = comments;
  }

  public String getCrust()
```

```
    {
      return crust;
    }

    public void setCrust(String crust)
    {
      this.crust = crust;
    }

    public String[] getToppings()
    {
      return toppings;
    }

    public void setToppings(String[] toppings)
    {
      this.toppings = toppings;
    }

    public String getToppingListString()
    {
      String toppingListString = "";
      StringBuffer toppingListStringBuffer;

      if (toppings != null)
      {
        toppingListStringBuffer = new StringBuffer();
        int i = 0;
        for (String topping : toppings)
        {
          toppingListStringBuffer.append(topping);
          if (i++ < toppings.length - 1)
          {
            toppingListStringBuffer.append(", ");
          }
        }
        toppingListString = toppingListStringBuffer.toString();
      }

      return toppingListString;
    }

}
```

As you can see, there is nothing special about this backing bean; it is simply a standard JavaBean. Of course, we need to declare this managed bean in the application's `faces-config.xml` file.

```
<faces-config xmlns="http://java.sun.com/xml/ns/javaee"
    xmlns:xsi="http://www.w3.org/2001/XMLSchema-instance"
    xsi:schemaLocation="http://java.sun.com/xml/ns/javaee http://
            java.sun.com/xml/ns/javaee/web-facesconfig_1_2.xsd"
    version="1.2">
    <application>
        <view-handler>com.sun.facelets.FaceletViewHandler</
                view-handler>
    </application>
    <managed-bean>
        <managed-bean-name>pizza</managed-bean-name>
        <managed-bean-class>
            net.ensode.glassfishbook.Pizza
        </managed-bean-class>
        <managed-bean-scope>request</managed-bean-scope>
    </managed-bean>
    <navigation-rule>
        <from-view-id>/index.xhtml</from-view-id>
        <navigation-case>
            <from-outcome>submit</from-outcome>
            <to-view-id>/confirmation.xhtml</to-view-id>
        </navigation-case>
    </navigation-rule>
</faces-config>
```

Again nothing special to make this work with Facelets; the managed bean is declared just as in any other JSF application.

While we are discussing the application's `faces-config.xml` file, it is worth taking a look at the navigation rule. The only peculiar thing about this navigation rule is that the view IDs end with `.xhtml`, where in standard JSF applications they end with `.jsp`. The reason for this is that the values for the `<from-view-id>` and `<to-view-id>` elements are the file names for the files containing the views. Since standard JSF uses JSP files and Facelets uses XHTML files, it shouldn't surprise us that the view IDs in this case end with `.xhtml`.

Notice that the XHTML previous markup file has the hardcoded value of `submit` as the value of its `action` parameter. Recall from Chapter 6 that this value is used to determine which page to navigate to when the form is submitted. In the navigation rule, we add this value to the `<from-outcome>` element, and set the `<view-id>` attribute to a page called `confirmation.xhtml`. We will take a look at this page next.

```
<?xml version="1.0" encoding="UTF-8" ?>
<!DOCTYPE html PUBLIC "-//W3C//DTD XHTML 1.0 Transitional//EN"
"http://www.w3.org/TR/xhtml1/DTD/xhtml1-transitional.dtd">
<html xmlns="http://www.w3.org/1999/xhtml"
  xmlns:h="http://java.sun.com/jsf/html">
<head>
<meta http-equiv="Content-Type" content="text/html; charset=UTF-8" />
<title>Confirmation</title>
</head>
<body>
<h2>Confirmation</h2>
<table cellpadding="0" cellspacing="0" border="0">
  <tr>
    <td align="right"><b>Crust:</b> </td>
    <td><span jsfc="h:outputText" value="#{pizza.crust}"><span
      jsfc="h:outputText" rendered=
                              "false">Thin</span></span></td>
  </tr>
  <tr>
    <td align="right"><b>Toppings:</b> </td>
    <td><span jsfc="h:outputText"
      value="#{pizza.toppingListString}"><span
      jsfc="h:outputText" rendered="false">Sausage,
                        Onions</span></span></td>
  </tr>
  <tr>
    <td align="right"><b>Comments:</b> </td>
    <td><span jsfc="h:outputText" value=
                  "#{pizza.comments}"><span
      jsfc="h:outputText" rendered="false">Love your stuff!</
                                      span></span></td>
  </tr>
</table>
</body>
</html>
```

As this page is a confirmation page, it contains no input fields. There is nothing new on this page. We again used the trick of setting the `rendered` attribute of some of the components to `false` so that the page previews properly when opening it directly in the browser, and also renders properly when it is being rendered by JSF.

The following screenshot shows how the file is rendered when opening it directly in the browser:

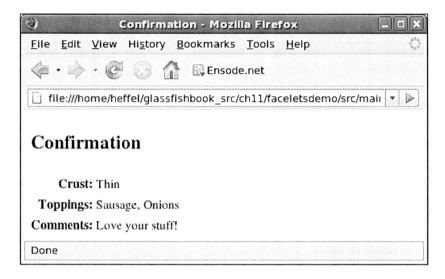

We are now done developing our simple application. After deploying it, we can test it by pointing the browser to `http://localhost:8080/faceletsdemo/index.jsf`.

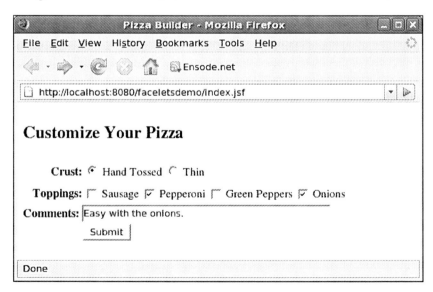

As we mentioned earlier, the rendered page is pretty much identical to the preview we saw by loading the XHTML file into the browser before deploying the WAR file. Submitting the form takes us to the rendered confirmation page.

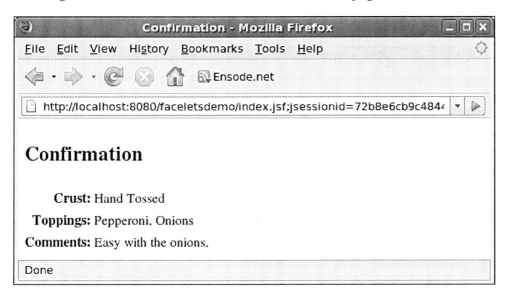

Again the rendered page looks pretty much identical to the version we previewed by opening the XML version in the browser.

Previewing pages in the browser without having to deploy an application is a great feature of Facelets; but of course, it only works if we don't use any custom components such as those found in JavaServer Faces component libraries like MyFaces Tomahawk or the Woodstock components. We can still use these components with Facelets, but they won't be rendered properly when loading the XHTML files in the browser. Before moving on, it is worth noting that JSF components can be used directly in Facelets XHTML. It is not necessary to convert standard XHTML components into JSF components via the `jsfc` attribute.

Facelets Templating

A typical web application contains several pages that share a look and feel. Sometimes customers want to make changes to the look and feel or layout of the application. For example, a customer may want to move a navigation menu from the left side of every page to the right side of every page. Facelets allow us to define the layout for all the pages in a web application in a template file. If we later need or desire to change the layout of all pages in the application, all we need to do is change the template; all other pages will automatically use the new layout.

The following example illustrates how to create a Facelets template page.

```
<?xml version="1.0" encoding="UTF-8" ?>
<!DOCTYPE html PUBLIC "-//W3C//DTD XHTML 1.0 Transitional//EN"
"http://www.w3.org/TR/xhtml1/DTD/xhtml1-transitional.dtd">
<html xmlns="http://www.w3.org/1999/xhtml"
  xmlns:ui="http://java.sun.com/jsf/facelets"
  xmlns:h="http://java.sun.com/jsf/html">
<head>
<meta http-equiv="Content-Type" content="text/html; charset=UTF-8" />
<title>Template Demo</title>
</head>
<body>
<h2>
  <ui:insert name="title">Title</ui:insert>
</h2>
<table cellspacing="0" cellpadding="0" border="1">
  <tr>
    <td width="160" valign="top"><b>Navigation</b><br />
    <a href="index.jsf">Home</a><br />
    <a href="articles.jsf">Articles</a><br />
    <a href="utilities.jsf">Utilities</a></td>
    <td width="100%" valign="top">
      <ui:insert name="body">Body goes here</ui:insert>
    </td>
  </tr>
</table>
</body>
</html>
```

A Facelets template needs to use a Facelets-specific component library; this library is declared by the xmlns:ui="http://java.sun.com/jsf/facelets" namespace. The `<ui:insert>` tag is what makes this page a template. A Facelets template must have at least one `<ui:insert>` tag. Each `<ui:insert>` tag has a required name attribute.

Pages using a template may declare a corresponding `<ui:define>` tag, which also has a name attribute. The body of the `<ui:define>` tag will be placed in the position of the corresponding `<ui:insert>` tag in the template; the name attribute of the `<ui:define>` tag must match the name attribute of the corresponding `<ui:insert>` tag in the template. If a page using a template is missing a `<ui:define>` tag corresponding to one of the template's `<ui:insert>` tags, then the body of the template page will be rendered in the appropriate position.

The following example illustrates how a page can use a template for its layout.

```
<?xml version="1.0" encoding="UTF-8" ?>
<!DOCTYPE html PUBLIC "-//W3C//DTD XHTML 1.0 Transitional//EN"
"http://www.w3.org/TR/xhtml1/DTD/xhtml1-transitional.dtd">
<html xmlns="http://www.w3.org/1999/xhtml"
  xmlns:ui="http://java.sun.com/jsf/facelets"
  xmlns:h="http://java.sun.com/jsf/html">
<head>
<meta http-equiv="Content-Type" content="text/html; charset=UTF-8" />
</head>
<body>
<ui:composition template="/template.xhtml">
  <ui:define name="title">
    <h:outputText>Welcome</h:outputText>
  </ui:define>

  <ui:define name="body">
    Welcome to the Facelets templating demo
    application.
  </ui:define>
</ui:composition>
</body>
</html>
```

We declare we are using a template by adding a `<ui:composition>` tag and specifying the template file as the value of its `template` attribute. `<ui:define>` tags need to be nested inside `<ui:composition>`. It doesn't matter in what order we place our `<ui:define>` tags, their bodies will be placed in the position corresponding to the matching `<ui:insert>` tag in the template.

The following screenshot illustrates how this markup is rendered after deploying the application's WAR file and pointing the browser to its URL.

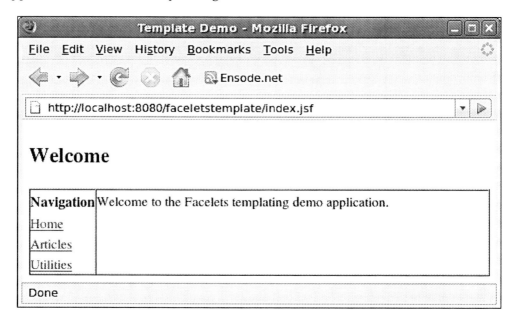

All pages using the template will display its title and body in the proper locations. Let's say we wish to center the title for every page, and that we would like to place the navigation links to the right of the page. All we need to do is modify the template page.

```
<?xml version="1.0" encoding="UTF-8" ?>
<!DOCTYPE html PUBLIC "-//W3C//DTD XHTML 1.0 Transitional//EN"
"http://www.w3.org/TR/xhtml1/DTD/xhtml1-transitional.dtd">
<html xmlns="http://www.w3.org/1999/xhtml"
  xmlns:ui="http://java.sun.com/jsf/facelets"
  xmlns:h="http://java.sun.com/jsf/html">
<head>
<meta http-equiv="Content-Type" content="text/html; charset=UTF-8" />
<title>Template Demo</title>
</head>
<body>
<h2 align="center">
  <ui:insert name="title">Title</ui:insert>
</h2>
```

```
<table cellspacing="0" cellpadding="0" border="1">
  <tr>
    <td width="100%" valign="top">
      <ui:insert name="body">Body goes here</ui:insert></td>
    <td width="160" valign="top"><b>Navigation</b><br />
    <a href="index.jsf">Home</a><br />
    <a href="articles.jsf">Articles</a><br />
    <a href="utilities.jsf">Utilities</a></td>
  </tr>
</table>
</body>
</html>
```

All we did to meet the new requirements was to add an `align` attribute to the `<h2>` tag and switch the order of the two table cells in the table used to lay out the page. After making these two changes and redeploying, the page now renders like this:

Of course all pages using the template will automatically use the new layout.

Ajax4jsf

Ajax4jsf is a library that greatly simplifies the task of developing AJAX-enabled applications. In essence, what Ajax4jsf allows us to do is to re-render one or more components in a page without having to submit the whole page. When a certain event occurs, for instance, a user enters a value on a text field or selects a value from a multiple select box, Ajax4jsf handles the event. It invokes a method on a managed bean then re-renders one or more components in the page. This allows us to create highly interactive AJAX-enabled applications.

More information about Ajax4jsf can be found at
`http://labs.jboss.com/jbossajax4jsf/`.

Downloading Ajax4jsf

Ajax4jsf can be downloaded by pointing the browser to `http://labs.jboss.com/jbossajax4jsf/downloads` and clicking on the **Download** link corresponding to the latest version.

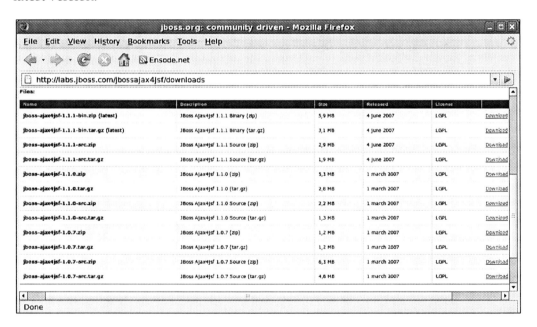

In order to start using Ajax4jsf in our applications, there are two JAR files that need to be extracted from the downloaded ZIP file. One of them will be named something like `ajax4jsf-1.1.0.jar`; the other one will be named something like `oscache-2.3.2.jar` (the exact names of these files will depend on the version of Ajax4jsf). These two JAR files need to be placed in the `WEB-INF/lib` directory of our web application.

Alternatively, if we are using Maven as our build tool, we can take advantage of Maven's dependency-management mechanism. The relevant sections of the `pom.xml` file will look like this:

```
<repositories>
    <repository>
      <id>repository.jboss.com</id>
      <name>Jboss Repository for Maven</name>
      <url>http://repository.jboss.com/maven2/</url>
      <layout>default</layout>
    </repository>
    <!-- Additional repositories can be added -->
</repositories>
<dependencies>
    <dependency>
      <groupId>org.ajax4jsf</groupId>
      <artifactId>ajax4jsf</artifactId>
      <version>[1.1.1,)</version>
    </dependency>
    <!-- Additional dependencies can be added -->
</dependencies>
```

The elements inside the `<repository>` element tell Maven what repository to download Ajax4jsf from. The elements inside the `<dependency>` element tell Maven that our application depends on the Ajax4jsf library. The first time we build our application, Maven will download Ajax4jsf from its repository along with all of its dependencies.

Configuring Our JSF Application for Ajax4jsf

Before we can use Ajax4jsf to AJAX enable our JSF application, we need to configure it by modifying its `web.xml` deployment descriptor.

```
<web-app xmlns="http://java.sun.com/xml/ns/javaee"
version="2.5"
  xmlns:xsi="http://www.w3.org/2001/XMLSchema-instance"
  xsi:schemaLocation="http://java.sun.com/xml/ns/
    javaee http://java.sun.com/xml/ns/javaee/web-app_2_5.xsd">
  <context-param>
    <param-name>javax.faces.STATE_SAVING_METHOD</param-name>
    <param-value>server</param-value>
```

```
    </context-param>
    <listener>
      <listener-class>
        com.sun.faces.config.ConfigureListener
      </listener-class>
    </listener>
    <servlet>
      <servlet-name>Faces Servlet</servlet-name>
      <servlet-class>javax.faces.webapp.FacesServlet</
                servlet-class>
      <load-on-startup>1</load-on-startup>
    </servlet>
    <servlet-mapping>
      <servlet-name>Faces Servlet</servlet-name>
      <url-pattern>*.jsf</url-pattern>
    </servlet-mapping>
    <filter>
      <filter-name>a4j</filter-name>
      <filter-class>org.ajax4jsf.Filter</filter-class>
    </filter>
    <filter-mapping>
      <filter-name>a4j</filter-name>
      <url-pattern>/*</url-pattern>
    </filter-mapping>
  </web-app>
```

All we need to do in our `web.xml` file is set up a filter that will intercept all requests. This filter is included with Ajax4jsf and contains functionality that allows the library to do its job.

Writing an AJAX-Enabled Application with Ajax4jsf

Once we have added the Ajax4jsf filter to the application's `web.xml` deployment descriptor, we are ready to develop our AJAX-enabled JSF web application. We will illustrate how to proceed with an example. The example is a page for a fictitious online computer store. The page we will develop allows a user to customize a laptop computer they are about to purchase; as they select different components for the laptop, its price is updated accordingly. The new price is immediately displayed on the page, without having to submit the whole page to the server.

Without further ado, let's look at the markup for this AJAX-enabled page.

```
<%@ taglib uri="https://ajax4jsf.dev.java.net/ajax" prefix="a4j"%>
<%@ taglib uri="http://java.sun.com/jsf/core" prefix="f"%>
<%@ taglib uri="http://java.sun.com/jsf/html" prefix="h"%>
<%@ page language="java" contentType="text/html; charset=UTF-8"
  pageEncoding="UTF-8"%>
<!DOCTYPE html PUBLIC "-//W3C//DTD HTML 4.01 Transitional//EN"
"http://www.w3.org/TR/html4/loose.dtd">
<html>
<head>
<meta http-equiv="Content-Type" content="text/html; charset=UTF-8">
<title>Customize Your Laptop</title>
</head>
<body>
<h2>Customize Your Laptop</h2>
<f:view>
  <h:form>
    <table cellpadding="0" cellspacing="0" border="0">
      <tr>
        <td align="right"><h:outputLabel for="screenField"
          value="Screen:"></h:outputLabel> </td>
        <td><h:selectOneMenu id="screenField"
          value="#{laptop.screen}">
          <a4j:support event="onchange"
                       action="#{laptop.recalculatePrice}"
                       reRender="priceText">
          </a4j:support>
          <f:selectItem itemLabel="14.1 inches" itemValue=
              "14.1 inches" />
          <f:selectItem itemLabel="15.4 inches" itemValue=
              "15.4 inches" />
          <f:selectItem itemLabel="17 inches" itemValue=
              "17 inches" />
        </h:selectOneMenu></td>
        <td align="right"> 
          <h:outputLabel for="processorField"
                         value="Processor:">
          </h:outputLabel> </td>
```

```
    <td><h:selectOneMenu id="processorField"
      value="#{laptop.processor}">
      <a4j:support event="onchange"
                action="#{laptop.recalculatePrice}"
                reRender="priceText"></a4j:support>
      <f:selectItem itemLabel="1 GHz" itemValue="1 GHz" />
      <f:selectItem itemLabel="2 GHz" itemValue="2 GHz" />
      <f:selectItem itemLabel="2.5 GHz" itemValue="2.5 GHz" />
    </h:selectOneMenu></td>
    <td align="right"> 
              <h:outputLabel for="memoryField"
      value="Memory:"></h:outputLabel> </td>
    <td><h:selectOneMenu id="memoryField"
      value="#{laptop.memory}">
      <a4j:support event="onchange"
                action="#{laptop.recalculatePrice}"
                reRender="priceText"></a4j:support>
      <f:selectItem itemLabel="512 MB" itemValue="512 MB" />
      <f:selectItem itemLabel="1 GB" itemValue="1 GB" />
      <f:selectItem itemLabel="2 GB" itemValue="2 GB" />
    </h:selectOneMenu></td>
    <td align="right"> <h:outputLabel for="priceText"
      value="Price:"></h:outputLabel> </td>
    <td>$
      <h:outputText id="priceText"
                value="#{laptop.price}">
      </h:outputText>
       USD
    </td>
  </tr>
  <tr>
    <td> </td>
    <!-- Dummy, "for looks only" button. -->
    <td colspan="7" align="left"><h:commandButton
      value="Submit"></h:commandButton></td>
  </tr>
  </table>
  </h:form>
</f:view>
</body>
</html>
```

All we had to do to AJAX-enable our page was add the Ajax4jsf tag library via the following line:

```
<%@ taglib uri="https://ajax4jsf.dev.java.net/ajax" prefix="a4j"%>
```

We then used the `<a4j:support>` tag from this library to add AJAX support to the three `<h:selectOneMenu>` components in the page. As you can see, we need to nest the `<a4j:support>` tag inside the elements we need to AJAX-enable.

The `<a4j:support>` tag contains three attributes that allow it to perform its functionality. The `event` attribute allows us to specify what event to tie the AJAX event to. In the example, we used `onchange`, but any valid event for the parent component such as `onblur`, `onmousover`, etc. can be used.

The next attribute we need to specify is the `action` attribute. This attribute's value must be a binding-value expression resolving to a managed bean's method. The method that this value expression resolves to must not have any arguments. Typically, this method will update one or more of a managed bean's properties, so that the new value(s) can be rendered on the page. In our example, the value of this attribute points to a method called `recalculatePrice()` in a managed bean named `laptop`. This method recalculates the laptop's price based on the user's selections.

The last attribute we need to specify is the `reRender` attribute. This attribute's value must contain one or more component IDs for components we need to re-render after the event specified in the tag's `event` attribute takes place. In our example, we used `priceText` as the value of this attribute, which matches the ID of the `outputText` component near the bottom of the page. If we need to specify more than one component ID as the value of the `reRender` attribute, we need to separate them with commas.

As you can see, all we really need to do to AJAX-enable our page is to nest an `<a4j:support>` element inside any components we would like to add AJAX support for.

Our page refers to a managed bean named laptop. Here is the code for that bean:

```
package net.ensode.glassfishbook;

public class Laptop
{
  private String screen;
  private String processor;
  private String memory;
  private int price;

  private static int BASE_PRICE = 500;
```

```java
public Laptop()
{
  price = BASE_PRICE;
  screen = "14.1 inches";
  processor = "1 GHz";
  memory = "512 MB";
}

public String getMemory()
{
  return memory;
}

public void setMemory(String memory)
{
  this.memory = memory;
}

public String getProcessor()
{
  return processor;
}

public void setProcessor(String processor)
{
  this.processor = processor;
}

public String getScreen()
{
  return screen;
}

public void setScreen(String screen)
{
  this.screen = screen;
}

public int getPrice()
{
  return price;
}

public void setPrice(int price)
{
  this.price = price;
}
```

```
public void recalculatePrice()
{
  price = BASE_PRICE;

  if (screen.equals("15.4 inches"))
  {
    price += 50;
  }
  else if (screen.equals("17 inches"))
  {
    price += 100;
  }

  if (processor.equals("2 GHz"))
  {
    price += 100;
  }
  else if (processor.equals("2.5 GHz"))
  {
    price += 150;
  }

  if (memory.equals("1 GB"))
  {
    price += 50;
  }
  else if (memory.equals("2 GB"))
  {
    price += 100;
  }
}
}
```

Other than the `recalculatePrice()` method, the bean simply consists of
a few properties and their corresponding getter and setter methods. The
`recalculatePrice()` method is the one that is automatically invoked every time a
user changes one of the options from any of the drop-down components. All it does
is check the value of the bean's screen, processor, and memory properties, which
are bound to the value of the drop-down components and therefore automatically
updated when the user picks a new value, and calculates a new price for the
laptop. This new price is automatically displayed on the page by Ajax4jsf, because
it is bound to the `<h:outputText>` component with ID of `priceText`, and this
component is the one we specified as the value of the `reRender` attribute of all
`<a4j:support>` tags in the page.

This bean, of course, needs to be declared in the application's `faces-config.xml` deployment descriptor.

```
<faces-config xmlns="http://java.sun.com/xml/ns/javaee"
    xmlns:xsi="http://www.w3.org/2001/XMLSchema-instance"
    xsi:schemaLocation="http://java.sun.com/xml/ns/javaee http://java.
                    sun.com/xml/ns/javaee/web-facesconfig_1_2.xsd"
    version="1.2">
  <managed-bean>
    <managed-bean-name>laptop</managed-bean-name>
    <managed-bean-class>
      net.ensode.glassfishbook.Laptop
    </managed-bean-class>
    <managed-bean-scope>request</managed-bean-scope>
  </managed-bean>
</faces-config>
```

As we can see, no special configuration needs to be done in this file to AJAX-enable the application.

After packaging the application into a WAR file, deploying it, and pointing the browser to its URL, we should see a page like the following:

The price at the right of the screen is updated automatically as the user selects different values for each of the dropdowns. A screenshot does not do this application much justice; in order to really appreciate the value of Ajax4jsf, readers are encouraged to download the source code for this application, and deploy it to see it in action.

As you can see, Ajax4jsf makes it almost too easy to add AJAX capabilities to our JSF applications, making it pretty much an obvious choice when we wish to add this kind of functionality to our applications.

Seam

Seam is a framework that simplifies the development of applications using JavaServer Faces (JSF) and the Java Persistence API (JPA). Seam was conceived by Gavin King, of Hibernate fame. Although Seam is distributed by JBoss, it is not tied to the JBoss Application server. Seam application can be deployed to any Java EE-compliant application server, such as GlassFish.

Seam provides a number of advantages over plain JSF, such as:

- Seam allows binding EJB components directly to JSF pages, which actually reduces/eliminates the glue code otherwise needed.

- Seam reduces the usage of XML required by plain JSF, as managed beans can be declared as such via annotations, eliminating the need to specify them in the `faces-config.xml` deployment descriptor.

- Seam can take advantage of Hibernate-specific functionality and easily integrate it into JSF applications.

Downloading Seam

Seam can be downloaded by pointing the browser to
`http://labs.jboss.com/jbossseam/download` and clicking on the
Download link for the latest stable Seam version.

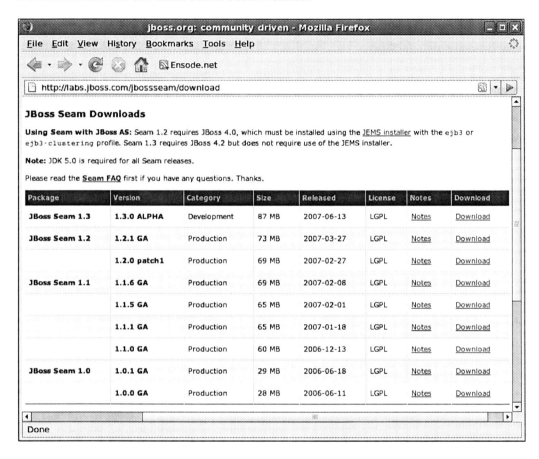

The downloaded file will be called `jboss-seam-1.2.1.GA.zip`, or similar,
depending on the exact version of Seam. We will be referring to this file simply as
"the Seam ZIP file" in the next few sections.

Seam applications typically consist of one or more JAR files containing Enterprise
JavaBeans, and a WAR file containing a web application. It is common practice
to package the EJB JAR file(s), the WAR file, and any of their dependencies in an
Enterprise Archive (EAR) file. The following JAR files from the Seam download must
be placed in the root directory of our EAR file:

- `jboss-seam.jar`
- `hibernate-all.jar`
- `thirdparty-all.jar`

`jboss-seam.jar` is the primary Seam library, containing classes needed for any Seam application. It can be found under the root directory of the Seam ZIP file. `hibernate-all.jar` contains classes needed when using Hibernate as the JPA provider for an application. It can be found under the `lib` directory of the Seam ZIP file.

> GlassFish comes preconfigured with Toplink Essentials as the default JPA provider. This default JPA provider can be swapped for another if we wish to do so. As Seam can take advantage of Hibernate-specific extensions to the JPA specification, Seam applications typically use Hibernate as their JPA provider.

`thirdparty-all.jar` contains several third-party libraries needed by Seam and/or Hibernate. It can be found under the `lib` directory of the Seam ZIP file.

Additionally, Seam includes a number of JSF components; these are included in a JAR file called `jboss-seam-ui.jar`. This file can be found under the root directory of the Seam ZIP file. If we wish to use Seam-specific components in our application, we need to include this file in the `WEB-INF/lib` directory of our WAR file.

In the following sections, we will be developing a modified version of the example discussed in the *Integrating JSF and JPA* section of Chapter 6. The application will be modified to take advantage of the Seam framework.

Configuring a Seam Application

Configuring a Seam application is not much different from configuring a standard application using JSF and JPA. In addition to the standard deployment descriptor, a Seam application can have an additional deployment descriptor called `component.xml`.

```
<?xml version="1.0" encoding="UTF-8"?>
<components xmlns="http://jboss.com/products/seam/components"
            xmlns:core="http://jboss.com/products/seam/core">
    <core:init
       jndi-pattern="java:comp/env/seamdemo/#{ejbName}/local" />
</components>
```

For our example, the only thing we need to set up in this file is the `<core:init>` element of this deployment descriptor. This element lets our web application know what JNDI name to use to look up EJBs used in the application.

The value of for the `jndi-pattern` for this element must always start with the string `java:comp/env`, as this is the standard Environment Naming Context (ENC) for Java EE applications. After that, we can use any pattern we wish, but the `#{ejbName}` string must be included in the pattern. This string will resolve to the value of the Seam-specific `@Name` annotation for the EJB in question. We will discuss this annotation in the next section.

The `components.xml` deployment descriptor must be placed in the `WEB-INF` directory of the web application's WAR file.

Just as for any Java EE web application, a `web.xml` deployment descriptor must be present in the `WEB-INF` directory of the application's WAR file at deployment time.

```xml
<?xml version="1.0" encoding="UTF-8"?>
<web-app version="2.5" xmlns="http://java.sun.com/xml/ns/javaee"
xmlns:xsi="http://www.w3.org/2001/XMLSchema-instance" xsi:
schemaLocation="http://java.sun.com/xml/ns/javaee http://java.sun.com/
xml/ns/javaee/web-app_2_5.xsd">
  <servlet>
    <servlet-name>Faces Servlet</servlet-name>
    <servlet-class>
      javax.faces.webapp.FacesServlet
    </servlet-class>
    <load-on-startup>1</load-on-startup>
  </servlet>
  <servlet-mapping>
    <servlet-name>Faces Servlet</servlet-name>
    <url-pattern>*.jsf</url-pattern>
  </servlet-mapping>
  <ejb-local-ref>
    <ejb-ref-name>
      seamdemo/CustomerController/local
    </ejb-ref-name>
    <ejb-ref-type>Session</ejb-ref-type>
    <local-home/>
    <local>
      net.ensode.glassfishbook.CustomerControllerLocal
    </local>
    <ejb-link>CustomerController</ejb-link>
  </ejb-local-ref>
</web-app>
```

As we can see, the `web.xml` deployment descriptor for a Seam application is not much different from a `web.xml` deployment descriptor for a JSF application not using Seam. The `<ejb-local-ref>` element is needed so that the code in the WAR file can perform JNDI lookups on the EJBs it depends on. One thing to notice is that the value of the `<ejb-ref-name>` element matches the pattern we declared in the `components.xml` deployment descriptor (minus the `java:comp/env` Environment Naming Context); in this case, the value of the `@Name` annotation for the EJB is used instead of the `#{ejbName}` expression.

As Seam applications are JSF applications, a `faces-config.xml` deployment descriptor must be present in the WAR file's `WEB-INF` directory.

```
<?xml version='1.0' encoding='UTF-8'?>

<faces-config version="1.2"
    xmlns="http://java.sun.com/xml/ns/javaee"
    xmlns:xsi="http://www.w3.org/2001/XMLSchema-instance"
    xsi:schemaLocation="http://java.sun.com/xml/ns/javaee http://java.
sun.com/xml/ns/javaee/web-facesconfig_1_2.xsd">

  <navigation-rule>
    <from-view-id>/save_customer.jsp</from-view-id>
    <navigation-case>
      <from-outcome>success</from-outcome>
      <to-view-id>/customer_saved.jsp</to-view-id>
    </navigation-case>
    <navigation-case>
      <from-outcome>failure</from-outcome>
      <to-view-id>/error_saving_customer.jsp</to-view-id>
    </navigation-case>
  </navigation-rule>

  <lifecycle>
    <phase-listener>
      org.jboss.seam.jsf.SeamPhaseListener
    </phase-listener>
  </lifecycle>
</faces-config>
```

When developing Seam applications, it is not necessary to declare managed beans in the `faces-config.xml` deployment descriptor; instead Seam-specific annotations are added to the managed beans.

Just as with any JSF application, navigation rules must be declared in the `faces-config.xml` deployment descriptor.

JSF phase listeners are Java classes implementing the `javax.faces.event.PhaseListener` interface. This interface has a number of methods that are invoked automatically either before a JSF life-cycle phase starts or after it ends. Seam provides a custom phase listener to implement its functionality. This phase listener must be declared in the `faces-config.xml` as shown in the preceding example.

The three preceding deployment descriptors are packaged and deployed with the application's WAR file.

The EJB JAR file for our EJB components must contain a `seam.properties` file. This file contains Seam-specific properties. Even if we don't need to add any properties, the file must still be there, because it lets Seam know that there are Seam components in the JAR file. This file must be placed in the `META-INF` directory of the EJB JAR file. Our example application does not need any properties; therefore it has an empty `seam.properties` file in this location.

JPA entities are typically packaged in the EJB JAR file of a Seam application, therefore a standard JPA `persistence.xml` deployment descriptor must be placed in the JAR file's `META-INF` directory; refer to Chapter 4 for details on this deployment descriptor.

 As we mentioned before, it is recommended to use Hibernate as a JPA provider when developing and deploying Seam applications. Simply adding the Hibernate libraries to the application's EAR file will allow the application to use Hibernate as a JPA provider. No special configuration is needed.

Finally, just as with any EAR file, an `application.xml` deployment descriptor must be present in the EAR file's `META-INF` directory.

```xml
<?xml version="1.0" encoding="UTF-8"?>
<application version="5" xmlns="http://java.sun.com/xml/ns/
javaee" xmlns:xsi="http://www.w3.org/2001/XMLSchema-instance" xsi:
schemaLocation="http://java.sun.com/xml/ns/javaee http://java.sun.com/
xml/ns/javaee/application_5.xsd">
  <display-name>Registration</display-name>
  <module>
    <web>
      <web-uri>seamdemo.war</web-uri>
      <context-root>/seamdemo</context-root>
    </web>
  </module>
  <module>
    <ejb>seamdemo.jar</ejb>
  </module>
</application>
```

As you can see, no Seam-specific configuration is needed in this deployment descriptor. It simply declares the web and EJB module(s) in the application.

Developing a Seam Application

One of the nice features of Seam is that it allows session beans to be managed beans in JSF applications. This allows us to take advantage of EJB features such as container-managed transactions and security in our managed beans.

Our application has two managed beans: one acts as a controller in the Model View Controller design pattern, the other one acts as the model. Our controller is a session bean; it is a modified version of the CustomerController class we saw in Chapter 6.

```java
package net.ensode.glassfishbook;

import java.sql.Connection;
import java.sql.PreparedStatement;
import java.sql.ResultSet;
import java.sql.SQLException;

import javax.annotation.Resource;
import javax.ejb.Stateless;
import javax.interceptor.Interceptors;
import javax.persistence.EntityManager;
import javax.persistence.EntityManagerFactory;
import javax.persistence.PersistenceUnit;
import javax.sql.DataSource;

import org.jboss.seam.annotations.In;
import org.jboss.seam.annotations.Name;

@Stateless
@Name("CustomerController")
@Interceptors({org.jboss.seam.ejb.SeamInterceptor.class})
public class CustomerController implements
    CustomerControllerLocal
{
  @Resource(name = "jdbc/__CustomerDBPool")
  private DataSource dataSource;

  @PersistenceUnit(unitName = "customerPersistenceUnit")
  private EntityManagerFactory entityManagerFactory;

  @In
  private Customer customer;

  public String saveCustomer()
  {
    String returnValue = "success";
    EntityManager entityManager =
```

```
      entityManagerFactory.createEntityManager();
    try
    {
      Long customerId = getNewCustomerId();
      customer.setCustomerId(customerId);
      entityManager.persist(customer);
    }
    catch (Exception e)
    {
      e.printStackTrace();
      returnValue = "failure";
    }
    return returnValue;
  }
  private Long getNewCustomerId()
  {
    Connection connection;
    Long newCustomerId = null;
    try
    {
      connection = dataSource.getConnection();
      PreparedStatement preparedStatement =
          connection.prepareStatement(
          "select max(customer_id)+1 as new_customer_id " +
          "from customers");
      ResultSet resultSet = preparedStatement.executeQuery();
      if (resultSet != null && resultSet.next())
      {
        newCustomerId = resultSet.getLong("new_customer_id");
      }
      connection.close();
    }
    catch (SQLException e)
    {
      e.printStackTrace();
    }
    return newCustomerId;
  }
}
```

The main differences between this controller class and the one we saw in Chapter 6 is that this version is a stateless session bean, as declared by the `@Stateless` annotation. Also, the Seam specific `@Name` annotation is used to declare the name of the session bean. This name is used in the `<ejb-ref-name>` element of the web application's `web.xml` deployment descriptor to access this session bean. Also, the `#{ejbName}` expression in the `<core:init>` element of the `component.xml` deployment descriptor resolves to the value of this annotation.

EJB interceptors are Java classes that contain a method annotated with the `@AroundInvoke` annotation, returning an instance of `java.lang.Object` and taking a single instance of `javax.ejb.InvocationContext` as a parameter. This method is invoked before and after any EJB that uses this interceptor. Interceptor usage in a bean is done via the `@Interceptors` annotation. This annotation takes an array of interceptor classes as a parameter. Alternatively, EJB interceptors can be declared in the EJB JAR's `ejb-jar.xml` deployment descriptor. This alternative approach is used when several EJBs need to use the same interceptor, as we don't need to decorate all of them with the `@Interceptors` annotation.

For Seam applications, session beans need to use a Seam-specific interceptor, defined in the `org.jboss.seam.ejb.SeamInterceptor` class.

The `Customer` class is a JPA entity containing customer information. In the previous version of the application, we declared a `getCustomer()` and a `setCustomer()` method to get and set the customer property of the controller. In this version, we took advantage of the Seam-specific `@In` annotation to inject an instance of the Customer class into the controller. The property name (`customer`, in this example) must match the value of the `@Name` annotation of the injected class.

The business interface for the `CustomerController` session bean is called `CustomerControllerLocal`. It is a standard session-bean business interface decorated with the `@Local` annotation.

The `Customer` class is a JPA entity and it is also used as a JSF managed bean.

```
package net.ensode.glassfishbook;

import java.io.Serializable;

import javax.persistence.Column;
import javax.persistence.Entity;
import javax.persistence.Id;
import javax.persistence.Table;

import org.jboss.seam.ScopeType;
import org.jboss.seam.annotations.Name;
import org.jboss.seam.annotations.Scope;

import org.hibernate.validator.NotNull;
```

```java
import org.hibernate.validator.Length;
@Entity
@Table(name = "CUSTOMERS")
@Name("customer")
@Scope(ScopeType.EVENT)
public class Customer implements Serializable
{
  @Id
  @Column(name = "CUSTOMER_ID")
  private Long customerId;

  @Column(name = "FIRST_NAME")
  private String firstName;

  @Column(name = "LAST_NAME")
  private String lastName;

  private String email;

  public Long getCustomerId()
  {
    return customerId;
  }
  public void setCustomerId(Long customerId)
  {
    this.customerId = customerId;
  }
  public String getEmail()
  {
    return email;
  }
  public void setEmail(String email)
  {
    this.email = email;
  }
  @NotNull
  @Length(min=2,max=10)
  public String getFirstName()
  {
    return firstName;
  }
  public void setFirstName(String firstName)
  {
    this.firstName = firstName;
  }
```

```
@NotNull
@Length(min=2,max=20)
public String getLastName()
{
   return lastName;
}
public void setLastName(String lastName)
{
   this.lastName = lastName;
}
}
```

The only difference between this version of the `Customer` class, and the one we saw previously, is the addition of some Seam- and Hibernate-specific annotations. The `@Name` annotation gives this class a name so that it can be injected into other classes via the Seam-specific `@In` annotation.

The `@Scope` annotation is a Seam-specific annotation that indicates the scope of the managed bean. Some of the valid values for this annotation are `ScopeType.EVENT`, which is equivalent to the request scope in standard JSF, `ScopeType.PAGE`, `ScopeType.SESSION`, and `ScopeType.APPLICATION`. These last three are equivalent to the page, session, and application scopes in standard JSF. There are also Seam-specific scopes that can be used as values for this annotation; consult the Seam documentation for details.

Some of the getter methods in the `Customer` class are annotated with Hibernate-specific annotations. These annotations allow Seam to validate values for the corresponding fields. The `@NotNull` annotation marks a field as required. The `@Length` annotation allows us to state the minimum and/or maximum length of a field. Seam integrates these annotations with JSF validation without us having to do any additional configuration or coding.

The `Customer` and `CustomerController` classes are deployed as part of an EJB JAR file. The application's WAR file contains only JSPs and deployment descriptors. There is nothing special we need to do to make the JSPs work with Seam. One thing worth mentioning is that value-binding expressions need to use the value of the `@Name` annotation of the EJB or entity in order to access its methods or properties, where in standard JSF the bean name is defined in the `<managed-bean-name>` element of the `faces-config.xml` deployment descriptor.

After compiling, packaging, and deploying our application, and pointing the browser to its URL, we should see a data-entry page for customer information.

Entering valid data where required results in a confirmation screen like the one shown in Chapter 6; however, entering invalid data results in the data entry page reloading and showing appropriate
error messages.

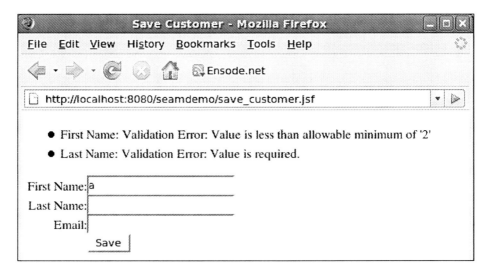

Here, we can see Seam's JSF and Hibernate validation annotation validation in action.

As we have seen in this section, Seam simplifies integration of JPA and JSF by providing custom annotations and a simpler programming model. When using standard JSF, it is not possible to use session beans as JSF managed beans, therefore if we need to take advantage of EJB features such as security or container-managed transactions, we need to invoke methods on session beans from JSF managed beans. By allowing session beans to become JSF managed beans, Seam reduces the number of classes we need to write considerably.

Summary

In this chapter, we covered some frameworks that build on top of the Java EE specification.

We covered how to use Facelets as an alternative view technology for JSF, including how to write pages in standard XHTML and have Facelets translate XHTML elements into JSF components via the `jsfc` attribute. We also covered how to separate a page's layout from its contents by taking advantage of Facelets templates.

Additionally, we covered how to easily AJAX-enable JSF web applications via the Ajax4jsf API.

Finally, we covered how to write applications using the Seam framework, a JBoss framework that integrates JavaServer Faces and EJB 3, including the Java Persistence API.

Sending Email from Java EE Applications

Applications deployed to GlassFish or any other Java EE-compliant application server frequently need the ability to send emails. Thanks to the JavaMail API, part of the Java EE 5 specification, sending emails from Java EE applications is fairly simple.

In order to implement the ability to send emails from a Java EE application, we need to have access to a mail server, typically one using the Simple Mail Transfer Protocol (SMTP)

GlassFish Configuration

Before we can start sending emails from our Java EE applications, we need to do some initial GlassFish configuration. A new JavaMail session needs to be added by logging into the GlassFish web console, expanding the **Resources** node in the tree at the left-hand side of the page, then clicking on the **JavaMail Sessions** node.

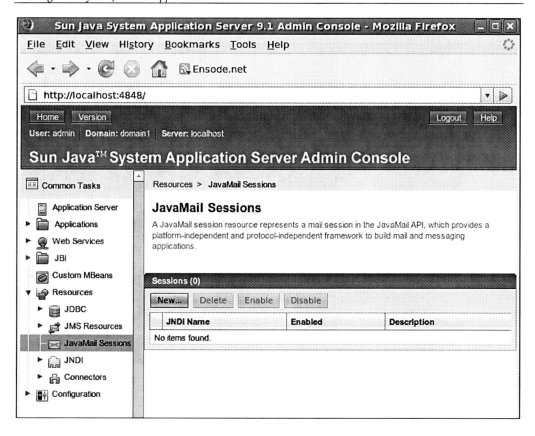

To create a new JavaMail session, we need to click on the **New...** button. The main area of the screen will look like the following screenshot:

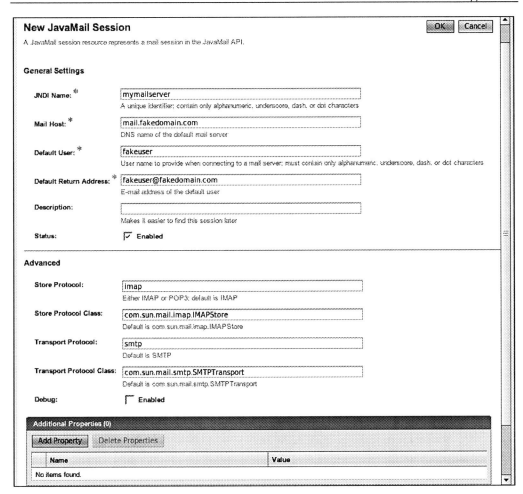

In the **JNDI Name** field, we need to provide a JNDI name for our JavaMail session. This name must be a valid, unique name of our choosing. Applications will use this name to access the mail session.

In the **Mail Host** field, we need to specify the DNS name of the mail server we will be using to send emails.

In the **Default User** field, we need to specify the default user name to use to connect to the mail server.

In the **Default Return Address** field, we need to specify the default email address that email recipients can use to reply to messages sent by our applications.

Specifying a Fake Return Address

The default return address does not have to be a real email address. We can specify an invalid email address here. Keep in mind that if we do this, then users will be unable to reply to emails sent from our applications, therefore it would be a good idea to include a warning in the message body letting the users know that they cannot reply to the message.

We can optionally add a description for the JavaMail session in the **Description** field.

The **Status** checkbox allows us to enable or disable the JavaMail session. Disabled sessions are not accessible by applications.

The **Store Protocol** is used to specify the value of the storage protocol of the mail server, which is used to allow our applications to retrieve email messages from it. Valid values for this field include **imap**, **imaps**, **pop3**, and **pop3s**. Consult your system administrator for the correct value for your server.

Store Protocol Ignored If Applications Only Send Emails

It is a lot more common to have our applications be required to send emails than it is to have them receive emails. If all applications using our mail session will only be sending emails, then the value of the Store Protocol field (and the Store Protocol Class field, discussed next) will be ignored.

The **Store Protocol Class** field is used to indicate the service provider implementation class corresponding to the specified store protocol. Valid values for this field include:

- `com.sun.mail.imap.IMAPStore` for a store protocol of IMAP
- `com.sun.mail.imap.IMAPSSLStore` for a store protocol of IMAPS
- `com.sun.mail.pop3.POP3Store` for a store protocol of POP3
- `com.sun.mail.pop3.POP3SSLStore` for a store protocol of POP3S

The **Transport Protocol** field is used to specify the value of the transport protocol of the mail server, which is used to allow our applications to send email messages through it. Valid values for this field include **smtp** and **smtps**. Consult your system administrator for the correct value for your server.

The **Transport Protocol Class** field is used to specify the service provider implementation class corresponding to the specified transport protocol. Valid values for this field include:

- `com.sun.mail.smtp.SMTPTransport` for a transport protocol of SMTP
- `com.sun.mail.smtp.SMTPSSLTransport` for a transport protocol of SMTPS

The **Debug** checkbox allows us to enable or disable debugging for the JavaMail session.

If we need to add additional properties to the JavaMail session, we can do so by clicking on the **Add Property** button near the bottom of the page, then entering the property name and value in the corresponding fields.

Once we have entered all the required information for our server, we need to click on the OK button at the top right of the page to create the JavaMail session. Once it is created, it is ready to be used by deployed applications.

Implementing Email Delivery Functionality

Once we have set up a JavaMail session as described in the previous section, implementing the email delivery functionality is fairly simple. The process is illustrated in the following code example:

```
package net.ensode.glassfishbook;

import javax.annotation.Resource;
import javax.mail.Message;
import javax.mail.MessagingException;
import javax.mail.Session;
import javax.mail.Transport;
import javax.mail.internet.AddressException;
import javax.mail.internet.InternetAddress;
import javax.mail.internet.MimeMessage;

public class FeedbackBean
{
  private String subject;
  private String body;

  @Resource(name = "mymailserver")
  Session session;

  public String sendEmail()
  {
```

```
        try
        {
          Message msg = new MimeMessage(session);
          msg.setRecipient(Message.RecipientType.TO,
              new InternetAddress(
              "customer@customerdomain.com"));
          msg.setSubject(subject);
          msg.setText(body);

          Transport.send(msg);
        }
        catch (AddressException e)
        {
          e.printStackTrace();
          return "failure";
        }
        catch (MessagingException e)
        {
          e.printStackTrace();
          return "failure";
        }
        return "success";
    }
    public String getBody()
    {
      return body;
    }
    public void setBody(String body)
    {
      this.body = body;
    }
    public String getSubject()
    {
      return subject;
    }
    public void setSubject(String subject)
    {
      this.subject = subject;
    }
}
```

This class is used as a managed bean for a simple JSF application. For brevity, other parts of the application are not shown, as they do not deal with email functionality. The full application can be downloaded from this book's website.

The first thing we need to do is inject an instance of the JavaMail session created as described in the previous section by adding a class-level variable of type `javax.mail.Session` and decorating it with the `@Resource` annotation. The value of the name attribute of this annotation must match the JNDI name we gave our JavaMail session when it was created.

We then need to create an instance of `javax.mail.internet.MimeMessage`, passing the session object as a parameter to its constructor.

Once we create an instance of `javax.mail.internet.MimeMessage`, we need to add a message recipient by invoking its `setRecipient()` method. The first parameter for this method indicates if the recipient is to be sent the message (TO), carbon copied (CC), or Blind Carbon Copied (BCC). We can indicate the type of recipient by using `Message.RecipientType.TO`, `Message.RecipientType.CC`, or `Message.RecipientType.BCC` as appropriate. The second parameter to the `setRecipient()` method indicates the email address of the recipient. This parameter is of type `javax.mail.Address`. This class is an abstract class, therefore we need to used one of its subclasses, specifically `javax.mail.internet.InternetAddress`. The constructor for this class takes a String parameter containing the email address of the recipient. The `setRecipient()` method can be invoked multiple times to add recipients to be sent, copied, or blind copied the message. Only a single address can be specified for each recipient type.

If we need to send a message to multiple recipients, we can use the `addRecipients()` method of the `javax.mail.Message` class (or one of its subclasses, like `javax.mail.internet.MimeMessage`). This method takes the recipient type as its first parameter, and an array of `javax.mail.Address` as its second parameter. The message will be sent to all recipients in the array. By using this method instead of `setRecipient()`, we are not limited to a single recipient per recipient type.

Once we have specified the recipient or recipients, we need to add the message subject and text by invoking the `setSubject()` and `setText()` methods on the message instance, respectively.

Once we have set the message subject and text, we are ready to send it. This can be accomplished by invoking the static `send()` method on the `javax.mail.Transport` class. This method takes the message instance as a parameter.

B
IDE Integration

GlassFish provides integration with two of the most popular Java IDE's: NetBeans and Eclipse. NetBeans, being a Sun Microsystems product, just like GlassFish, provides GlassFish integration "out of the box". GlassFish provides an Eclipse server adapter.

NetBeans

NetBeans Standard and Full editions contain "out of the box" support for GlassFish. When installing one of these editions of NetBeans, GlassFish is also installed. NetBeans can be downloaded from `http://www.netbeans.org`.

NetBeans has several project categories; Java EE applications can be created from the Web and Enterprise categories.

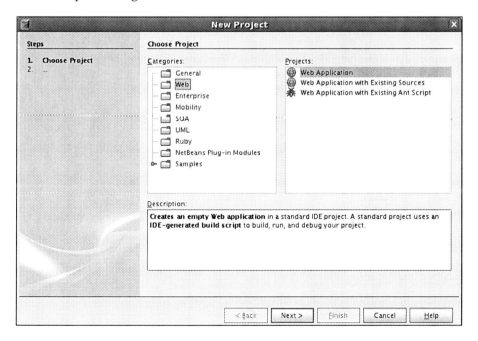

For most project types in the Enterprise or Web categories, NetBeans requires us to select an application server where the project will be deployed. GlassFish is labeled **Sun Java System Application 9** in the drop-down box used to select a server.

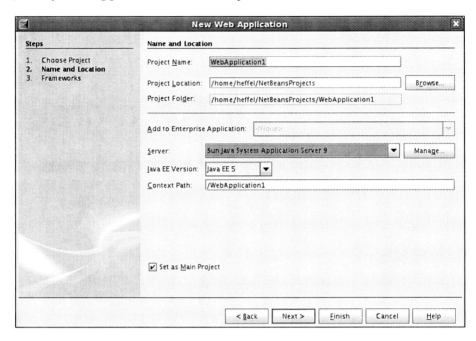

Once we create the project and we are ready to deploy it, we simply need to right-click on the project and select **Deploy Project** from the resulting pop-up menu.

The project will be automatically built, packaged, and deployed. For web applications, we also get the **Run Project** and **Debug Project** options. Both of these options, in addition to building, packaging, and deploying the project, automatically open a new browser window and point it to the application's URL. When we select **Debug Project**, GlassFish will be started in debug mode, if necessary, and we can use the NetBeans debugger to debug our project.

Eclipse

Unlike NetBeans, Eclipse does not come with GlassFish support out of the box. Fortunately, it is very easy to add GlassFish support. Eclipse can be downloaded from `http://www.eclipse.org`.

The first step to follow in order to add GlassFish support is to install the Web Tools Project Eclipse plug-in. This plug-in can be easily installed via the Eclipse Update Manager, refer to the Web Tools Project website at `http://www.eclipse.org/webtools/main.php`.

After installing the Web Tools Project plug-in, we need to create a Java EE project by clicking on **File | New | Project...** then selecting a Java EE project type from the list of project categories. Most projects under the EJB, J2EE, JPA, and Web categories are Java EE projects that need to be deployed to an application server such as GlassFish.

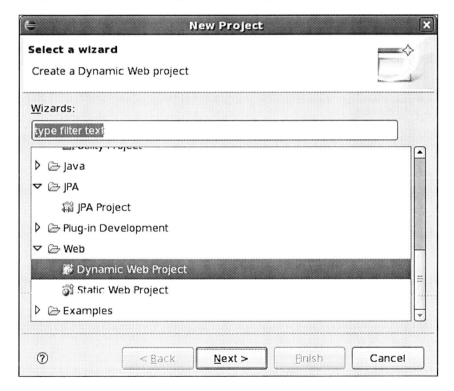

In our example, we will use a project of type **Dynamic Web Project**, but the procedure is very similar for other Java EE project types.

After selecting the project type and clicking **Next >**, Eclipse will ask, among other things, for the **Target Runtime** for the project. **Target Runtime** is "Eclipse Speak" for a Java EE application server.

At this point we should click on the **New...** button in order to select a new target runtime.

In order to add GlassFish integration, we need to click on the **Download additional server adapters** link.

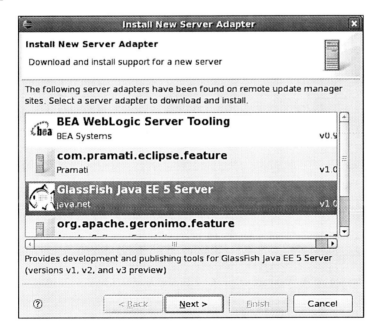

At this point, a number of additional server adapters will be listed, with GlassFish being one of them. Selecting Glassfish and clicking on the button labeled **Next >** will download the GlassFish server adapter. Once it is downloaded, Eclipse will ask to be restarted. It is recommended that we do so.

Once Eclipse restarts, we need to start creating the project once again. This second time around, there will be an option to select GlassFish as the server runtime when clicking on the **New...** button next to the target runtime selection dropdown.

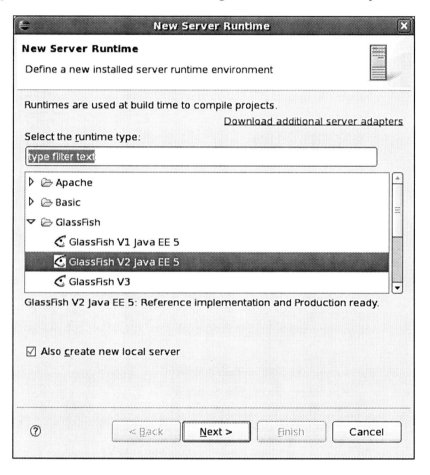

The next couple of windows will ask for a Java Runtime Environment to use with GlassFish, the directory where GlassFish is installed, and for the server address, port, domain name, etc. Sensible defaults are presented for all fields.

At this point, we can continue going through the wizard and creating our project.

We should now see GlassFish in the servers view, which is typically at the bottom of the screen.

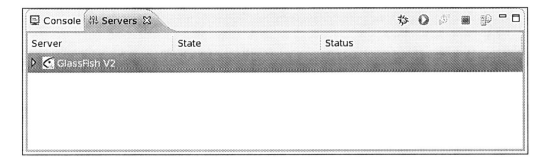

If the servers view is nowhere to be seen, it can be opened by clicking on **Window | Show View | Servers**.

At this point, we are ready to start developing our application. When we are at a point where we need to deploy it, we can do so by clicking on the GlassFish server icon in the Servers view, and selecting **Publish**.

At this point, Eclipse will build, package, and deploy the application.

For web applications, we can execute the application as soon as it is deployed by right-clicking on the project and selecting **Run As | Run on Server**.

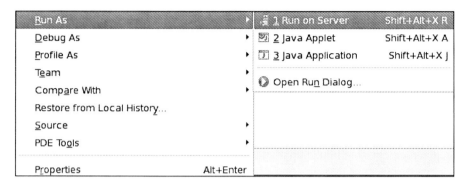

At this point, Eclipse will build, package, deploy the application, and open it in a browser window embedded in Eclipse.

If we wish to debug the application using Eclipse's debugger, we can do so by right-clicking on the project and selecting **Debug As | Debug on Server**. This will cause Eclipse to start or restart GlassFish in debug mode, if necessary, and deploy the application. We can then debug it using Eclipse's built in debugger.

Index

logical operator 149
life cycles, EJB
  about 308
  message driven bean life cycle 313
  stateful session bean life cycle 308
  stateless session bean life cycle 312

M

many to many relationships 128
message driven bean life cycle 313
message driven beans 301, 302
message queues
  about 228
  browsing 237
  messages, adding 228
  messages, retrieving from 232
  messages, sending to 228
  messages receiving asynchronously 234
  message types 231
message styles, customizing 192, 193
message text, customizing 193
message topics
  durable subscribers, creating 243
  messages, receiving from 241
  messages, sending to 239
  pub/sub domain 239
  pub/sub domain,disadvantage 243
method binding expression 179
Model View Controller 62

N

NetBeans 395, 396

O

one to many relationships 122
one to one relationships 116
operators
  arithmetic operator 150
  logical operator 149
  relational operator 148

P

persisting application data across requests
  about 58

object,retrieving 57
predefined security realms
  about 248
  admin-realm 249
  certificate realm 265
  file realm 251
  file realm authenticating 252
pub/sub domain
  about 239
  disadvantages 243

R

realms. *See* **security realms**
receiving messages asynchronously from
    message queue 234-237
receiving messages from a message topic
    241, 242
relational operator 148
relationships. *See* **entity relationships**
remote business interface 293
response redirection
  about 53
   disadvantage 53
  illustrating 53
retrieving messages from message queue
    232-234

S

Seam
  about 373
  advantages over JSF 373
  application, configuring 375-379
  application, developing 379-384
  downloading 374, 375
securing, web services 341-343
securing web services, EJB 343-345
security, EJB
  about 316-320
  client, authenticating 320
security realms
  about 247
  additional certificate realms 274
  additional file realms 273
  additional realms 273
  custom realms 283

Thank you for buying
Java EE 5 Development using GlassFish Application Server

Packt Open Source Project Royalties

When we sell a book written on an Open Source project, we pay a royalty directly to that project. Therefore by purchasing Java EE 5 Development using GlassFish Application Server, Packt will have given some of the money received to the GlassFish project.

In the long term, we see ourselves and you—customers and readers of our books—as part of the Open Source ecosystem, providing sustainable revenue for the projects we publish on. Our aim at Packt is to establish publishing royalties as an essential part of the service and support a business model that sustains Open Source.

If you're working with an Open Source project that you would like us to publish on, and subsequently pay royalties to, please get in touch with us.

Writing for Packt

We welcome all inquiries from people who are interested in authoring. Book proposals should be sent to authors@packtpub.com. If your book idea is still at an early stage and you would like to discuss it first before writing a formal book proposal, contact us; one of our commissioning editors will get in touch with you.

We're not just looking for published authors; if you have strong technical skills but no writing experience, our experienced editors can help you develop a writing career, or simply get some additional reward for your expertise.

About Packt Publishing

Packt, pronounced 'packed', published its first book "Mastering phpMyAdmin for Effective MySQL Management" in April 2004 and subsequently continued to specialize in publishing highly focused books on specific technologies and solutions.

Our books and publications share the experiences of your fellow IT professionals in adapting and customizing today's systems, applications, and frameworks. Our solution-based books give you the knowledge and power to customize the software and technologies you're using to get the job done. Packt books are more specific and less general than the IT books you have seen in the past. Our unique business model allows us to bring you more focused information, giving you more of what you need to know, and less of what you don't.

Packt is a modern, yet unique publishing company, which focuses on producing quality, cutting-edge books for communities of developers, administrators, and newbies alike. For more information, please visit our website: www.PacktPub.com.

PUBLISHING

Business Process Management with JBoss jBPM

ISBN: 978-1-847192-36-3   Paperback: 300 pages

Develop business process models for implementation in a business process management system

1. Map your business processes in an efficient, standards-friendly way

2. Use the jBPM toolset to work with business process maps, create a customizable user interface for users to interact with the process, collect process execution data, and integrate with existing systems

3. Use the SeeWhy business intelligence toolset as a Business Activity Monitoring solution, to analyze process execution data, provide real-time alerts regarding the operation of the process, and for ongoing process improvement

BPEL Cookbook: Best Practices for SOA-based integration and composite applications development

ISBN: 1-904811-33-7   Paperback: 188 pages

Ten practical real-world case studies combining business process management and web services orchestration

1. Real-world BPEL recipes for SOA integration and Composite Application development

2. Combining business process management and web services orchestration

3. Techniques and best practices with downloadable code samples from ten real-world case studies

Please check **www.PacktPub.com** for information on our titles

Business Process Execution Language for Web Services Second Edition

An architect and developer's guide to orchestrating web services using BPEL4WS

Matjaz B. Juric   Benny Mathew Poornachandra Sarang

PACKT

Business Process Execution Language for Web Services 2nd Edition

ISBN: 1-904811-81-7   Paperback: 350 pages

An Architects and Developers Guide to BPEL and BPEL4WS

1. Architecture, syntax, development and composition of Business Processes and Services using BPEL

2. Advanced BPEL features such as compensation, concurrency, links, scopes, events, dynamic partner links, and correlations

3. Oracle BPEL Process Manager and BPEL Designer Microsoft BizTalk Server as a BPEL server

Building Websites with
Joomla! 1.5 Beta 1

The best-selling Joomla tutorial guide updated for the latest download release

Hagen Graf   PACKT

Building Websites with Joomla! 1.5 Beta 1

ISBN: 978-1-847192-38-7   Paperback: 380 pages

The bestselling Joomla tutorial guide updated for the latest download release

1. Install and configure Joomla! 1.5 beta 1

2. Customize and extend your Joomla! site

3. Create your own template and extensions

4. **Free eBook upgrades up to 1.5 Final Release**

5. Also available covering Joomla v1

Please check **www.PacktPub.com** for information on our titles

Printed in the United Kingdom
by Lightning Source UK Ltd.
124364UK00001B/280/A